D1609853

HOW STATES THINK

HOW STATES THINK

The Rationality of
Foreign Policy

John J. Mearsheimer
and Sebastian Rosato

Yale

UNIVERSITY PRESS

NEW HAVEN & LONDON

Published with assistance from the Mary Cady Tew Memorial Fund.

Yale University Press books may be purchased in quantity
for educational, business, or promotional use. For information, please e-mail
sales.press@yale.edu (U.S. office) or sales@yaleup.co.uk (U.K. office).

Set in Yale and Alternate Gothic No2 type by IDS Infotech Ltd.
Printed in Great Britain by TJ Books Limited, Padstow, Cornwall.

Library of Congress Control Number: 2022949565
ISBN 978-0-300-26930-7 (hardcover : alk. paper)

A catalogue record for this book is available from the British Library.

10 9 8 7 6 5 4 3 2 1

MIX
Paper from
responsible sources
FSC® C013056

For our fellow international relations theorists

CONTENTS

PREFACE

It is widely believed in the West that Russian president Vladimir Putin's decision to invade Ukraine was not a rational act. On the eve of the invasion, British prime minister Boris Johnson suggested that perhaps the United States and its allies had not done "enough to deter an irrational actor and we have to accept at the moment that Vladimir Putin is possibly thinking illogically about this and doesn't see the disaster ahead." U.S. senator Mitt Romney made a similar point after the war started, noting that "by invading Ukraine, Mr. Putin has already proved that he is capable of illogical and self-defeating decisions."[1] The assumption underlying both statements is that rational leaders start wars only if they are likely to win. By starting a war he was destined to lose, the thinking went, Putin demonstrated his nonrationality.[2]

Other critics argue that Putin was nonrational because he violated a fundamental international norm. In this view, the only morally acceptable reason for going to war is self-defense, but the invasion of Ukraine was a war of conquest. Russia expert Nina Khrushcheva asserts that "with his unprovoked assault, Mr. Putin joins a long line of irrational tyrants," and she goes on to argue that he "seems to have succumbed to his ego-driven obsession with restoring Russia's status as a great power with its own clearly defined sphere of influence." Bess Levin of *Vanity Fair* describes Russia's president as "a power-hungry megalomaniac who harbors imperial ambitions, so much so that he decided to attack a neighboring country." Former British ambassador to Moscow Tony Brenton argues that Putin's "assault on Ukrainian sovereignty . . . [and] almost clinical obsession with bringing the country to heel" reveal that he is an "unbalanced autocrat," not the "rational actor" he once was.[3]

These claims rest on common understandings of rationality that are intuitively plausible but ultimately flawed. Contrary to what many people think, we cannot equate rationality with success and nonrationality with failure. Rationality is not about outcomes. Rational actors often fail to achieve their goals, not because of foolish thinking but because of factors they can neither anticipate nor control. There is also a powerful tendency to equate rationality with morality since both qualities are thought to be features of enlightened thinking. But that too is a mistake. Rational policies can violate widely accepted standards of conduct and may even be murderously unjust.

So what is "rationality" in international politics? Surprisingly, the scholarly literature does not provide a good definition. For us, rationality is all about making sense of the world—that is, figuring out how it works and why—in order to decide how to achieve certain goals. It has both an individual and a collective dimension. Rational policymakers are theory-driven; they are *homo theoreticus*. They have credible theories—logical explanations based on realistic assumptions and supported by substantial evidence—about the workings of the international system, and they employ these to understand their

HOW STATES THINK

situation and determine how best to navigate it. Rational states aggregate the views of key policymakers through a deliberative process, one marked by robust and uninhibited debate. In sum, rational decisions in international politics rest on credible theories about how the world works and emerge from a deliberative decision-making process.

All of this means that Russia's decision to invade Ukraine was rational.

Consider that Russian leaders relied on a credible theory. Most commentators dispute this claim, arguing that Putin was bent on conquering Ukraine and other countries in Eastern Europe to create a greater Russian empire, something that would satisfy a nostalgic yearning among Russians but that makes no strategic sense in the modern world. President Joe Biden maintains that Putin aspires "to be the leader of Russia that united all of Russian speakers. I mean . . . I just think it's irrational."[4] Former national security adviser H. R. McMaster argues, "I don't think he's a rational actor because he's fearful, right? What he wants to do more than anything is restore Russia to national greatness. He's driven by that."[5]

But the fact is that Putin and his advisers thought in terms of straightforward balance-of-power theory, viewing the West's efforts to make Ukraine a bulwark on Russia's border as an existential threat that could not be allowed to stand. Russia's president laid out this logic in a speech explaining his decision for war: "With NATO's eastward expansion the situation for Russia has been becoming worse and more dangerous by the year. . . . We cannot stay idle and passively observe these developments. This would be an absolutely irresponsible thing to do for us." He went on to say, "For our country, it is a matter of life and death, a matter of our historical future as a nation. This is not an exaggeration; this is a fact. It is not only a very real threat to our interests but to the very existence of our state and to its sovereignty. It is the red line which we have spoken about on numerous occasions. They have crossed it."[6] In short, this was a war of self-defense aimed at preventing an adverse shift in the balance of power.

It is worth noting that Moscow preferred to deal with the growing threat on its borders through aggressive diplomacy, but the United States and its allies were unwilling to accommodate Russia's security concerns.[7] This being the case, Putin opted for war, which analysts expected to result in the Russian military's overrunning Ukraine. Describing the view of U.S. officials just before the invasion, David Ignatius of the *Washington Post* wrote that Russia would "quickly win the initial, tactical phase of this war, if it comes. The vast army that Russia has arrayed along Ukraine's borders could probably seize the capital of Kyiv in several days and control the country in little more than a week."[8] Indeed, the intelligence community "told the White House that Russia would win in a matter of days by quickly overwhelming the Ukrainian army."[9]

The Russian decision to invade was also the product of a deliberative process. Again, many observers dispute this point, arguing that Putin operated alone without serious input from civilian and military advisers, who would have counseled against his reckless bid for empire. As Senator Mark Warner, the chair of the Senate Intelligence Committee, puts it, "He's not had that many people having direct inputs to him. So we're concerned that this kind of isolated individual [has] become a megalomaniac in terms of his notion of himself being the only historic figure that can rebuild old Russia or recreate the notion of the Soviet sphere." Former ambassador to Moscow Michael McFaul suggests that one element of Russia's nonrationality is that Putin is "profoundly isolated, surrounded only by yes men who have cut him off from accurate knowledge."[10]

The available evidence tells a different story: Putin's subordinates shared his views about the nature of the threat confronting Russia, and he consulted with them before deciding on war. The consensus among Russian leaders regarding the dangers inherent in Ukraine's relationship with the West is reflected in a 2008 memorandum by then ambassador to Russia William Burns; it warned that "Ukrainian entry into NATO is the brightest of all redlines for the Russian elite (not just Putin). In more than two and a half years of conversations with key Russian players, from knuckle-draggers in the dark recesses of the Kremlin to Putin's sharpest liberal critics, I have yet to find anyone who views Ukraine in NATO as anything other than a direct challenge to Russian interests. . . . I can conceive of no grand package that would allow the Russians to swallow this pill quietly." Nor does Putin appear to have made the decision for war alone. When asked whether the Russian president consulted with his key advisers, Foreign Minister Sergey Lavrov replied, "Every country has a decision-making mechanism. In that case, the mechanism existing in the Russian Federation was fully employed."[11] All of this is to say that the Russian decision to invade most likely emerged from a deliberative process.

Not only was Russia's decision to invade Ukraine rational, but it was also not anomalous. Many great powers are said to have acted nonrationally when in fact they acted rationally. The list includes Germany in the years before World War I and during the July Crisis, as well as Japan in the 1930s and during the run-up to Pearl Harbor. This is not to say that states are always rational: the British decision not to balance against Nazi Germany in 1938 was not rational, nor was the American decision to invade Iraq in 2003. But those cases are the exceptions. Against the increasingly common view among students of international politics that states are often nonrational, we argue in this book that most states are rational most of the time.

This argument has profound implications for both the study and the practice of international politics. Neither can be coherent in a world where nonrationality prevails. Inside the academy, our argument affirms the rational actor assumption, which has long been a fundamental building block for understanding world politics even if it has recently come under assault. If nonrationality is the norm, state behavior can be neither understood nor predicted, and studying international politics is a futile endeavor. For practitioners, rationality enables states to devise effective foreign policies. Only if those other states are rational actors can one anticipate how friends and enemies are likely to behave in a given situation and thus formulate policies that will advance one's interests.

We first discussed the possibility of writing something on the rational actor assumption in international politics in November 2019. At the time, we planned to write an article, which we outlined over the next four months in a series of day-long meetings at the University of Chicago Booth School of Business. The only insight we had in those early days that has survived over the course of producing this book was that theory-driven thinking is the hallmark of rationality.

In March 2020, the pandemic hit, putting an end to our meetings but not our endeavors. Rosato produced the first draft of the article on 8 May, at which point Mearsheimer set out to write a second draft. When he ran into trouble, we started meeting daily on Zoom to resolve the issues that were stumping him and soon found ourselves writing the second draft together. We completed that version on 31 July and circulated it to a number of colleagues, with whom we then met on Zoom — usually two at a time — to get feedback on our ideas. We also presented the draft at two virtual workshops: the Notre Dame International Relations Workshop and the University of Chicago Workshop on International Politics.

Virtually everyone who read the draft had major reservations about the project, and we realized that despite our best efforts we did not have a good handle on the rationality issue. There is usually a temptation to quit in such situations, but we decided to double down and write a book, not only because we believed we had something important to say, but also because almost all of our interlocutors were captivated by the subject.

So beginning in October 2020, we met on Zoom for four hours a day almost every day until we produced the first draft of the book on 17 June 2021. Our meetings followed a regular pattern: we spent the first fifteen, sometimes thirty, minutes shooting the breeze before going to work, using the share-screen function to write, read, and research together. We then circulated the book draft to a host of colleagues — some of whom had read the article version — and followed up in a series of Zoom conversations, many of which lasted several hours. We also took advantage of loosening pandemic restrictions to have two in-person meetings with some of our Chicago and Notre Dame colleagues in Hyde Park.

Although we went into those meetings thinking, not for the first time, that we had our arguments down, we did not. Once again our interlocutors pointed out major problems with the manuscript, though a number of them told us they thought we were onto something and had the makings of an important book.

In late September 2021, we began a complete overhaul, meeting on Zoom for four hours a day, seven days a week — including

Thanksgiving and New Year's Day but not Christmas – until we had a new version on 5 March 2022. The difference between this draft and the previous one, conceptually, theoretically, and empirically, was profound. Having exhausted our list of interlocutors, we shared the manuscript with William Frucht, our editor at Yale University Press, who sent it out for review. The extensive comments we received from him and the reviewers led us to go back on Zoom full-time and rewrite the manuscript once again. We completed the final draft on 15 August, two years and nine months to the day since we had embarked on the project.

As should be clear, *How States Think* is a child both of the pandemic, which confined us to our homes, and by putting the rest of our lives on hold, afforded us the time we needed to think and write, and of Zoom, which allowed us to spend some three thousand hours working together and meeting with colleagues around the world. Strange as it may seem, we cannot imagine having completed the book under any other circumstances, and even if we had, we suspect it would have taken us much longer to write and the end product would not have been as good.

It is a great pleasure to thank the many smart and talented people who made this a better book. We owe a special debt to those individuals who met with us on Zoom and offered many challenging and insightful comments, including Jasen Castillo, Dale Copeland, Eliza Gheorge, Charles Glaser, Brendan Green, Mariya Grinberg, Dominic Johnson, Sean Lynn-Jones, Nuno Monteiro, Lindsey O'Rourke, Brian Rathbun, John Schuessler, Jack Snyder, Janice Gross Stein, Marc Trachtenberg, Stephen Walt, and Alexander Wendt. We are equally indebted to Joshua Byun, Moritz Graefrath, Robert Gulotty, William Howell, Eric Oliver, and Duncan Snidal, who met with us in person, offering sage advice on the entire manuscript.

PREFACE

We benefited greatly from presenting our early thoughts on rationality at the Notre Dame International Relations Workshop and the University of Chicago Workshop on International Politics. We are grateful to all the participants at those workshops, especially Austin Carson, Michael Desch, Eugene Gholz, Alec Hahus, Rosemary Kelanic, Dan Lindley, Joseph Parent, Jazmin Sierra, and Diana Wueger, for their helpful questions, comments, and suggestions.

We very much appreciate the conversations and e-mail exchanges we had with Bryce Adam, Sener Aktürk, Ólafur Björnsson, Sean Braniff, Kevin Bustamante, Arthur Cyr, Amitava Dutt, Christian Godwin, Gary Goertz, Peter Katzenstein, Samuel Leiter, Jennifer A. Lind, Ramzy Mardini, James Morrow, Bangchen Ruan, Yubing Sheng, Lei Sun, Robert Trager, Mike Wolcott, and especially Robert Keohane.

Finally, we thank the three anonymous reviewers for the seriousness with which they read and critiqued the manuscript. Our sincere apologies to anyone we might have forgotten to mention here.

We are fortunate to have received excellent administrative and financial support. Special thanks go to Elyse Boldt, David Mearsheimer, and Burak Tan for their first-rate research assistance. Mearsheimer's research was facilitated by a small grant from the Valdai Discussion Club that he received in conjunction with his book *The Great Delusion*, winning the club's best book award for 2019. Rosato's work on the book was funded in part by the College of Arts and Letters at Notre Dame.

This is the second book each of us has published with Yale University Press. We could not have asked for a better editor than William Frucht, who was enthusiastic throughout the process and also did a wonderful job line editing the manuscript. We also thank Amanda Gerstenfeld for logistical support, Bojana Ristich for superb copyediting, and Joyce Ippolito for guiding us seamlessly through production.

The process of writing a book is all-consuming for the authors and thus inevitably has a profound effect on those close to them. Because of the pandemic, this was especially true for Pamela and David Mearsheimer and for Susan, Anna, and Olivia Rosato, who were forced to experience the enterprise up close on a daily basis. Yet in spite of everything, they were unfailingly patient, supportive, and encouraging, for which we are deeply grateful.

Chapter 1

THE RATIONAL ACTOR ASSUMPTION

It has become commonplace for American leaders to describe their foreign adversaries as nonrational. At some point over the past twenty-five years, Saddam Hussein, Mahmoud Ahmadinejad, Hugo Chávez, Muammar Gaddafi, Kim Jong-un, and Vladimir Putin, among others, have been branded "irrational," "illogical," "crazy," "delusional," or "mad," and in some cases they have been likened to Adolf Hitler, who is often portrayed as the poster child of nonrationality.[1]

The view that individuals, including policymakers, are nonrational may be even more influential in academic circles, where it is said that "a new behavioral revolution has swept across the social sciences in the last few decades."[2] Building on the work of psychologists, many students of politics and economics maintain that human beings — from ordinary consumers to heads of state — frequently act in ways that are at odds with the dictates of rationality.

If these claims are true, then traditional international relations scholarship is in trouble since so much of it is based on the assumption that states are rational actors.[3] A finding that they are regularly

---

nonrational would undermine many of the central arguments and insights in the field and arguably cast doubt on the entire enterprise.[4] It would also make it impossible for state leaders to design effective foreign policies. After all, they would not be able to anticipate how other states were likely to behave. In short, the academic and real world stakes could hardly be higher.

Our aim in this book is to examine the rational actor assumption in world politics. We seek to answer two related questions. First, what is rationality? Any discussion of the rational actor assumption must begin with a proper understanding of what it means for states to think and act rationally and, conversely, what it means for them to think and act nonrationally. Without a compelling definition, it is impossible to establish a baseline that can be used to distinguish rational from nonrational thought and action. Second, are states actually rational actors? That is, does the empirical record show that they are routinely rational or routinely nonrational?

Rationality is all about making sense of the world for the purpose of navigating it in the pursuit of desired goals.[5] In the foreign policy realm, this means it has both individual and state-level dimensions. Rational decision makers are theory-driven — they employ credible theories both to understand the situation at hand and to decide the best policies for achieving their objectives. A state is rational if the views of its key decision makers are aggregated through a deliberative process and the final policy is based on a credible theory. Conversely, a state is nonrational if it does not base its strategy on a credible theory, does not deliberate, or both. A careful review of the historical record shows that judged by these criteria, states are regularly rational in their foreign policy.

Our arguments stand in marked contrast to the existing literature on rationality in international relations.[6] In the two perspectives that dominate the debate — rational choice and political psychology — there is surprisingly little discussion of how individuals make sense of the world, a step that is an essential component of rationality. Scholars working in the rational choice tradition, whom one would expect to speak volumes on this issue, simply do not consider how policymakers employ their critical faculties to figure out the way the world works. Political psychologists are also largely silent when it comes to how policymakers seek to comprehend the world around them.

Instead, both rational choice theorists and political psychologists focus on the narrower issue of how individuals decide among alternative policy options. Rational choice scholars claim that rational individuals act "as if" they aim to maximize their expected utility. This approach does not consider how individuals actually think about their choices. Political psychologists, meanwhile, do examine how individuals actually make decisions, and thus they take a view on what rational choice looks like. But their understanding is different from ours; whereas we emphasize the use of credible theories, they say that rational individuals make choices by using the expected utility maximization formula.

Rational choice theorists and political psychologists have even less to say about what rationality is at the state level than at the individual level. While they acknowledge that the making of foreign policy is a collective enterprise, they say hardly anything about how the views of different decision makers are aggregated to produce a rational or nonrational strategy.

Turning to the empirical question of whether states are in fact rational actors, rational choice scholars and political psychologists dispute our claim that rationality is commonplace. To be clear, a number of rational choice theorists do not address the question.

Those who do take a position on the matter maintain that states are often nonrational. Political psychologists also claim that nonrationality is widespread in international politics.

All of this is to say that ours is a radical intervention in the debate. For one thing, we offer a meaningful definition of rationality in international politics where none existed. Moreover, rather than merely asserting that states are routinely rational, we make the case.

Strategic Rationality and Uncertainty

Before we can define "rationality" in international politics, it is important to delineate some key facets of the relevant actors and the environment in which they operate. There is an important distinction between policymakers and states. Therefore, it is essential to consider what it means for individuals to think and act rationally, as well as what it means for collectivities to do so. Moreover, judgments about rationality apply both to the goals that policymakers and states set for themselves and the strategies they adopt to realize them. There is a difference between what we call "strategic rationality" and "goal rationality," though the debate on rationality in the international relations literature focuses almost exclusively on whether a state's strategies are rational and pays little attention to evaluating the rationality of its goals.

The world in which states operate is characterized, above all, by uncertainty. In other words, international politics is an information-deficient enterprise; much of the data policymakers require to make decisions is lacking, and what information does exist may not be reliable. Policymakers confront information deficits about their own state, about other states—both friends and enemies—and about potential interactions between their state and others. These problems, all intractable in the present, are even more daunting when one tries to anticipate the future.

Individual Rationality

At the individual level, rationality is a mental process. To say that individuals are rational or nonrational is thus to make a statement about the character of their thinking. How do they, first, make sense of the world and, second, make decisions about specific issues that confront them?[7]

Rational individuals employ a thought process that is appropriate for making sense of the world in which they operate. They use their critical faculties to answer questions such as these: What goals should they pursue and why? What factors matter most for shaping their world? What are the causes and effects of those various factors? Why do those causes and effects obtain? What are the causes and effects of particular actions? What explains why those causes produce those effects? In other words, making sense of the world—which is the essence of rationality—involves explaining how the world works and why it works the way it does. In performing this task, rational policymakers are aware that international politics is a social world, one that is information-deficient and therefore uncertain.

When rational individuals make decisions about how to deal with specific issues, they choose what they think is the best strategy for achieving their goals, taking into account that they are operating in an uncertain world. Rational decision-making also has an important informational dimension. As they make their decisions, rational individuals carefully assess the situation at hand, a process that involves gathering and analyzing the available evidence. Moreover, having made a choice, they are open to modifying their views if new information becomes available.

Collective Rationality

Rationality at the collective level is all about how the decision makers who formulate foreign policy work together to come up with goals and strategies for achieving them. It is this collection of individuals rather than the state itself that makes policy. A state's rationality thus depends on how the views of its key policymakers are aggregated.

A rational aggregation process has two key features. The first is a mechanism that allows for systematic consideration of the available options. In practice, this means that the members of the policymaking group put their preferred options — which derive from their understandings of the world — on the table, and all those options are discussed, as are each policymaker's views about them. Such methodical examination is essential if the aggregation process is to be rational because in the uncertain world in which states operate, it is often not obvious what they should aim for or how best to get there. The second feature is a procedure for deciding among the available options. After all, only an aggregation process that produces a decision is rational; one that fails to produce a decision is nonrational.

A final word is in order about the rational actor concept. One might think that the foregoing discussion about the individual and collective processes that lead to a policy means that we have little to say about the rational actor assumption, which is ostensibly about action. Since policy and action are analytically distinct concepts, it might seem that we are focusing on the former and ignoring the latter. That would be wrong. Although policy and action are analytically distinct, they are inextricably linked. Simply put, states act on the basis of policies. To the extent that their policies are rational, therefore, so too are their actions. In short, our analysis is all about the rational actor assumption.

———

To conclude, the requirements for a sound definition of rationality in international politics are straightforward. At both the individual and state level, it must describe a process appropriate to an uncertain world that allows those actors to make sense of their situation and make decisions as issues arise.

Defining Strategic Rationality in World Politics

Although international relations scholars often invoke the rational actor assumption in referring to states as rational or nonrational, there is surprisingly little discussion in the literature of what rationality entails. Therefore, we provide a definition of strategic rationality and explain why it is superior to the most commonly used alternative.[8]

Credible Theory and Deliberation

As noted, we define a state as rational if its strategy is based on a credible theory and is the result of a deliberative process. Rational policymakers are theory-driven; they employ credible theories to make sense of the world and decide the best way to achieve some goal. Rational states aggregate the views of different policymakers in two steps: a robust and uninhibited debate and a policy choice made by an ultimate decider.

Rational policymakers who seek to make sense of the world adopt credible theories; we can call them *homo theoreticus*. Because theory and policy are inextricably linked, decision makers who employ such theories ultimately advocate rational policies. Individuals have in their heads different theories — probabilistic statements made up of assumptions, causal logics, and supporting evidence — about various aspects of international politics. Many of these theories are credible, which is to say their assumptions are realistic, their causal stories are logically consistent, and their claims find substantial support in the historical record. Some theories, however, are noncredible on suppositional, logical, or empirical grounds (or all three), in which case the policy prescriptions that flow from them are nonrational. So, too, are strategies based on any form of nontheoretical thinking.

When confronted with the need to make a decision on a particular issue, rational policymakers once again rely on credible theories. Because they explain the way the world works, these theories help policymakers decide the best strategy for dealing with the situation at hand. To be sure, no credible theory applies to all problems, and even if it applies in one instance, it may not do so later if circumstances change. In other words, rational policymakers are strongly wedded to their theories, but they also assess whether those theories apply in the relevant case, and they are willing to change their minds in the face of powerful new evidence.

Rational states aggregate the views of key policymakers through deliberation. As should be clear, in any given situation, each decision maker is likely to have a preferred theory and will be inclined to believe that it best captures the way the world works and thus provides the approved solution for dealing with the problem at hand. Sometimes these theories will significantly overlap, and at other times there will be sharp disagreements. Some policymakers may even favor noncredible theories, although most will not. Thus the aggregation issue looms large.

Deliberation is the hallmark of a rational aggregation process at the state level. It involves robust and uninhibited debate in which each decision maker gets to weigh in on the strengths and weaknesses of the different policies under consideration without resorting to or falling victim to coercion or deception, and a policy choice by an ultimate decider. In effect, the discussion approximates a classic marketplace of ideas where the group seeks to understand the situation. The debate can play itself out in three ways. First, policymakers, including the ultimate decider, discuss the situation confronting them in a comprehensive manner and easily reach a consensus because their theories largely overlap. Second, they champion different theories and associated policies but resolve their disagreements because the debate leads some to reconsider their views. Third, the participants disagree, no side can convince any other, and the ultimate decider settles the dispute.

Conversely, a state is nonrational if the aggregation process that yields the chosen policy is nondeliberative — that is, some members of the decision-making group engage in silencing, coercion, suppression, lying, or the withholding of information. This is true even if the final policy turns out to be based on a credible theory. And, of course, a state is nonrational if its chosen strategy rests on a noncredible theory or no theory regardless of the nature of the aggregation process.

Our definition of "strategic rationality" — states are rational if their policies are based on credible theories and result from a deliberative decision-making process — captures the essential meaning of that concept. At the individual level, credible theories — which are mental constructs — are the most appropriate way to make sense of an uncertain world, though they are by no means perfect. They are also well suited for making decisions about how best to move forward in the face of serious information deficits. At the collective level, deliberation provides a mechanism for both the systematic review of policy options, which is essential in an uncertain world where it is not clear what the best strategy is, and a procedure for deciding among those options.

Expected Utility Maximization

Most students of international relations treat rationality as synonymous with expected utility maximization, which is basically a data-driven enterprise. According to this method — championed by rational choice scholars — rational individuals first identify the set of possible outcomes that can result from their interactions with other actors. They then rank those potential outcomes in order of preference and assign them particular utilities or values. Next, they multiply the utility of each possible outcome by the probability that it will occur — which they establish by examining the available data — to calculate the expected utility of the various actions under consideration. Finally, they optimize, choosing the action that maximizes their expected utility. This view of rationality is routinely employed in mainstream economics, which is why individuals who maximize or optimize by engaging in expected utility calculations are often referred to as *homo economicus*.

It is important to note that there are two views in the literature about rationality and expected utility maximization. Rational choice theorists argue that rational individuals act as if they were maximizing their expected utility. They do not assume that rational actors actually calculate the expected utility of the available actions in order to make decisions. Indeed, they are silent about the mental process in which individuals engage to choose how to act. Political psychologists take a different perspective. While they also identify rationality with optimization, they take that to mean that rational individuals actually perform expected utility calculations in their heads when deciding what to do.

This definition of rationality in international relations is incomplete; it deals only with how individuals make choices, stipulating that rational deciders choose actions that maximize their expected utility. The definition says little about how these individuals make sense of the world prior to being confronted with a problem that requires a decision. It also says little about what a rational aggregation process looks like at the state level.

Even on the particular matter of individual choices, expected utility maximization is a flawed definition of rationality. Rational choice scholars say hardly anything about the mental process of choice. Instead, they merely assume that rational individuals act as if they were maximizing their utility, not that they are actually doing so. Because thought processes are at the heart of rationality, this means that rational choice theorists ultimately say nothing about rational decision-making. Political psychologists, who argue that rational policymakers actually think in expected utility terms, do not face this problem. Nevertheless, like rational choice scholars, political psychologists are vulnerable to a further criticism: expected utility maximization is not a rational approach to making foreign policy decisions. It is a good way to decide how to achieve one's objectives in an information-rich world where reliable data is abundant, but international politics is information-deficient and uncertain.

Assessing Strategic Rationality in World Politics

Once rationality has been defined, we can assess whether states are rational actors. In essence, there are two positions on the matter. We argue that states are routinely rational, while political psychologists claim they are routinely nonrational. Analyses of both sets of arguments, as well as the historical record, reveal that rationality is commonplace in international politics.

———

Routine Rationality

Given our definition of rationality as credible theories plus deliberation, we find that generally speaking, states are rational actors. Individual policymakers typically employ credible theories to inform their understanding of international politics and decisions about the issues at hand and deliberate among themselves to formulate strategies for reaching their goals.

Our analysis of the historical record focuses on a series of prominent cases in which great powers formulated grand strategies and managed crises. We examine instances in which those states are said to have thought and acted in a nonrational fashion. The reason is simple: if the great powers were rational in these cases of alleged nonrationality, then they are likely to have been rational at most other times as well. We have not, of course, analyzed the entire historical record. That is impossible as there are innumerable cases of states making foreign policy decisions and scant evidence on many of them. Nevertheless, we believe our approach goes some way toward addressing the problem.

It is important to note that in many of the cases we examine, the chosen policy failed, sometimes disastrously. This does not mean that the state in question was nonrational. There is a crucial conceptual distinction between process and outcomes, and rationality is about the former, not the latter. Rational states seek to make sense of the world and systematically consider the strategies available to them. It does not follow that the policies they choose will be successful. States can be committed to theory-driven deliberation yet fail to reach their desired outcome because of some exogenous constraint or unforeseen circumstance. By the same token, there are several reasons — such as chance or overwhelming superiority — why nonrational states may achieve their objectives. To sum up, states can be

—

rational and unsuccessful as well as nonrational and successful. It therefore makes little sense to equate rationality with outcomes. Nevertheless, a state that pursues a rational strategy is more likely to succeed than fail since it has a good understanding of international politics and has carefully pondered how to proceed.

None of this is to say that rationality is ubiquitous in international politics. Indeed, we identify a number of instances of nonrationality, where states either failed to deliberate, failed to base their policy on a credible theory, or both.

There is a simple explanation for why states routinely think and act rationally when making foreign policy. International politics is a dangerous business. States operate in a system where there is no higher authority to protect them and where other states can and may want to do them grave harm. Consequently, they have a strong interest in finding the best strategies to address the problems they confront. This leads individual policymakers to employ credible theories to make sense of the world and decide what to do, as well as to deliberate among themselves to settle on a strategy for moving forward. This is not to deny that states will sometimes think and act nonrationally when devising grand strategies or navigating crises. But the high costs of failure mean that such cases are likely to be uncommon.

All Shortcuts All the Time

Although both political psychologists and rational choice scholars rivet on the rational actor issue, the latter say hardly anything about whether states are in fact rational. After all, they largely ignore the individual mental processes that underpin state behavior. Instead, they merely assume that rational decision makers act as if they are employing expected utility maximization. Political psychologists assert that states are routinely nonrational. Based on their notion of rationality as optimization, they conclude that states frequently deviate from that idealized notion of strategic decision-making. Specifically, they claim that the historical record is filled with instances in which policymakers failed to employ expected utility maximization and instead acted in nonrational ways. According to political psychologists, the primary cause of nonrationality or bias in international relations is that state leaders employ mental shortcuts, including analogies and heuristics, to make policy — they are *homo heuristicus*. Crucially, these simplifying devices — some of which are hardwired and some of which are learned — are not theories because they do not involve explanations for why the world works the way it does.

Decision makers are said to employ mental shortcuts because of situational and cognitive limitations. They may lack the time or information required to think through a problem or may have limited computational capacities that hinder their ability to calculate the optimal strategy for addressing a problem. All of these limitations, which necessitate the use of analogies and heuristics, are synonymous with the concept of bounded rationality.

There are good reasons to doubt these empirical claims about the prevalence of nonrationality in international politics. To begin with, political psychologists define rationality in such a way as to guarantee that decision makers are nonrational. Rationality, in their story, calls for individuals to actually choose policies that maximize their expected utility, but this is asking them to perform impossible tasks. Policymakers can never identify all of the possible outcomes of their interactions with other states, let alone assign them meaningful utilities and probabilities. In essence, rationality is defined out of existence.

Although their definition of rationality should lead political psychologists to see only nonrationality, they ultimately argue that states are nonrational most but not all of the time. This more quali-fied claim appears to rely on a different definition of rationality — one based on outcomes rather than how decision makers think and act. Political psychologists tend to focus on disastrous outcomes — such as defeat in war — and reason backward to argue that the under-lying decision was based on analogies or heuristics, thus making it nonrational. This approach is wrongheaded. To repeat, one cannot assess whether states are rational or nonrational by considering outcomes.

It is also not clear that political psychologists have a good ex-planation for all of this purported nonrationality. In particular, there is little reason to think that decision makers employ mental short-cuts when making foreign policy. There is no question that individ-uals regularly resort to rules of thumb in their daily lives. When the stakes are high, however, as in matters of national security, they have powerful incentives to think in theoretical terms.

These issues aside, political psychologists do not in fact pro-vide much historical support for their headline claim that states sel-dom think and act rationally. Indeed, it is striking that despite their rhetoric about widespread nonrationality, they collectively provide only a handful of prominent examples in international politics. To be sure, they suggest that decision makers employed a variety of cognitive shortcuts, but they fixate on the same small set of cases. And even these signal cases are not compelling examples of nonra-tionality. On close inspection, the relevant policymakers were ratio-nal, employing credible theories to make sense of the world and decide how to move forward. Nor is there any evidence that they relied on analogies or heuristics to make decisions. In short, contrary to the views of political psychologists, the historical record is mainly populated by *homo theoreticus* rather than *homo heuristicus*.

———

Goal Rationality

Up to this point, we have focused on whether states are rational in devising their foreign policies. This debate regarding strategic rationality dominates the international relations literature about the rational actor assumption. Yet a comprehensive discussion needs to consider goal rationality as well.

The key question here is whether states are rational with respect to their goals. Nobody disputes that rational states can have multiple objectives, including security, prosperity, and promoting their way of life around the world. We maintain, however, that to be considered rational, a state must rank survival as its number one goal. After all, a credible theory will inevitably place survival above all other objectives. It is a matter of incontrovertible logic and evidence that survival is a prerequisite for pursuing any other goals a state might have. Other goals can be ranked in whatever order a state chooses since credible theories can be constructed to justify any ranking.

Although few scholars dispute the conceptual point that rational states rank survival as their preeminent goal, some identify historical instances in which states are said to have recklessly risked or cared little about their survival and were therefore nonrational. We disagree with their interpretation of those cases. On careful review, states have almost always privileged survival above their other objectives.

Roadmap

The next three chapters are theoretical and conceptual. Chapter 2 discusses the meaning of strategic rationality at a general level, focusing on the fact that international politics is an information-deficient realm and that rational actors — both policymakers and states — seek to make sense of it for the purpose of making wise strategic decisions.

In chapter 3, we lay out our definition of strategic rationality, arguing that what distinguishes rational from nonrational policymakers is whether or not they base their policy choices on credible theories. The same is true of states but with the added criterion that the policy must emerge from a deliberative decision-making process.

In chapter 4, we examine other arguments about rationality in international politics. We focus most of our attention on the dominant definition of strategic rationality — proposed by rational choice scholars and accepted by political psychologists — and find it wanting. We then offer theoretical and conceptual reasons to doubt the claims, put forward by political psychologists, that states are routinely nonrational.

Next we take up the empirical question: are states actually strategically rational? To support our argument that they routinely think and act rationally, we describe five cases of grand strategic decision-making in chapter 5 and five cases of crisis decision-making in chapter 6. Each of these ten cases has been offered at some point as an example of nonrationality. Yet we show that in every instance the relevant decision-making process was deliberative and resulted in a policy based on a credible theory. This is not to say that states have always been rational: in chapter 7, we describe four examples of strategic nonrationality.

Chapter 8 switches the focus away from strategic rationality and zeroes in on goal rationality. We begin by explaining that whether states are goal-rational depends on how they think about survival. Specifically, do they place survival above all other goals?

We then show that contrary to the claims of some scholars, there is scant evidence of states subordinating their self-preservation to other objectives, ignoring the survival imperative, or recklessly putting their survival at risk.

In Chapter 9, we explore the implications of our arguments for the theory and practice of international politics.

Chapter 2

STRATEGIC RATIONALITY AND UNCERTAINTY

This chapter begins our discussion of what it means to say that states are strategically rational. To that end, we perform three tasks. First, we provide a framework for thinking about strategic rationality that informs the rest of our analysis, to include our definition of the term and our evaluation of its alternatives, in subsequent chapters. We distinguish between individual and collective rationality and explain what it means for individuals and collectivities — in this case policymakers and states — to be rational. Second, because comprehending and deciding how to deal with the real world is the essence of strategic rationality, we describe the defining feature of international politics. In a word, that feature is uncertainty. Much of the information required to understand and navigate the world is lacking, and what relevant information does exist may not be reliable. Finally, we provide four historical examples that illustrate how decision makers invariably have to contend with serious information deficits when formulating foreign policy.

Strategic Rationality

When thinking about strategic rationality in international relations — which, again, is all about making sense of the world for the purpose of navigating it in the pursuit of desired goals — it is essential to consider what the term entails for both policymakers and states.

Individual Rationality

Individual rationality is a mental attribute. To say an individual is rational or nonrational is to make a statement about his or her thought process. As Herbert Simon observes, rationality is a "process" and a "product of thought," meaning that any assessment of individual rationality "must give an account [of] . . . *procedural rationality* — the effectiveness, in light of human cognitive powers and limitations, of the *procedures* used to choose actions."[1] Debra Satz and John Ferejohn call this "the *internalist interpretation*" of rationality, noting that "from this perspective, mental entities (for example, preferences and beliefs) are thought to be causally related to choice, in the sense of being reasons for an agent's having made the choice."[2]

Individuals employ their critical faculties for two main purposes: to make sense of the world and to decide what to do when faced with particular problems.[3] With respect to understanding how the world works and why it works that way, rational individuals seek to detect the driving forces at play and grasp the most important cause-effect relationships. In doing so, they consider the amount and quality of information available to them. Specifically, rational individuals tasked with making foreign policy understand that international politics is a social and hence information-deficient world.

This view of individual rationality, as trying to make sense of an uncertain world, is not especially controversial. According to Max

Weber, explains Stephen Kalberg, "However much they may vary in content, mental processes that consciously strive to master reality are common to all the types of rationality. . . . All of these processes systematically confront, for Weber, social reality's endless stream of concrete occurrences, unconnected events, and punctuated happenings. In mastering reality, their common aim is to banish particularized perceptions by ordering them into comprehensible and 'meaningful' regularities."[4]

When particular issues arise, individual rationality involves deciding how to move forward. As David Lake and Robert Powell put it, "[rational] actors make purposive choices . . .[;] to the best of their ability, [they] choose the strategy that best meets their subjectively defined goals."[5] To be more specific, rational individuals take account of the world in which they are operating and choose what they think is the best policy for addressing the situation at hand. In international politics, this means employing a decision-making process that is mindful of uncertainty.

In making choices, rational individuals are attentive to information. In order to decide what to do, they gather and analyze whatever information is available to them. Then, after choosing a strategy, they are prepared to change their minds if they become aware of important new facts. Brian Rathbun makes this point forcefully: "Rational thinking requires an active approach to information gathering. This process is continuous; it does not end after settling on a particular conclusion. Thus rational thinking is open-minded in nature. The rational thinker never closes himself or herself off from new evidence. Such a person is always willing to reconsider his or her beliefs, even if comfortable with previous conclusions. Rationalists call this 'updating,' the process by which incomplete information becomes more complete as more data are collected."[6]

———

Collective Rationality

When discussing collective rationality in world politics, it is important to note that it is a state's executive that is rational or nonrational, not the state itself. A leadership group, in turn, is made up of several officials — typically the head of the government plus a handful of ministers and advisers — who act collectively to formulate state policy. As Sidney Verba observes, "It is a truism that all action within the international system can be reduced to the action of individuals. It is also true, however, that international relations cannot be adequately understood in terms of individual attitudes and behaviors. Models of the international system usually deal with larger units, nation states, as prime actors."[7] Whether a state is rational thus depends on the aggregation process that translates the views of individual policymakers into a final decision.[8]

A rational aggregation process has two dimensions. First, there is a procedure for assuring systematic evaluation of the possible strategies. Given that states operate in an uncertain world, it is often not clear what the best policy is for dealing with a particular problem. The rational solution is to ensure methodical consideration of all the options. All views held by the various decision makers are presented and debated in what is effectively a marketplace of ideas among the small group in the room. Stanley Ingber makes a similar point with reference to the marketplace that is said to operate in the broader society: "This theory assumes that a process of robust debate, if uninhibited . . . will lead to the discovery of truth, or at least the best perspectives or solutions for societal problems. . . . The quality of the public exchange of ideas promoted by the marketplace advances the quality of . . . government."[9] Second, there is a procedure for choosing among the policies on the table. A state that fails

---

22

to settle on a guiding strategy is nonrational. It follows that a rational state has a mechanism for making that decision.

In sum, strategic rationality in international relations refers to both policymakers and states who recognize that they operate in an uncertain world. When faced with particular problems, rational policymakers make sense of that world and decide the best way to proceed, while rational states evaluate the strategies available to them and choose which one to adopt.

An Uncertain World

What does it mean to say that uncertainty is the defining feature of international politics? It is commonplace in the literature on rationality to describe the world that actors face as one of certainty, risk, or uncertainty.[10] In a certain world, all the information required to make a decision is known. There is no doubt about the consequences of pursuing any given strategy, even if complicated calculations and a great of deal of information are required to reach those conclusions. All the requisite information is available. Hardly anyone would argue that policymakers or states exist in such a world.

In a risk world, decision makers do not know the consequences of pursuing any given strategy, but they can acquire the information needed to calculate the odds of various outcomes. There are two ways to arrive at a probability judgment. The first is by logical deduction, or what Frank Knight calls "a priori calculation."[11] This method applies in games of chance, where the likelihood of all possible outcomes is known, even if one cannot know which outcome will occur. For example, someone rolling a fair die knows that there is a one in six chance of rolling each number but does not know what number will come up in any given roll.

The second way of arriving at a probability judgment in a risk world is by gathering available data and using statistics to evaluate it. This process, which Knight labels "the empirical method of applying statistics to actual instances," is employed in the insurance industry.[12] Insurance companies possess extensive data that allows them to calculate the likelihood of various events, from house fires to accidental deaths.

In an uncertain world, actors cannot acquire the information needed to evaluate the likely consequences of pursuing different strategies. When "knowledge" is "uncertain," observes John Maynard Keynes, "there is no scientific basis on which to form any calculable probability whatever." In addition, he notes that when uncertainty obtains, the information required to specify the costs and benefits, or what he calls "prospective advantages and disadvantages," associated with different policies is not available. Regarding these factors, "we simply do not know."[13]

The difference between worlds of risk and uncertainty — or what are called "small" and "large" worlds — cannot be overemphasized.[14] It is a distinction between situations in which information relevant for making policy is abundant and dependable, on the one hand, and scarce and unreliable, on the other. Yet many social scientists assume that there is no meaningful difference between the informational features of small and large worlds. John Kay and Mervyn King point out the prevalence of such thinking in economics: "Over the last century economists have attempted to elide that historic distinction between risk and uncertainty, and to apply probabilities to every instance of our imperfect knowledge of the future."[15] In doing so, they mistakenly conflate two fundamentally different worlds.

International relations happens in an uncertain world. Policymakers do not have access to abundant information about the

issues confronting them, and what relevant data they can acquire is not always reliable. Carl von Clausewitz makes these points with respect to war, the most extreme form of international politics. Because "all information and assumptions are open to doubt," he writes, "war is the realm of uncertainty; three quarters of the factors on which action in war is based are wrapped in a fog of greater or lesser uncertainty."[16]

Policymakers confront serious information deficits regarding most of the elements that matter for designing grand strategies or navigating crises. The farther they peer into the future, the larger these deficits become. Among other things, policymakers may not have good data about their own people's resolve or how their weaponry and combat forces will perform in a war. Additional uncertainties apply when it comes to assessing other states, friends as well as enemies. It is difficult to measure the military assets, objectives, intentions, and strategies of other states, especially since states often conceal or misrepresent their capabilities and thinking.[17] Taken together, these information deficits mean that decision makers are bound to have limited knowledge about how their states' interactions with other states are likely to play out and to what outcome. To further compound these problems, unforeseen factors sometimes shape events in significant ways.

Uncertainty at Play

Makers of foreign policy are mainly concerned with handling crises or developing grand strategies. Crisis management is a short-term enterprise that requires policymakers to address a serious dispute with another state. Among other options, they can decide to negotiate a settlement, back down, capitulate, stand fast, escalate, or go to war. For example, Europe's great powers elected to go to war during the July Crisis of 1914. Conversely, British and French leaders fashioned a settlement with Nazi Germany to end the Munich Crisis in the fall of 1938. France backed down in the Fashoda Crisis of 1898 and the Soviet Union did the same in the 1948 Berlin Crisis.

Formulating grand strategy is a long-term endeavor in which decision makers develop a "plan for making [their state] secure."[18] Famous examples of grand strategic debates include Britain's choice between retreating into splendid isolation versus accepting a continental commitment in the first half of the twentieth century and the debate in the United States during the late 1930s and early 1940s about how to deal with the great powers in Europe and Asia.

Policymakers invariably face uncertainty when handling crises or devising grand strategies. We illustrate these informational problems with two examples of grand strategic decision-making – U.S. policy toward Europe after World War II and toward East Asia after the Cold War – and two examples of crisis decision-making: Japan's thinking during its crisis with the United States in 1941 and U.S. thinking during the 1962 Cuban Missile Crisis.

American Policy toward Europe after World War II

In the five years after Germany's defeat in World War II, American policymakers had to decide the best strategy for dealing with Europe. They had to do so in the face of significant information deficits about how Europe would evolve after the devastation of the war, what policy options would be available to the United States, and the likely consequences of those policies.

Germany, which was principally responsible for starting both World War I and World War II, was destroyed, leaving a power vacuum in the heart of the continent. Yet it had the potential to rebuild itself and return to the ranks of the great powers. The Soviet Union, which had been a close ally of the United States during the war, was the dominant military power in Europe, but it had been ravaged by its conflict with Nazi Germany. Britain was badly damaged economically and burdened by the demands of empire. France confronted similar economic and imperial problems and was also in political turmoil, in part because it had a formidable Communist party. Italy was wracked by economic and political problems. There was also substantial uncertainty about the United States itself. It was not clear whether isolationism and the depression, which profoundly affected America's role in the world in the 1930s, were things of the past or harbingers of the future. Complicating matters even further, at the time Germany surrendered, in May 1945, it was impossible to know how and when the war against Japan would end.

American policymakers could not know how the situation in Europe would evolve. It was not clear to what extent Germany would recover from the war. The Allies had divided it into four occupation zones; would Germany remain divided or be reunified, and if so, when? Would it be neutral, and if not, with whom would it ally? As for the Soviet Union, no one knew whether it could make a full economic recovery and if it did, whether it would remain an ally or at least continue to have cordial relations with the United States and Western Europe. Nor was there any way to estimate the economic prospects of Britain and France, determine whether they would commit to maintaining their empires, or predict the consequences of these decisions for the politics of Europe. Moreover, the domestic political situations in both France and Italy, especially the role their powerful Communist parties would play, were shrouded in doubt.

By 1948, most American policymakers believed that the Soviet Union posed a threat to Western Europe and thus to the United States itself. Yet they still did not have enough reliable data to assess Moscow's intentions, objectives, and strategies. These unknowns in turn made it difficult to evaluate the nature of the Soviet threat and decide how best to address it. It was hard to say whether Moscow mainly represented an ideological threat to Western Europe in the form of communism or a military one in the shape of the Soviet army. The absence of such information, coupled with the substantial uncertainties about American and West European options, capabilities, and resolve, made it difficult for Washington to chart the best way forward.

Nonetheless, American policymakers had no choice but to develop a strategy for dealing with Europe, and they debated four broad options. The first of these was isolationism, in which case the United States would pull its forces out of Europe and pay little attention to the Soviet threat. A second was offshore balancing, a strategy that called for getting the states of Western Europe to balance against the Soviet Union while the United States stood over the horizon ready to help if needed. A third option was containment: American forces would remain in Europe, and Washington would take the lead in balancing against the Soviet Union. Finally, the United States could pursue an ambitious rollback strategy, which would seek to undermine Moscow's control over Eastern Europe and possibly weaken the Soviet Union itself.

The uncertainties American policymakers faced about the Soviet Union, the West Europeans, and even the United States meant that the best choice among these options was not clear. How would the Soviet Union react to each of the strategies and to what effect? Was the division of Germany sustainable or would the

Germans demand unification? If Germany remained divided, would the West Germans be reliable allies, and if it reunified, what would Germany's foreign policy look like? What could the United States expect of Britain, France, and Italy? Would the American public support a military commitment to Europe, and could the U.S. economy sustain that effort? These were just a few of the relevant questions to which there were no easy answers.

American Policy toward East Asia after the Cold War

With the end of the Cold War in 1990 and the collapse of the Soviet Union a year later, the United States became the lone great power on the planet. One of the central issues facing American policymakers was to devise a strategy for dealing with East Asia. Their task was complicated by important information deficits about the emerging politics of the region, the strategies the United States might employ, and their likely outcomes.

Russia, the Soviet Union's successor, was crippled both economically and militarily, but it had a robust nuclear arsenal and the raw ingredients to eventually regain its position as a major power – a large, skilled population and abundant natural resources. China's economy had grown impressively during the 1980s, but it was still a developing country. Although it had nuclear weapons, it was not a first-rank military power. Japan, which then had the second largest economy in the world, was the wealthiest state in the region by some distance, yet it was militarily weak and heavily dependent on the United States for its security. As for the United States, it was deeply committed to the region, maintaining a large-scale military presence there and providing nuclear deterrence for key allies, including Japan and South Korea. Washington also had deep ties with all of the leading East Asian economies.

There was great uncertainty about how the politics of East Asia would evolve. It was difficult to know whether Russia would recover and if so, how powerful it would become, both militarily and economically. It was not evident how its relationships with the United States and other countries in the region would develop. It was even harder to forecast whether China would continue its impressive economic growth and if it did, whether it would convert that newfound economic might into military might. Nor could anyone know what Beijing's political and economic goals would be and how it would interact with its neighbors and the United States. Regarding Japan, no one could say where its military and economic relations with Washington were headed. The same was true of Tokyo's historically complex relationships with other East Asian countries.

Many American policymakers believed Japan would be the main threat to U.S. interests in East Asia. By the end of the 1990s, however, it was clear that these expectations were wrong and that China was more likely to emerge as the United States' primary rival. Yet Washington's lack of dependable information about Beijing's prospects and thinking made it difficult for American policy elites to assess the contours of the China threat and formulate a response.

Faced with the need to craft a strategy, American policymakers had three options. With isolationism, the United States would ignore balance-of-power politics and withdraw its military forces from East Asia. Nevertheless, it would remain involved economically and politically with China and the rest of the region. The second option, engagement, would mean promoting Beijing's economic growth, fostering its political liberalization, and further integrating it into international institutions, with the expectation that China would become a responsible stakeholder in the American-led international order. Finally, containment called for expanding U.S.

alliances in East Asia and maintaining a robust military presence there while trying to limit China's economic growth.

Given the information deficits surrounding China, Japan, Russia, and other states in East Asia, it was hard to know which of the three strategies would be best for the United States. How would China respond to each strategy? If American forces were withdrawn from the region, would China bid for regional hegemony? How would other regional powers like Japan and Russia respond, and what would be the consequences for the United States? If the United States engaged China, would Beijing become a force for international stability, or would it become a dangerous rival? If Washington balanced against China, would that strategy restrain Beijing, or would it prompt an intense security competition that might lead to war? In either case, how would Russia and America's allies react and with what effects? There were no ready answers to these questions, making it hard to determine the most promising strategy.

Japanese Policy before Pearl Harbor

Japan, which had long been an imperial power in East Asia, began expanding its empire on the mainland in 1931, when it conquered Manchuria. In 1937, it invaded northern China. Three years later, it seized northern Indochina, and in July 1941, it occupied southern Indochina. At that point, the United States and its partners, Britain and Holland, embargoed the delivery of petroleum and petroleum products to Japan. Because Tokyo was heavily dependent on imports of those goods, the embargo threatened to strangle Japan's economy and undermine its ability to wage its ongoing war in China. Japanese policymakers concluded that if their country was to remain a great power and preserve its empire, they had to find some way to end the embargo.

They had four possible strategies for solving their oil problem. First, Japan could negotiate with the United States and reach a mutually acceptable end to the embargo. Second, it could restore the flow of oil by capitulating to whatever demands the United States might make regarding its empire. Third, Tokyo could strike southward with its military forces and seize the oil-rich Dutch East Indies. Fourth, it could pair an assault on the oilfields of Southeast Asia with an attack on the United States at Pearl Harbor.

Given the serious uncertainties surrounding each of these options, it was difficult for Japanese policymakers to choose among them. Regarding a negotiated settlement, it was not clear that the United States wanted to negotiate, much less what its demands would be. Nor could Japanese policymakers know how their American counterparts would interpret Tokyo's willingness to strike a deal and what effect the discussions would have on subsequent U.S. policy.

In the months between July and December 1941, it seemed that the United States had little interest in negotiating an end to the embargo, so Japan began to pay increasing attention to the other three options. These were all plagued by information deficits of their own. It was difficult to determine, for example, what capitulation entailed. There was evidence that the Americans wanted Japan to withdraw completely from northern China, but what demands they would have beyond that, and how these would evolve with respect to Manchuria, Korea, and Indochina, were unknown. Nor did Japan have a good sense of how capitulation would affect its economic and military power and its diplomatic position in East Asia.

Similar uncertainty surrounded the two military options. A strike into the Dutch East Indies, if successful, would break the embargo and secure the oil that Japan desperately needed to maintain

both its great power status and its empire. The danger, of course, was that the United States would view this move as a casus belli and Japan would be at war with a much more powerful adversary. The crucial question, then, was how the United States would react, and on this there was no clear answer. There were reasons to believe both that the United States would stand aside and that it would declare war.

A simultaneous attack on Pearl Harbor and the Dutch East Indies might not only break the embargo, but might also make it harder for Washington to wage war against Tokyo. If Japan destroyed the U.S. fleet and expanded its defense perimeter, the United States would face the prospect of fighting a long and bloody war across the Pacific. The great unknown was how U.S. leaders, as well as the American public, would react to such a prospect. There was little doubt that even after a major setback at Pearl Harbor, the United States would regroup and fight back. But it was not clear that Washington had the resolve to wage a protracted war in Asia given isolationist sentiments at home and the fact that its top priority was defeating Nazi Germany. Furthermore, if the Americans continued to fight, it was difficult to know whether they would inflict a limited or decisive defeat on Japan, what the costs of such a defeat would be, and what a postwar settlement might look like. There was a chance Japan could lose the war and yet retain much of its empire.

American Policy during the Cuban Missile Crisis

In October 1962, the John F. Kennedy administration learned that the Soviet Union had placed nuclear missiles in Cuba. There was unanimous agreement among key officials that this move could not be allowed to stand.

American policymakers had two strategic options. First, they could attempt to coerce the Soviets into withdrawing their missiles by drawing a line in the sand and threatening military escalation. In response, Moscow might capitulate to U.S. demands or be forced to the negotiating table, where a mutually acceptable deal could be worked out. Second, the United States could skip the negotiations and solve the problem by force. It could simply bomb the missile sites or do so in conjunction with an invasion of Cuba.

There was a great deal of uncertainty about both options. The coercive strategy would combine a naval blockade around Cuba with a threat to attack the Soviet missiles or conquer the island, moves that would raise the prospect of further escalation. It was difficult to know, however, whether this strategy would succeed or fail. Would the Soviet Union capitulate or negotiate a deal, or would it try to break the blockade, precipitating a war between the superpowers? Assuming the Soviets were prepared to negotiate, it was hard to say how the negotiations would unfold, especially since American policymakers faced political constraints at home and abroad, and Moscow's resolve and objectives were unclear. Furthermore, if a bargain were struck, it was not apparent how the settlement would affect U.S. relations with either the Soviet Union or its own allies in the future.

The military options — bomb the missile sites or invade Cuba — were also plagued by information deficits. To begin with, American policymakers did not know how the Soviets would respond. A crucial unknown was whether Moscow would retaliate by blockading Berlin or, worse, using military force there. If a conflict broke out, the Americans could not know whether the Soviets would escalate it or where that process would lead. More generally, it was hard to determine whether and how nuclear weapons would figure in an escalating crisis in either the Caribbean or Europe. Would either side threaten or even initiate nuclear use? What was the balance of resolve between Washington and Moscow in the two most likely theaters of conflict? What was the military balance? While the United States had a marked advantage at the strategic nuclear level, it was not clear whether it had a splendid first-strike capability (meaning that it could take out the entire Soviet arsenal in one fell swoop) and if it did, how that affected its options. Nor was it easy to determine whether the Soviet Union had a viable nuclear option.

Uncertainty Writ Large

It should be apparent that policymakers routinely confront serious information deficits when formulating grand strategy or managing a crisis. We should also note that the decision makers in the four cases discussed above confronted many more uncertainties beyond those described. Moreover, what might seem obvious to us today, with the benefit of hindsight, was not obvious to them at the time. They could not fully grasp the situation facing them, nor could they know where their decisions would lead.

Even in retrospect, with many additional facts at their disposal, scholars still do not agree about significant aspects of past decisions. Debates continue, for example, about Soviet objectives in the late 1940s, whether the Franklin D. Roosevelt administration was prepared to consider a mutually agreeable settlement with Japan in the fall of 1941, whether the United States had a splendid first-strike capability during the Cuban Missile Crisis, and the consequences of engaging China early in the twenty-first century.[19]

The Meaning of Strategic Rationality

Strategic rationality in international politics is all about how policy-makers and states make sense of their situation and decide the way forward in an uncertain world. The key task for us now is to specify what are good, or rational, versus bad, or nonrational, ways to do that.

Chapter 3

DEFINING STRATEGIC RATIONALITY

In the uncertain world of international politics, credible theories and deliberation provide the most appropriate means of making sense of the world and deciding how to navigate it in the pursuit of desired goals.[1] At the individual level, strategically rational policymakers are theory-driven, employing credible theories not only to understand the way the world works, but also to choose the best policy for achieving their goals. Conversely, policymakers who rely on noncredible theories, or do not use theories at all, are nonrational. At the state level, where the views of individual decision makers are aggregated, rationality also involves deliberation. Strategically rational states evaluate the views of the principal policymakers in a thoroughgoing fashion and ultimately choose a policy based on a credible theory. A nonrational state fails to deliberate, bases its strategy on either a noncredible theory or no theory, or suffers from both of these pathologies.

Credible theory runs like a red skein through our discussion of rationality. We should begin, therefore, by unpacking our understanding of theory and policy. What is a theory? What are the virtues of theoretical thinking in an uncertain world? What is the connection between theory and policy? What makes theories credible or noncredible? What are the inventories of credible and noncredible theories? And what does nontheoretical thinking look like? After addressing these questions, we define rationality at the level of both the policymaker and the state. Finally, we look at the relationship between rationality and outcomes. Strategically rational states do not always achieve their desired outcomes, but policies based on credible theories maximize their chances of surviving and thriving, which is why they rely on them.

Theory

Theories are simplified descriptions of reality that explain how some facet of the world works. They are made up of empirical claims, assumptions, and causal logics. Empirical claims in the international relations literature stipulate a robust, though not absolute, relationship between an independent and a dependent variable. A typical claim holds that independent variable A is a likely or probable cause of dependent variable B. For example, balance of threat theory claims that states regularly build up their capabilities against threatening competitors, where threat is mainly a combination of capabilities and intentions.[2] Democratic peace theory, on the other hand, maintains that democracies rarely fight wars against each other.[3]

Assumptions and the causal logics that flow from them provide explanations for empirical claims – that is, they describe how independent variables affect dependent variables. Assumptions are descriptive statements about decision makers or their environments. Most international relations theories, including balance of threat theory and democratic peace theory, implicitly or explicitly assume that states are the principal actors in world politics, that they aim to survive, and that they are rational actors. Moreover, those states are assumed to operate in an anarchic system in which there is no higher authority that sits above them.

A causal logic builds on a set of assumptions and elaborates one or more chains of causal mechanisms that connect an independent and dependent variable. A simple causal logic might take the following form: A causes B because A causes x, which causes y, which causes z, which causes B. The main causal logic underpinning balance of threat theory argues that states move to protect themselves against powerful rivals that are judged to have malign intentions because those states endanger their survival and there is no night watchman to whom they can turn for help. A prominent causal logic behind democratic peace theory maintains that elections and free speech make leaders accountable to domestic constituencies that may oppose war, which in turn means democracies are constrained from fighting each other.

The Virtues of Theory in an Uncertain World

As we have emphasized, international politics is an information-deficient world. Whether policymakers are handling crises or formulating grand strategies, they invariably have to assess situations and make decisions based on limited and flawed data. Among other things, they lack abundant and reliable information about the interests, intentions, resolve, and capabilities of other states. Nor do they know how their interactions with those states will play out. Nevertheless, they have little choice but to settle on the strategy they think is most likely to achieve their aims.

Philosophers have identified two typical ways in which actors can use their critical faculties to acquire knowledge about the world around them. The first is logical deduction. In order to address a situation, individuals make assumptions – known as premises – from which they then deduce conclusions. "A tool with such power," writes Steven Pinker, "allows us to discover new truths about the world . . . and to resolve disputes about the many things people don't agree on."[4] The second form of reasoning is empirical. In this case, individuals discover solutions to issues by examining the relevant evidence in an objective manner. According to Brian Rathbun, this inductive approach privileges "data-driven analysis" and yields "an accurate understanding of the world."[5]

Each approach, in its pure form, has only limited utility for understanding the workings of world politics and informing decisions on how best to pursue particular goals. Pure logic merely ensures that if the premises policymakers make about international relations are true, then the conclusions are also true. It says nothing, however, about whether those premises are true, a determination that can be made only by assessing the empirical record. Pure empiricism is equally untenable. Since the evidence policymakers can glean about the workings of the international system is often complex, ambiguous, contradictory, unavailable, messy, or all of the above, no amount of objectivity can reveal the truth. "Pure empiricism is impossible," writes Robert Jervis. "Facts do not speak for themselves. It is not wise – indeed it is not possible – to . . . 'sit down before fact[s] as a mere child.'"[6]

Thinking theoretically is the best, though by no means perfect, way to deal with the uncertain world of international politics. Simply put, it combines the strengths of the purely logical and empirical approaches while avoiding their weaknesses. Theorizing is all about developing logically consistent explanations that are based on empirically verified assumptions and tested against the facts.[7] As the

Prussian strategist Carl von Clausewitz, who was acutely aware of the uncertain nature of international politics, put it: "Theory cannot equip the mind with formulas for solving problems, nor can it mark the narrow path on which the sole solution is supposed to lie by planting a hedge of principles on either side. But it can give the mind insight into the great mass of phenomena and of their relationships, then leave it free to rise into the higher realms of action."[8]

Theory and Policy

One might think that theory has little relevance for policy and is an enterprise properly confined to academia. Former U.S. policymaker Robert Zoellick, for example, maintains that "American diplomacy has focused on achieving results in particular matters, not on applying theories."[9] That view is wrong. Virtually all policymakers depend on theories to formulate grand strategies and navigate crises. Some realize it, and some do not; some admit it, and some do not; some do so explicitly, and some do not. But there is little doubt that they use theories as they go about their business.

Former U.S. State Department official Roger Hilsman highlights the importance of theory to national security policymakers: "It seems obvious that all thinking involves notions of how and why things happen. Even the 'practical' man who despises theory has a number of assumptions and expectations which lead him to believe that when certain things are done, certain results follow. . . . It is this 'theory' that helps a problem solver select from the mass of facts surrounding him those which he hopes are relevant."[10] In a detailed analysis of the link between the academy and the policy world, Michael Desch makes a similar point, noting that policymakers "use theory in analyzing situations and assessing their alternatives. . . . They depend on the academy for the raw data—whether quantitative or historical — that they use in decision making. They also rely on the social sciences for the theories they use to analyze and make sense of this data."[11]

This line of argument about the relationship between theory and policy has deep roots in the economic world, which is sometimes described as a realm of "radical uncertainty."[12] Hilsman, in fact, was paraphrasing John Maynard Keynes's famous comment that "the ideas of economists and political philosophers, both when they are right and when they are wrong, are more powerful than is commonly understood. Indeed the world is ruled by little else. Practical men, who believe themselves to be quite exempt from any intellectual influences, are usually the slaves of some defunct economist. Madmen in authority, who hear voices in the air, are distilling their frenzy from some academic scribbler of a few years back."[13]

Examples are not hard to find. Binyamin Appelbaum writes in *The Economists' Hour,* an account of the relationship between economic theories and American economic policy between 1969 and 2008, that Richard Nixon "was not well versed in economics but, like most Americans of his generation, his basic frame of reference was Keynesianism. He believed the government faced a choice between inflation and unemployment, and he knew what he wanted to order from the menu." Ronald Reagan, by contrast, was heavily influenced by Milton Friedman's monetarist theories, going so far as to write a leading journalist that he could not embrace a policy proposal that "one of my favorite people Milton F. opposed." More generally, Appelbaum makes it clear that the evolution of American economic policy over the decades he covers was influenced at every turn by competing theories.[14]

Much like its economic policy, America's foreign policy since the Cold War has relied on the same theories that populate academia. The United States adopted a policy of liberal hegemony after the superpower competition ended and the world became unipolar. That policy was based on the "big three" liberal theories of international relations: liberal institutionalism, economic interdependence theory, and democratic peace theory. Its aim was to expand membership in the international institutions that were created in the West during the Cold War, foster an open world economy, and spread democracy around the globe, all in the belief that such measures would create a safer and more prosperous world. The main critics of liberal hegemony were informed by realism, and policy debates between the two sides were often conducted in the language of those rival theoretical traditions.

Take NATO expansion, one of the major policy issues of the 1990s. Deputy Secretary of State Strobe Talbott, a key proponent of moving the alliance eastward, argued that the "enlargement of NATO would be a force for the rule of law both within Europe's new democracies and among them." Moreover, it would "promote and consolidate democratic and freemarket values," further contributing to peace.[15] But George Kennan, the architect of the post–World War II policy of containment, opposed expansion on realist grounds: "I think it is the beginning of a new cold war. I think the Russians will gradually react quite adversely and it will affect their policies. I think it is a tragic mistake. There was no reason for this whatsoever. No one was threatening anybody else."[16] In short, policymaking is a theoretical enterprise at its core, although many do not see it that way.

Policymakers' reliance on theories is unsurprising, as it is the only viable way they can do business. The essence of policymaking is determining the consequences of different strategies. Decision makers operate in a world where "if, then" logic is constantly at play. As Robert Dahl notes: "To be concerned with policy is to focus on the attempt to produce intended effects. Hence policy-thinking is and must be causality-thinking."[17] Moreover, as noted, their world is information-deficient, which means they never have all the relevant facts at their disposal. They need to figure out cause and effect from limited information, which is what theory does.

Credible Theories

What makes a theory credible? For starters, we should emphasize that although theories are powerful instruments for making sense of and deciding how to act in the world, there are limits to the explanatory power of even the best international relations theories. For any theory, there will always be cases that contradict its main claims. No theory can explain every relevant case. The reason for these anomalies is straightforward: theories simplify an enormously complicated reality by omitting certain factors that are judged to be less important for explaining a particular phenomenon while privileging other factors that are thought to be more important. Economic interdependence theory, for example, assumes that concerns about prosperity are crucial for explaining the outbreak of war while concerns about the balance of power are less significant. Meanwhile, structural realist theories ignore individual leaders and domestic politics in explaining security competition among the great powers. It is this simplicity that makes theories such useful guides for policymakers — but simplification has its costs. When the factors a theory omits actually matter greatly in a given situation, that theory will explain little.

The credibility of a theory rests on an evaluation of its assumptions, causal logics, and empirical claims. There is a debate about whether a credible theory has to rest on realistic assumptions.[18] Some scholars argue that assumptions need not reflect reality; what matters is whether a theory based on a particular set of assumptions makes claims that are supported by the empirical record. Friedman went so far as to maintain that the best theories "will be found to have 'assumptions' that are wildly inaccurate descriptive representations of reality, and, in general, the more significant the theory, the more unrealistic the assumptions."[19] This assertion is implausible: a theory whose starting assumptions are descriptively false is unlikely to offer a good explanation of how the world works. As Ronald Coase wrote in response to Friedman's claim, "Realism in our assumptions is needed if our theories are ever to help us understand why the system works in the way it does. Realism in assumptions forces us to analyze the world that exists, not some imaginary world that does not."[20]

A credible theory must not only rest on realistic assumptions, but it must also derive a logically consistent causal story from them.[21] The theory must elaborate one or more causal mechanisms that explain how the independent variable exerts an effect on the dependent variable. A compelling causal logic is essential if the theory is to offer an accurate understanding of key aspects of international politics. The claim is sometimes made that the best way to deduce such logics is to employ formal models because mathematization ensures "superior clarity and consistency."[22] There is no question that formalization can help facilitate logical consistency, but it is neither necessary nor sufficient. One can achieve a sound logic without mathematics, and mathematization is not a foolproof method for producing clarity and consistency.[23]

None of this is to deny that all causal logics have gaps and inconsistencies. Kenneth Waltz, for example, argues in *Theory of International Politics* that the two leading powers in a bipolar world will compete hard in the periphery. Yet he also contends that peripheral areas have little strategic value, which raises the question: why would great powers compete there at all?[24] Or take liberal institutionalism, which says that international institutions are a force for peace because they solve the cheating problem between states, which is a serious obstacle to cooperation. Yet that theory largely ignores relative gains — the fact that others may benefit disproportionately from cooperating — which is the other major impediment to international cooperation.[25] Still, these logical flaws are marginal. It would be wrong to condemn these two theories as noncredible. Such a verdict only applies to theories whose causal logics are plagued by serious oversights or contradictions.

Finally, to be credible, a theory must receive evidentiary support. There must be substantial evidence on which to judge the theory, and proponents of the theory must make a plausible case that the preponderance of the evidence supports it. After all, a theory that does not mesh with actual cases cannot explain events in the real world. Maurice Allais made the point well in accepting the Nobel Prize in economics: "Mere logical, even mathematical[,] deduction remains worthless in terms of an understanding of reality if it is not closely linked to that reality. . . . Any theory whatever, if it is not verified by empirical evidence, has no scientific value and should be rejected."[26] Evidentiary support takes two forms: evidence for the theory's empirical claims about the relationship between the independent and dependent variables and evidence that the assumptions and mechanisms that comprise the theory's causal logic capture what is actually going on.

Determining whether a particular theory has sufficient evidentiary backing to qualify as credible is a challenging task because even in the best-documented cases, the relevant evidence is scanty and unreliable. Take World War I, which looms large in many theories of war and peace. Some realists maintain that Germany's decision to start that war was a deliberate attempt to gain hegemony in Europe. Other realists argue that World War I was a preventive war initiated by Germany to thwart Russia's rise. Still other realists maintain that Berlin's decision is best explained by domestic political considerations since it made no sense for Germany to attempt to dominate Europe. And even among this last set of scholars, there is disagreement about which domestic factors caused Germany to go to war.[27]

Consider too the debate between realists and liberal international relations theorists on what World War I says about democratic peace theory. Liberal proponents of the democratic peace claim that the composition of the rival alliances in the Great War is consistent with their theory because it involved illiberal Germany fighting against four liberal great powers — Britain, France, Italy, and the United States. A number of realist scholars, however, argue that Germany was also a liberal democracy; thus liberal democracies fought against each other, contradicting democratic peace theory.[28]

These evidentiary issues explain why international relations scholarship is populated by multiple credible theories, not a single theory that dominates all others.[29] As Paul Krugman notes, "In the social sciences, it is much harder to [distinguish] . . . between serious ideas and pseudoscience. . . . Partly this is because one cannot perform controlled experiments: evidence in social science is always historical evidence, and history is complicated enough that its lessons are seldom unambiguous."[30] We should thus require a modest evidentiary benchmark in determining whether a theory crosses the credibility threshold. There should be substantial evidence — ideally generated by statistical or process-tracing techniques applied to the historical record — corroborating the theory's empirical claims as well as its assumptions and causal logic.[31]

—

There is another reason why there are multiple credible theories of international politics. Because they are probabilistic statements, it is difficult to dismiss them when they are contradicted in particular cases. Jonathan Kirshner puts the point well: "If a theory suggests that a certain outcome has a 70 percent chance of occurring, it means the theory holds that that outcome will not happen 30 percent of the time. So when a failure is observed, is it the result of a flawed model or bad luck? Either is possible; it is very difficult to determine which occurred with very small heterogeneous samples. As a result, competing theories are not easily selected out."[32]

There is an exception to the foregoing discussion. Some theories address international phenomena that have never happened, so there is no evidence against which to test them. For example, substantial bodies of theory deal with nuclear escalation and nuclear war fighting, but save for the two atomic bombs dropped on Japan at the end of World War II, nuclear weapons have never been employed in wartime. Nor has there been a large-scale conventional war between two nuclear-armed states that might have escalated to the nuclear level.[33] There was also, early in the nuclear age, little evidence on which to assess theories of nuclear coercion and nuclear deterrence, although that situation changed over time. And there was limited evidence with which to examine theories of unipolarity at the start of the unipolar moment in 1991. In such instances, judgments about a theory's credibility rest largely on whether its assumptions are realistic and its causal logic is sound.

An Inventory of Credible Theories

Policymakers appraise their situations and formulate their strategies using two sets of credible international relations theories: realism and liberalism.[34] These bodies of theory originate in academia, where they have long dominated the discourse, and find their way into the minds of aspiring decision makers before those individuals begin to make policy. How they come by their guiding theories varies. Some study the relevant literature. Others are exposed to various ideas simply because it is impossible for anyone interested in international politics to avoid such exposure. Regardless of the acquisition process, however, international relations theories effectively become policymakers' theories.

The realist and liberal traditions each include a number of different theories.[35] What makes it possible to identify two broad traditions is that the theories that fall under each heading are based on certain common premises. This overlap does not mean that theories in the same family share identical core assumptions. They can also have different causal logics, either because they differ on an assumption or because they make different deductions. This, in turn, means that theories in the same tradition sometimes make different empirical claims.

Realist theories share the premise that the architecture of the international system is the main driver of state behavior. "Realism," Kevin Narizny notes, "is a top-down paradigm. Every realist theory must start with a specification of systemic imperatives; only then can it address other factors."[36] States, the principal actors in international politics, seek survival above all else in a dangerous world that lacks a central authority able to settle disputes among them and protect them from each other. This situation forces them to pay serious attention to the balance of power. After all, how much power they have, relative to their rivals, largely determines their ability to protect themselves and to pursue other interests.[37]

These crucial similarities notwithstanding, there are a variety of realist theories of international politics.[38] Defensive realists claim that the structure of the system incentivizes states to compete for power but limits that competition in important ways. They employ two lines of argument. The first holds that war rarely pays because it is typically easier to defend than to attack and because potential victims have powerful incentives to balance together against a state that threatens them. Still, defensive realists recognize that states sometimes behave aggressively, launching major wars to increase their power or even dominate the system. This kind of behavior, they argue, is usually a consequence of factors such as miscalculation, the prevailing political order, civil-military relations, and organizational politics.[39]

The second defensive realist line of argument is that states satisfied with the status quo can sometimes communicate that fact to each other and greatly reduce the intensity of their competition. When status quo powers cannot signal each other, however, they continue competing for power as usual. The same is true if one or more states want to revise the status quo.[40]

Offensive realism posits that the international system pushes states to compete more intensely than defensive realism suggests because aggression sometimes pays and states cannot divine each other's interests and intentions. The knowledge that other states might have the capability and desire to hurt or even destroy them leads states to want as much power as possible. States are always on the lookout for opportunities to shift the balance of power in their favor—through arms buildups, alliances, or war—with hegemony as their ultimate goal.[41]

Hegemonic realism also says that states aim to dominate the system and may go to war to reach or remain in that position. It differs from offensive realism, however, on the question of why a state wants to be the hegemon. It says that states seek unrivaled power

DEFINING STRATEGIC RATIONALITY

not only to ensure their security, but also to pursue more ambitious goals: to shape the world in ways that maximize their political, economic, ideological, and other interests.[42]

Because realists pay much attention to the role of military power in international politics, they have developed a number of theories dealing specifically with deterrence, coercion, and the use of force, at both the conventional and nuclear levels.

Regarding the success or failure of conventional deterrence, different theories highlight the importance of factors such as the balance of forces, clever strategies, and the offense-defense balance.[43] In the nuclear realm, the debate centers around mutual assured destruction (MAD). Some theorists maintain that MAD is inescapable and provides abundant deterrence for all states that have a secure second-strike capability, whereas other theorists argue that a state may develop counterforce war-fighting capabilities that allow it to break out of a MAD world and fight and win a nuclear war.[44]

As for coercion, there are several schools of thought about the best strategy for changing an adversary's behavior in peacetime. Theories of conventional coercion emphasize diplomacy combined with threats of force against an adversary's regime or military assets.[45] Theories of nuclear coercion revolve around the threatened use of nuclear weapons against another state's population centers, economic infrastructure, or military forces.[46]

The actual use of force may take a variety of forms. At the conventional level, it can involve a ground assault, a naval blockade, an amphibious landing, or air strikes, among other actions. In more extreme cases, it can include major land, sea, and air campaigns. This diversity means there are many possible theories of victory. What experts agree on, however, is the importance of having a strategy that offers a reasonable chance of success, along with the forces needed to execute that strategy.[47] Regarding nuclear war, theorists identify three paths to victory: states can eliminate the other side's nuclear arsenal with a splendid first strike; they can engage in counterforce exchanges, retaining the upper hand as they go up the escalation ladder; or they can use nuclear weapons in a limited fashion so as to force an adversary to reverse course for fear of further escalation and possible devastation.[48]

Liberal theories posit that state interests are the main driver of state behavior. In doing so, they take the opposite position from the realist contention that the system is the motivating force of international politics. Liberalism, Narizny writes, "'rests on a 'bottom-up' view of politics in which the demands of individuals and societal groups are treated as analytically prior to politics.' Every liberal theory must start with a specification of societal actors and their preferences; only then can it address other factors."[49] While liberals recognize that the international system constrains states, they maintain that interests weigh more heavily in the decision-making process.[50] This emphasis on interests such as peace and prosperity has important consequences. Liberals argue that the pursuit of those interests can engender significant cooperation among states, a perspective that contrasts with the realist emphasis on interstate competition.

The liberal tradition revolves around three sets of theories. Democratic peace theory comes in normative and institutional variants. The normative argument holds that democracies share common interests and values and therefore trust and respect each other. The institutional argument says that elected governments are accountable to various domestic constituencies that oppose war — including the general public and different interest groups — and therefore have an interest in peace. These differences aside, both

---

variants explain why democracies rarely fight each other.[51] Economic interdependence theories are predicated on the belief that states are profoundly concerned about their prosperity. Although these theories differ in some ways, they all agree that this interest in prosperity incentivizes states not only to cooperate, but also to avoid security competition and war.[52] Liberal institutionalism focuses on rules of behavior, established by states, that stipulate how they should interact with each other. Because following those rules is in their best interests, states are strongly inclined to obey them, which is to say cooperate with each other.[53]

Although the "big three" theories dominate the liberal tradition, other theories also focus on interests as the key drivers of state behavior. These additional liberal theories emphasize the domestic features of states — including their political systems, cultures, and ideologies — that define their interests in important ways. When states share common interests, they are likely to cooperate with each other. According to one well-known set of theories, states want their ideologies to spread across the globe and therefore cooperate with other states that share their legitimating principles.[54] Another set of liberal theories holds that some cultures promote peaceful interests. For example, some argue that Confucian states are interested in promoting justice and harmony and are therefore powerfully inclined to behave peacefully.[55]

Beyond realism and liberalism, the two bodies of thought on which policymakers generally rely to understand the world and decide how best to navigate it, there is another body of academic theories — social constructivism — that sheds light on the way international politics works.[56] There are two threads that tie the different theories in this tradition together. First, social constructivists argue that ideational rather than material factors are the key drivers of state behavior. Second, those factors — especially ideas and identities — are created and recreated through social interaction. Several of these theories are credible. Moreover, policymakers sometimes use them to aid their thinking about international politics. Yet these theories seldom appear to guide their grand strategic or crisis decision-making.

Although this inventory is large, this is not a consequence of setting a low bar for determining what counts as a credible theory. After all, each of the theories listed is a logical explanation derived from realistic assumptions and backed by substantial empirical evidence. They have cleared a high bar. Moreover, students of international politics have fiercely debated the merits and demerits of liberal and realist theories for centuries, and it is reasonable to think that the noncredible theories among them would have been weeded out by now. Finally, there are many perspectives on international relations that do not clear the credibility bar, including noncredible theories and nontheoretical ideas such as analogies and heuristics.

Noncredible Theories

A theory is noncredible if it commits one or more of the following errors. First, it rests on unrealistic assumptions. To be clear, these assumptions need not capture reality perfectly since they are simplifications of some aspect of international politics, but for a theory to be credible, the assumptions must be at least reasonably accurate. Second, a theory is noncredible if its causal story is logically inconsistent. As we have noted, minor issues are hardly fatal: theories always have some gaps, contradictions, and ambiguities. But a theory that contains a serious contradiction in its causal logic is noncredible. Third, theories are noncredible if there is little evidentiary support for their causal logics, overarching claims, or both.

———

Determining whether the pieces of a causal logic fit together in a cogent fashion is a straightforward matter that leaves little room for disagreement. Theories with significant logical inconsistencies are thus likely to be weeded out before they achieve prominence in either academic or policy circles. Judgments about the empirical truth of a theory's assumptions, causal logics, and overarching claims are a different matter. Given the scanty and unreliable nature of historical evidence, there is substantial room for disagreement on these issues. That said, some theories embraced by scholars and policymakers rest on clearly unrealistic assumptions or find little evidentiary support for their causal logics or overarching claims. They are therefore noncredible.

An Inventory of Noncredible Theories

A handful of noncredible theories rely on unrealistic assumptions. For example, the clash of civilizations thesis rests on the premise that civilizations are the highest-level social groups of real significance for people around the world. Conflicts thus occur along civilizational lines, either between states in different civilizations or within states where large fractions of the population belong to rival civilizations.[57] The fact is, however, that nations, not civilizations, are the largest social groups that command intense loyalty. Nationalism, not civilizationism — whatever that may be — is the most powerful political ideology on the planet. It is therefore not surprising that the empirical record provides little support for the claim that conflicts in the modern world are largely driven by civilizational differences.[58]

Racial theories, accepted by many international relations scholars in the 1930s, were based on the assumption that there is a biologically rooted racial hierarchy among peoples and nations.

These noncredible theories maintained that white people are naturally superior to people of color, whom the theorists described as "savage peoples," members of a "child race," or of "inferior stock." Although the assumptions behind "scientific racism" had already been repudiated, political scientists continued to use it to account for colonial empires; in essence, racial superiority was said to lead to political superiority. This false and racist premise was also the basis for determining how to administer colonies and for justifying colonialism as a noble enterprise.[59]

Neoclassical realism as described by Norrin Ripsman, Jeffrey Taliaferro, and Steven Lobell is another noncredible theory, though in this case it is so because there is a serious contradiction at the heart of its causal logic. On the one hand, Ripsman, Taliaferro, and Lobell maintain that for states "survival is the most important national interest in an anarchic realm." On the other hand, they also argue that political considerations can push states to satisfy the interests of domestic groups "at the expense of international ones" and pursue strategies that "jeopardize [their] primary security interests."[60] In other words, the theory holds that survival is and is not the primary goal of states at the same time. As Narizny points out, this makes it "a jumble of contradictions."[61]

Other theories are noncredible because their causal stories or overarching claims lack evidentiary support. Democratization and war theory maintains that elites in emerging democracies with weak political institutions have both the incentive and opportunity to gin up nationalist fervor, which in turn makes their states likely to start wars.[62] Yet a comprehensive review of the evidence finds that "there are no instances of an incomplete democratizer with weak institutions participating in, let alone initiating, an external war since World War I." In the century before 1914, there are six cases of emerging democracies with weak political institutions participating in external wars, but the incomplete democratizer initiated only one of them. Even in that one case – the 1879 War of the Pacific, waged by Chile against Bolivia and Peru – there are reasons to doubt that Chile was an unstable regime. All of this means that "there has not been a single instance of an incomplete democratizer with weak institutions initiating war between 1816 and 1992."[63]

Audience costs theory holds that democratically elected leaders – unlike their nondemocratic counterparts – are especially good at signaling their resolve in crises because they can make public commitments to act in particular circumstances, on which they are then obliged to follow through.[64] A number of studies have shown, however, that there is hardly any evidence that the causal logic underpinning audience costs theory works as advertised. As one scholar concludes, "The basic finding is quite simple. There is little evidence that the audience costs mechanism played a 'crucial' role in any [crisis]. Indeed, it is hard to identify any case in which that mechanism played much of a role at all."[65] Another analysis, which focuses on "the easiest cases for audience costs theory," nevertheless turned up "so little evidence of audience costs mechanisms . . . that the significance of the theory needs to be reassessed."[66] In short, audience costs theory is noncredible.

Forcible democracy promotion theory posits that a state can use military force to topple a nondemocratic leader and transform the target state into a democracy.[67] The argument is that since publics around the world yearn for democracy and only tyrants stand in their way, a democracy can use its military to do large-scale social engineering in another country. But there is hardly any evidence that this strategy ever succeeds – although this is not to deny that states can promote democracy abroad in nonmilitary ways. Several studies

DEFINING STRATEGIC RATIONALITY

note that the United States, which has frequently tried to impose democracy abroad, has routinely failed in these efforts. A major analysis notes that between World War II and 2004, "the United States intervened more than 35 times in developing countries around the world. . . . In only one case — Colombia after the American decision in 1989 to engage in the war on drugs — did a full-fledged, stable democracy . . . emerge within 10 years. That's a success rate of less than 3%."[68] This dismal record continues into the present, showing that forcible democracy promotion theory is noncredible.

Nuclear coercion theory says that a state with nuclear weapons can use them to threaten a non-nuclear state — or even a nuclear-armed state with a small arsenal — and force its outgunned rival to change its behavior.[69] In the early years of the Cold War, it was reasonable to think that nuclear coercion might work as advertised. As the theory was tested empirically, however, a scholarly consensus developed that it was noncredible. The most comprehensive study of the issue identifies nineteen cases in which one could plausibly argue that nuclear-armed states tried to coerce their rivals, and the only case that might be considered a success is the Cuban Missile Crisis of 1962. Even there, however, it is hard to make a persuasive case that the United States used nuclear threats to coerce the Soviet Union, let alone that it did so successfully.[70]

Finally, bandwagoning theory maintains that states facing a powerful and threatening rival typically align with that state rather than balance against it, either because they hope to appease the threat and avoid an attack or because they want to share in the spoils of victory when that state goes on the offensive.[71] Perhaps the most famous variant of this argument is the domino theory, first articulated publicly by President Dwight Eisenhower in 1954 to justify

American efforts to prevent a Communist takeover of South Vietnam. According to the theory, if one country fell to communism, its neighbors would quickly follow suit, and soon most of the world would be engulfed by communism. Domino theory was credible in the 1950s and early 1960s, when the United States seriously escalated its commitment to defending South Vietnam, because at the time there was little evidence on which to judge it. Over time, however, evidence accumulated against domino theory and against bandwagoning theory more generally; by the mid-1980s, it was apparent that both theories were noncredible.[72]

The case of domino theory shows that theoretical credibility is historically contingent. The march of real world events can markedly change the evidentiary base, rendering credible theories noncredible and vice versa. As the physicist Steven Weinberg reminds us, "the Hellenistic astronomers Apollonius and Hipparchus developed the theory that the planets go around the Earth on looping epicyclic orbits by using only the data that had been available to them."[73] Their theory — credible when it was first developed — was later rendered noncredible as new evidence became available.

Nontheoretical Thinking

Although policymakers are theoretical animals, they sometimes formulate grand strategies or manage crises based on nontheoretical thinking. In such cases, they act on the basis of either data-driven or emotion-driven thinking.

Data-driven thinking includes the use of either expected utility maximization or analogies and heuristics. Expected utility maximizers survey the empirical record to establish the probabilities of various phenomena — to include the likelihood that another actor is benign or malign and the chances that certain events will occur — and they then plug their findings into a formula that tells them what course of action to choose in order to maximize their utility. Analogical thinkers also observe the historical record, but instead of examining many cases, they focus on a small number of past events and assume that if they resemble a contemporary one, then the earlier events prescribe the appropriate course of action in the present. Policymakers who employ heuristics think in a similar fashion, drawing selectively on the past—for example, focusing on events that come to mind easily or that are judged to be similar to the current situation—to inform their decisions.

Philosophers and psychologists observe that there is no agreed-upon definition of emotions and that emotions are an amorphous concept.[74] Our definition, which is broadly consistent with much of the literature, is that an emotion is a feeling that represents an unconscious response to a given situation. Scholars frequently identify the emotions of fear, anger, anxiety, hope, pride, and humiliation. These feelings are, in turn, triggered by stimuli that are biologically or culturally driven.[75] All of this is to say that emotional thinking is nontheoretical thinking as it does not entail a conscious and proactive effort to understand the world.

Although emotions are nontheoretical, the neuroscientist Antonio Damasio argues that they are essential to rational thought.[76] This view is now broadly accepted among scholars, including students of international politics.[77] As Janice Gross Stein writes in a review of the relevant research, "What we have learned in the last two decades is that without emotion, there is no rationality."[78] Likewise, Dominic Johnson notes: "Considerable evidence now shows that rational decision-making actually *requires* emotion to function properly. . . . Specific emotions may even improve decision-making processes."[79]

In a detailed analysis of the role that emotions play in coercive diplomacy, Robin Markwica lends support to Damasio's view that emotions typically work hand-in-hand with reason. His examination of the thinking of Soviet premier Nikita Khrushchev during the Cuban Missile Crisis and Iraqi leader Saddam Hussein during the 1990–91 Gulf War suggests that emotions did not hinder their reasoning but complemented it. Khrushchev's and Saddam's emotions, Markwica writes, "shaped" and "influenced" their thought processes. More generally, "The term emotional choice theory and the way I contrast this action model with the rational choice paradigm may create the impression that I cast emotion in opposition to rationality. This is certainly not the case. I do not see feeling and thinking as separate or antithetical processes."[80]

Nevertheless, there are times when decision makers are driven mainly by emotions rather than theories. Stein and Richard Ned Lebow argue that in some circumstances policymakers can become "emotionally upset," which causes them to "avoid, dismiss, and deny warnings that increase anxiety and fear" and leads to misguided decisions.[81] Similarly, Philip Tetlock writes that during crises "the ebb and flow of human emotions" can interfere with "dispassionate calculations" and that the attendant stress "impairs complex information processing." Emotional thinking, he adds, is "not cold, rational, and calculating, but . . . self-righteous, moralistic, and simplistic," causing policymakers to pursue risky strategies.[82] Meanwhile, Rathbun claims that "our emotions often get the better of our deliberative functions."[83] Jonathan Mercer sums up the basic point: emotion "can undermine rationality even while it is necessary to rationality."[84]

Yet these instances of emotions driving the train are rare. Scholars who argue that policymakers are sometimes strongly

influenced by their emotions point to only a few cases to substanti-
ate their claim, and even these examples do not support the notion
that leaders are vulnerable to emotional thinking. Consider
Tsar Nicholas II of Russia, who is said to have been "paralyzed
by indecision" during the July Crisis leading up to World War I
and thus failed to respond forcefully to Austria's provocative
actions against Serbia.[85] It is hard to square this story with the facts.
There is scant evidence in the scholarly literature that Nicholas was
paralyzed by stress on the eve of the Great War. To be sure, he
wanted to avoid what he thought would be a devastating conflict,
but he authorized general mobilization as soon as it was clear
that Germany was bent on war and might secure an advantage by
moving first.[86]

There are also cases where policymakers under extreme pressure are overwhelmed by their emotions and robbed of their critical
faculties. For example, General Helmuth von Moltke, the chief of
the German General Staff at the start of World War I, suffered a ner-
vous breakdown shortly after Germany launched the Schlieffen Plan
in August 1914.[87] It also appears that Soviet leader Josef Stalin became profoundly depressed and withdrawn in the days immediately
after Germany invaded the Soviet Union in June 1941.[88] General
Yitzhak Rabin, the chief of staff of the Israel Defense Forces, was
similarly overcome by his emotions in June 1967 just before the
start of the Six Day War.[89]

In these cases, however, other decision makers quickly moved
to ensure that their emotionally overwhelmed colleagues did not de-
rail the policy process. Stalin's temporary incapacitation led his key
subordinates—Vyacheslav Molotov, Lavrentiy Beria, Georgy
Malenkov, and Kliment Voroshilov—to create the State Defense
Committee, a supreme authority for overseeing the Soviet war

effort. Moltke was dismissed, and Rabin was removed from the chain of command until he recovered.

The imperative of preventing overwrought leaders from influencing the decision-making process is so powerful that other policymakers sometimes move preemptively to sideline them. In the summer of 1974, when President Richard Nixon was under tremendous pressure from the Watergate investigations, some of his advisers feared he might have an emotional breakdown. Secretary of Defense James Schlesinger took measures to ensure that Nixon could not circumvent the chain of command and initiate a nonrational policy.[90] Decades later, General Mark Milley, the chairman of the Joint Chiefs of Staff, feared that President Donald Trump might be emotionally overwhelmed by his defeat in the November 2020 presidential election. He coordinated with other administration officials and his Chinese counterparts to minimize the chances that Trump would start a war between the United States and China.[91]

Individual Rationality

What, then, does it mean for policymakers to be rational? Rational policymakers are *homo theoreticus:* they employ credible theories to make sense of the world and decide how to act in particular circumstances. Nonrational policymakers employ noncredible theories, or no theory at all, to deal with the situations facing them.

It is rational to rely on credible theories to understand how international politics works because they are the most appropriate, though by no means perfect, instruments for that task. They identify the factors that matter most for shaping the world, as well as the causes and effects of various international political phenomena. And they do so in a logically consistent and empirically supported fashion that maximizes the chances that policymakers will make accurate assessments of how events are likely to unfold. For these reasons, leaders are strongly wedded to their preferred theories and consider them superior to competing theories, whether credible or noncredible.

It is also rational to rely on credible theories to make decisions about what is the best strategy when a problem arises. Because such theories are all about identifying the probable consequences of different strategies, they not only help policymakers make sense of the world, but they also help them decide how to move forward.

There is a crucial informational dimension to individual decision-making. Policymakers invariably confront an abundant and ever-changing set of facts and must figure out which matter most, both as they decide what needs to be done and after they have made their initial decision. The rational way to sort through these facts is to rely on credible theories since they are powerful tools for identifying which facts to focus on and deciding what they mean within the overall situation. Policymakers whose theories cause them to ignore contradictory facts or distort the facts of a case are of course nonrational, even if those theories are credible. But as long as they do not employ theories in this way, they are rational.

State Rationality

Enough said about individual rationality. In world politics, it is not single policymakers but states — groups of policymakers — that design grand strategies and try to manage crises. All those involved in the decision-making process will of course have their own preferred theories and will advocate the policies that follow from them. The theories that decision makers bring to the table may not all be the same and may not all be credible. The key issue, however, is not what particular individuals think but how the state aggregates their views and what policy it ultimately adopts.

A state's policy is rational if it is based on a credible theory or some combination of credible theories and is the product of a deliberative process. Policies that do not rest on credible theories or are not the products of a deliberative process are not rational.

Deliberation is a two-step aggregation process involving robust and uninhibited debate among key decision makers, followed by a final policy choice by an ultimate decider. Discussion alone is not enough to yield a rational collective decision. Policymakers must exchange their views and compare their merits in a vigorous and unconstrained fashion. They can have strong opinions, of course, but they must be willing to listen to their colleagues and weigh the strengths and weaknesses of the options before them. At the same time, they cannot conceal or lie about relevant information or shut down debate by threatening or coercing their colleagues.

While robust and uninhibited debate is a necessary feature of state rationality, it is not sufficient. A rational state must also choose a guiding policy. This means there are three paths to a rational strategy. First, most or all of the relevant policymakers—including the ultimate decider—come into the room with the same credible theory in mind, and once they have discussed the situation at hand, they have little difficulty reaching a consensus on the appropriate strategy.

Second, the principal decision makers start with different theories and engage in a robust and uninhibited debate, after which they settle on a guiding policy based on a credible theory or theories. In effect, the discussion shifts the balance of power among the competing options, resulting in victory for a particular theory or theories. There are two ways the balance of power within the decision-making group can shift. Most obviously, the proponents of one policy can persuade their opponents to change their minds. Alternatively, new information may emerge that brings the two sides into agreement on the best policy. In either case, the ultimate decider, who has participated in the debate, ratifies the agreement, and it becomes policy.

Third, the policymakers in the room engage in a vigorous and unconstrained debate but fail to agree on a strategy, in which case the ultimate decider determines the way forward. Deadlock is not unusual. Individual decision makers are often firmly wedded to their theories, and there is little agreement in academic and policy circles about how to rank credible theories. Moreover, although new information invariably comes to light when policy issues are being debated, such information is rarely dispositive. Yet a decision has to be made. This responsibility falls to the ultimate decider, who has to adjudicate the debate rather than ratify a consensus or agreement.

One might conclude that this third path is nondeliberative and therefore nonrational, but that would be wrong. For one thing, there is no shortage of debate about the merits of competing credible theories. And there is a clear mechanism for making a decision, which must be made if the process is to be rational. Indeed, the necessity of decision is one of the key reasons why states are organized in hierarchies.

Process versus Outcomes

Rationality is often judged in terms of outcomes. In this view, a policy is rational if it brings success and nonrational if it fails. Rational thinking is associated with good outcomes, such as victory in war, and nonrational thinking with bad outcomes, such as defeat.[92]

But rationality is about process rather than outcomes. Rational actors employ their critical faculties to figure out how to operate in an uncertain world. This does not ensure that the policies they come up with will meet with success. Exogenous constraints or unforeseen circumstances may keep them from achieving their objectives even though their policies are based on credible theories that emerge from a deliberative process.

Consider, first, that credible theories are imperfect instruments. Given that they simplify a complex reality, they are bound to be wrong some of the time because the significant factors in an event may turn out to be ones they omitted. When that happens, the policies based on those theories will not work as expected. For example, a state that thought in terms of economic interdependence theory, as described by Norman Angell in his classic book *The Great Illusion*, would have anticipated a peaceful resolution to the July Crisis in 1914. But what happened was World War I.[93]

Even if the theory underpinning a state's decision fits well with the situation at hand, the policy may still fail because decision makers either do not have enough information about the circumstances confronting them or else have bad information. It is difficult to assess relative capabilities before they are employed in combat. Intangible factors such as intentions, preferences, and resolve are even harder to measure. To make matters worse, states have powerful incentives to conceal and misrepresent both their capabilities and their thinking in order to gain advantage over each other. Whatever the reason, information deficits can lead states to conclude that they are secure when in fact they are threatened, that they should appease when it would be wiser to deter, and that victory is at hand when they are on the verge of defeat.

Finally, policies derived from credible theories sometimes fail because circumstances change in important and unexpected ways — what Niccolò Machiavelli calls fortune and both Thucydides and Clausewitz call chance.[94] A state could employ an appropriate theory and also have good information yet fail to reach its objective because a rival undergoes an unexpected regime change or develops a new technology that alters the balance of power.

By the same token, exogenous constraints and unforeseen circumstances may help nonrational states to achieve their objectives despite flaws in their understanding and decision-making. All of this means that rational states can fail and nonrational states can succeed, thus making it impossible to define rationality in terms of outcomes.

None of this is to say that rationality and outcomes are unrelated. Rational policies are more likely to succeed than fail. They rest on credible theories that enable states to make logical and evidence-based predictions about where a given policy is likely to lead. Conversely, nonrational policies are more likely to fail than succeed because they are based on a poor understanding of the way the world works, a nondeliberative decision-making process, or both.

Credible Theories and Deliberation

Strategic rationality in international politics means making sense of the world and deciding how best to proceed in pursuit of a particular goal. It is both an individual and state-level phenomenon. Rational policymakers employ credible theories to understand the situation they face and decide what to do. In contrast, nonrational decision makers rely on noncredible theories or no theories at all to make policy. As for rational states, they not only base their policies on credible theories, but they also engage in deliberation. This two-part process includes robust and uninhibited debate among the policymakers in the room, as well as a final policy choice by an ultimate decider. Meanwhile, nonrational states do not base their policies on credible theories or are nondeliberative, either because their internal debates are not vigorous and unconstrained or because they do not make a final policy decision. Now that we have presented our definitions of "rationality" and "nonrationality," it is time to describe and evaluate the main alternative definitions in the literature.

Chapter 4

CONTENDING DEFINITIONS

There are two bodies of scholarship that explore the rational actor assumption in international politics. Rational choice scholars and political psychologists both think about rationality in terms of expected utility maximization, which is basically a data-driven enterprise. But they emphasize different issues: the former focus on rationality while the latter focus on nonrationality.

Rational choice scholars ostensibly define "rationality" as expected utility maximization. On close inspection, however, they say little about the concept. For starters, they pay scant attention to how rational policymakers make sense of the world or how rational states aggregate the views of those individuals. They do examine how individuals make choices, as one would expect from scholars who describe themselves as rational choice theorists. Yet they do not discuss the mental processes by which rational policymakers make decisions. Instead, they assume that those individuals act "as if" they were expected utility maximizers. Thus they do not offer a definition of individual rational choice in international politics since that requires an account of what actually takes place in decision makers' heads.

Rational choice theorists might adopt a fallback definition, abandoning the "as if" assumption and claiming that rational policymakers actually employ the expected utility maximization formula when deciding what to do. The problem with this approach is simple: it is not rational to use expected utility in uncertain realms such as international politics.

Political psychologists define nonrationality as deviation from expected utility maximization, which they call bias.[1] Focusing almost exclusively on how individuals make choices, they argue that policymakers routinely rely on mental shortcuts — primarily analogies and heuristics — that lead to biases. This definition of nonrational choice at the individual level is implausible because it implies that leaders are almost always nonrational. Moreover, political psychologists say hardly anything about how individual leaders comprehend the world or how their views are aggregated to produce a state's foreign policy. In other words, their definition of "nonrationality" in international relations is both flawed and incomplete.

The bulk of this chapter is devoted to elaborating our claim that rational choice scholars and political psychologists fail to offer compelling definitions of "rationality" and "nonrationality" respectively.[2] Then, because political psychologists maintain that analogies and heuristics are the principal driving forces behind nonrationality, we critique their claims about those mental shortcuts.

Expected Utility Maximization

Expected utility maximization, a concept at the heart of the rational choice enterprise, is widely considered the canonical definition of strategic rationality. Rational actors, so the argument goes, maximize or optimize their expected utility, defined as benefit or value. Nonrational actors do not. As Bruce Bueno de Mesquita — a leading figure in this literature — explains, "The particular form of rationality I am postulating is that of expected-utility maximization. . . . Being rational simply implies that the decision maker uses a maximizing strategy in calculating how best to achieve his goals."[3] Similarly, in their evaluation of rational choice theory in political science, Donald Green and Ian Shapiro note that "the first assumption about which there is widespread agreement among rational choice theorists is that rational action involves *utility maximization*."[4] Arthur Stein makes the same point, noting that for decision theorists and rational choice theorists, rationality means "optimizing and maximizing actor preferences."[5] Emilie Hafner-Burton and her colleagues write: "All rationalist theories of international relations rest on important assumptions about the environment and the actors. Individuals are assumed to maximize expected utility."[6]

Expected utility theory, with its emphasis on maximization, originates in economics, mainly in the famous theorem described in John von Neumann and Oskar Morgenstern's 1944 book *Theory of Games and Economic Behavior.*[7] At least initially, the approach von Neumann and Morgenstern described was largely normative — that is, it was designed to help individuals choose those actions that best enabled them to attain their goals. As Jon Elster explains, that enterprise is, "before it is anything else, a normative theory. It tells us what we ought to do in order to achieve our aims as well as possible."[8] Indeed, Charles Glaser explicitly calls his rational choice theory of international politics a "prescriptive, normative theory" of how states should make policy choices rather than a "positive, explanatory theory" of how they actually decide what to do.[9]

Over time, however, many adherents of expected utility theory have come to use the method for descriptive or explanatory purposes. Observing that "at a common-sense level, rationality is a *normative* concept," John Harsanyi adds, "but even at a common-sense level, this concept of rationality does have important *positive* (non-normative) applications: it is used for *explanation,* for *prediction,* and even for mere *description* of human behavior."[10] Arthur Stein captures this evolution in his summary of the strategic-choice framework, which is grounded in expected utility theory: "Ironically, the strategic-choice approach offered here as a retrospective explanation for behavior and outcome began as part of a normative enterprise intended to improve decisions, not explain them."[11]

It should be apparent that the term "expected utility theory" is something of a misnomer in that "expected utility maximization" is not a theory but is instead an approach to making decisions. It describes a specific formula that individuals must employ if they are to maximize their expected utility. David Lake and Robert Powell say this explicitly: "The strategic-choice approach is, to state the obvious, an approach or orientation, rather than a theory."[12] This is not to say that scholars who treat states as utility maximizers cannot come up with their own "rationalist" theories of international relations. Many do. But when our goal is to define rationality, we should not focus our inquiry on these theories but rather on the expected utility maximization formula itself.

The unit of analysis in expected utility theory is the individual actor. Green and Shapiro observe that "[a key] assumption that commands widespread agreement among rational choice theorists is that the relevant maximizing agents are *individuals.*"[13] This being the case, scholars of international politics who equate rationality with optimization either focus their attention on especially powerful leaders or treat states as unitary actors. Bueno de Mesquita adopts the first approach, "assuming that decision making regarding war is dominated by a single leader." He views German foreign policy in the 1930s as the product of Adolf Hitler's actions, which he describes as "completely consistent with the behavior of a rational expected-utility maximizer."[14] For the most part, however, expected utility theorists adopt the second approach and identify states as unitary actors. Powell notes, "The actors in the bargaining model are not individuals . . . [but] states. Indeed, the actors in most IR models and theories are not individuals. They are aggregates that are assumed to behave as if they were unitary actors with well-defined preferences."[15]

Expected utility maximization involves following a set of rules that stipulate how to make decisions. As von Neumann and Morgenstern explain, "The immediate concept of a solution is plausibly a set of rules for each participant which tell him how to behave in every situation which may conceivably arise."[16]

What are the specific rules that an individual must employ when faced with the need to make a decision?[17] Rational decision makers first consider different states of the world—all the factors relevant to the problem they confront that are beyond their control—and analyze the pertinent data so as to establish the probability that those states of the world are true. At the same time, they consider what actions or policies are available to them. These states of the world and available actions are then combined to identify a set of possible outcomes. In a simple situation where there are two states of the world and two available actions, there are four possible outcomes. Having identified this set of outcomes, the decider ranks them in order of preference. These preferences are transitive—that is, if outcome A is preferred over outcome B, and B is preferred over

C, then A is preferred over C. After that, each outcome is assigned a utility or value, with the largest number assigned to the most preferred outcome. With ordinal utilities, the differences between the assigned numbers are meaningless, but with cardinal utilities those differences are meaningful.

Once the decision makers are armed with these inputs, the next step is to calculate the expected utility of each available action or policy. To do that, the probabilities of the different states of the world are multiplied by the utilities of the different outcomes. The resulting numbers are the expected utility of each available action. Maximization simply means selecting the action with the highest expected utility. In short, as one group of scholars puts it, the optimization approach involves "determining the payoffs attached to all possible outcomes, assessing their probabilities, updating information on those probabilities, and choosing the strategy with the highest expected return."[18]

For a look at expected utility maximization in action, consider how American decision makers might have used this method to identify a rational policy for dealing with the Soviet Union in early Cold War Europe.[19] The key issue was the nature of the Soviet Union's goals. In this regard, there were two possible states of the world: Moscow was either a status quo power or an expansionist power. The United States, in turn, had two available actions or policies: it could withdraw from Europe or remain there. Taken together, these states of the world and actions yielded four possible outcomes: if Moscow was status quo and the United States withdrew, the outcome would be a cheap balance of power in Europe; if Moscow was status quo and the United States remained, the outcome would be a costly balance of power in Europe; if Moscow was expansionist and the United States remained, the outcome would be a war between the superpowers; and if Moscow was expansionist and the United States withdrew, the outcome would be Soviet hegemony in Europe.

Let us assume the following. First, American policymakers examined the data available to them and estimated there was a 60 percent chance that the Soviet Union was expansionist and a 40 percent chance that it was status quo. Second, they ranked the four possible outcomes, from most preferred to least preferred, as cheap balance of power, costly balance of power, superpower war, and Soviet hegemony. Third, they assigned these outcomes cardinal utilities of 1, .75, .25, and 0 respectively, reflecting their belief that a balance of power—however it was achieved—would best serve U.S. security, whereas war, and especially Soviet hegemony, would undermine it.

Given these probabilities and utilities, the rational decision was for the United States to remain in Europe because the expected utility of remaining was greater than the expected utility of withdrawing. That conclusion was based on the following calculations:

Expected utility remain = (probability USSR expansionist) (utility superpower war) + (probability USSR status quo) (utility costly balance of power) = (.6)(.25) + (.4)(.75) = .45

Expected utility withdraw = (probability USSR expansionist) (utility Soviet hegemony) + (probability USSR status quo) (utility cheap balance of power) = (.6)(0) + (.4)(1) = .40

A Non-Definition of Individual Rationality

As hard as it might be to believe from the previous discussion, it turns out that rational choice scholars do not have a definition of individual rationality in international relations. They neither describe how rational policymakers make sense of the world around them nor how they make decisions about what to do.

Any definition of individual rationality in international politics must start with an explanation of how rational policymakers make sense of the world. One cannot identify a rational way to move forward without first understanding the problem at hand. Yet rational choice theorists pay almost no attention to how rational policymakers go about comprehending the world in which they operate. As for choices, any definition of individual rationality must also describe the mental process by which rational policymakers make decisions. One might think that expected utility maximization would provide such a description since the method is said to identify the way to choose among policy alternatives. It says that rational individuals choose the strategy that maximizes their expected utility.

On close inspection, however, expected utility maximization does not describe a mental choice process — it does not describe how rational decision makers think — and therefore does not offer a definition of individual rational choice. It ignores what goes on in policymakers' minds and instead asks whether their chosen actions are consistent with what the formula recommends. The issue is not whether rational decision makers "actually think" according to the formula but rather whether they act "as if" they were employing it. Bueno de Mesquita writes: "The [rationality] assumption is intended to convey the notion that choices between war and peace are made *as if* to maximize the strong leader's welfare." He further argues, "If we find that policymakers act as if they are rational expected-utility maximizers, then the assumption is realistic."[20] Christopher Achen and Duncan Snidal also employ the "as if" claim in describing how rational actors operate, noting, "Rational deterrence is agnostic about the actual calculations decision makers undertake. It holds that they will act *as if* they solved certain mathematical problems, whether or not they actually solve them."[21] This understanding of rational choice is rooted in economics and identified with Milton Friedman, who maintains that "under a wide range of circumstances individual firms behave *as if* they were seeking rationally to maximize their expected returns."[22]

This argument, that expected utility maximization does not describe how rational individuals employ their critical faculties to make decisions, is not controversial. In a statement that still rings true today, Herbert Simon noted in 1978 that "economics has largely been preoccupied with the *results* of rational choice rather than the *process* of choice."[23] Indeed, rational choice theorists are explicit on this point. In his discussion of the rational choice approach, James Morrow states, "We do not assume the decision process is a series of literal calculations," adding that "utility theory is not an attempt to explain the cognitive process of individuals."[24] Similarly, Achen and Snidal assert that "rational deterrence is implicitly misconstrued as a theory of how decision makers think." Furthermore, "The axioms and conclusions of utility theory refer only to choices. Mental calculations are never mentioned: the theory makes no reference to them."[25] Milton Friedman is more emphatic: "Now, of course, businessmen do not actually and literally solve the system of simultaneous equations in terms of which the mathematical economist finds it convenient to express this hypothesis."[26]

A Flawed Fallback Definition of Individual Rationality

The rational choice literature provides a possible fallback definition of how rational individuals make decisions (though not of how they make sense of the world). Rational choice theorists could abandon the "as if" assumption and define rational decision-making as the actual employment of the expected utility maximization method to choose among strategic options. This approach has certain virtues, but it ultimately fails because expected utility maximization is simply not rational in an uncertain world such as that of international politics.

There are good reasons to define rational policymakers as actual expected utility maximizers. By describing a mental process, this move addresses how individuals actually make choices. Absent such a description, any definition of rational choice is wanting, as there is no story about how decisions are made. As Brian Rathbun, Joshua Kertzer, and Mark Paradis explain, "Rational choice is not possible without rational thought. . . . Instrumental rationality is not possible without procedural rationality. Procedural rationality includes all of those cognitive processes we associate with rational decision making, such as thorough search for relevant data, unbiased consideration of information, and careful deliberation. This is rational thought or reason."[27]

Once the imperative to have a story about process is recognized, it is plausible for rational choice theorists to argue that rational policymakers actually are expected utility maximizers. After all, applying the expected utility maximization formula is a fairly straightforward matter, and while it may be too difficult for the average person to use this approach, it is surely not beyond the capabilities of most high-level policymakers. Indeed, there is abundant evidence that individuals in other walks of life — including scholars and businessmen — identify what they believe is the maximizing strategy by employing some version of the formula. To be sure, the required calculations can sometimes be especially complicated, but policymakers can always call on experts to perform the analyses.

———

It is therefore unsurprising that rational choice theorists themselves sometimes imply that rational decision-making actually involves a mental process revolving around expected utility maximization. Consider Bueno de Mesquita's claim that "being rational simply implies that the decision maker uses a maximizing strategy in calculating how best to achieve his goals."[28] He also writes, "Each decision maker and each individual or group trying to influence decisions looks ahead, contemplating what the likely responses are if they choose this action or that action. Then they choose the action that they believe, based on looking ahead and working back to the current situation, will give them the best result."[29] Similarly, Glaser asserts that "acting rationally means that states are purposive actors that make at least reasonable efforts to choose the strategy that is best suited to achieving their goals. States are assumed to be able to identify and compare options, evaluating the prospects that they will succeed, as well as their costs and benefits."[30] Elster maintains that "rational choice involves three optimizing operations. The action that is chosen must be optimal, given the desires and beliefs of the agent. The beliefs must be optimal, given the information available to the agent. The amount of resources allocated to the acquisition of information must be optimal."[31] As Rathbun notes, "That is a lot of thinking for an approach that claims not to have a theory of decision-making process."[32]

This fallback position has several merits. It provides a clear definition of individual rational choice: actors who choose the policy that promises to maximize their expected utility are rational, whereas those who do not are nonrational. Furthermore, it rigorously specifies a method for establishing which of the various policy options maximizes expected utility. As Arthur Stein observes, the method offers impressive "analytical coherence and rigor."[33] In other words, actual expected utility maximization gives individuals a well-defined, straightforward procedure for determining the optimal strategy for achieving their goals. Hence Elster's laudatory observation: "There is no alternative to rational-choice theory as a set of normative prescriptions. It just tells us to do what will best promote our aims, whatever they are."[34]

The greatest virtue of the fallback definition, however, is that expected utility maximization is rational choice in a small world — that is, a world characterized by certainty or risk. In such circumstances, it is the ideal way for individuals to decide what option best achieves their goals. In a certain world — one where the outcomes that will follow from each course of action are known for sure — the expected utility maximization formula enables individuals to choose the policy that best achieves their objectives. Indeed, Morrow points out that from the perspective of expected utility theory, "decisions under certainty are trivial."[35] The formula is also ideally suited for making decisions about how to move forward in a risk world, where decision makers can assign probabilities by logical or statistical means.

But in an uncertain world, expected utility maximization is a defective approach for making decisions. When data is scarce and unreliable, it is impossible to use statistical methods to assign probabilities. This means that in international politics, expected utility maximization is a nonrational way to make decisions. After all, the international system is an information-deficient, uncertain world, not an information-rich, certain or risk world.

The expected utility maximization approach involves identifying states of the world and available actions, combining them to create a list of possible options, rank ordering those options and giving them utilities, calculating the expected utility of each option, and choosing the strategy that yields the highest expected utility. Probabilities are at the heart of this enterprise; they are assigned to the different states of the world at the outset, and they underpin the subsequent calculations of expected utility. To be clear, not any probability will do if the formula is to identify the best way forward. Probabilities must be objective: they must accurately capture the prevailing states of the world. That is, they must identify the true likelihood that a rival power is aggressive, peaceful, resolved, and so on. Making that assessment requires abundant and dependable data that lends itself to statistical analysis.

Yet international politics is an uncertain world where information is scarce and unreliable. The point that the social world — including almost all of politics and economics — is characterized by uncertainty has been made forcefully by two of the twentieth century's most influential economists. Frank Knight, who introduced the distinction between "risk" and "uncertainty," argued that "the best example of uncertainty is in connection with the exercise of judgment or the formation of those opinions as to the future course of events, which opinions (and not scientific knowledge) actually guide most of our conduct. . . . Life is mostly made up of uncertainties."[36] John Maynard Keynes asserted that "our knowledge of the future is fluctuating, vague and uncertain. . . . The sense in which I am using the term is that in which the prospect of a European war is uncertain, or the price of copper and the rate of interest twenty years hence, or the obsolescence of a new invention, or the position of private wealthowners in the social system in 1970."[37] Jonathan Kirshner maintains that what is true in economics is even more so in international politics. "War, as well as many of the steps taken toward its approach," he writes, "is a plunge into radical uncertainty and rational experts can and will disagree, profoundly, with regard to their expectations about its cost, course, and consequence, even in the most complete and symmetrical information environments imaginable."[38]

Actual expected utility maximization is thus not a recipe for rational choice in international politics. Foreign policy decision makers are condemned to operate with scarce and unreliable information and cannot determine objective probabilities. This problem in turn means that they cannot calculate the expected utilities of alternative actions, let alone identify the one that yields the highest expected utility. In other words, the expected utility maximization method cannot be used as the basis for acting purposively in the international system. It would be nonrational for policymakers to adopt it as a guide to action.

To illustrate the shortcomings of the expected utility maximization approach, let us return to the example of early Cold War American policy toward the Soviet Union described above. It is impossible to attach meaningful probabilities to different states of the world and, on that basis, assign meaningful expected utilities to various policy options. Consider the contention that there was a 60 percent probability that the Soviet Union was expansionist and a 40 percent probability that it was a status quo power and therefore that it was best for the United States to remain in Europe rather than withdraw. There was, in fact, no way either to calculate the true probability that Moscow was either expansionist or status quo or to know the relative expected utility of each available strategy. Decision makers in an uncertain world can do no better than guess what likelihoods to attach to possible states of the world and what costs and benefits to attach to different policies. The problem is so intractable that even today, with the benefit of hindsight, scholars cannot establish the actual probabilities and expected utilities that obtained in the early Cold War.[39]

Given that it is impossible to assign objective probabilities and expected utilities in an uncertain world and given that international politics is an information-deficient realm, expected utility theory cannot be employed to make rational decisions. But proponents of this method do just that, and it raises the obvious question: How do they defend this move?

Rational choice scholars deal with this problem by introducing the concept of subjective probability.[40] They acknowledge that there is a fundamental distinction between a risk world and an uncertain world, and that, as Morrow puts it, "Most [policy] decisions are made under the condition of uncertainty."[41] They also recognize that one cannot determine objective probabilities in information-deficient environments. Nevertheless, rational choice advocates argue that decision makers can come up with subjective probabilities—personal estimates of the probability of different states of the world—which they can then plug into the expected utility maximization formula to determine the best way forward. Noting the difference between "risk" and "uncertainty," Jeffrey Friedman maintains that in uncertain realms, individuals employ subjective probabilities, which he defines as "probability assessments with respect to an analyst's personal convictions."[42] As Elster explains, this claim reflects the belief that "we always have some information, however vague and diffuse, which we can use to assess the probabilities of the various outcomes. More specifically, they point to the existence of procedures that will elicit the agent's subjective probabilities in any choice situation that he confronts." He adds that "once these probabilities are given, the principle of maximizing expected utility can be applied as before."[43] All of this means that there is no meaningful difference in how rational individuals make choices under uncertainty and under risk.

How, then, does one assign subjective probabilities? Several scholars have explained how it can be done. The key is to employ a data-driven approach, accumulating what information is available and analyzing it with statistical reasoning. Philip Tetlock and Peter Scoblic find that certain people are "naturally numerate and open-minded" and can "think probabilistically." These individuals, they argue, "would approach seemingly intractable questions by decomposing them into parts, researching the past frequency of similar (if not precisely analogous) events, adjusting the odds based on the uniqueness of the situation, and continually updating their estimates as new information emerged." In doing so, they "transmuted uncertainty into measurable risk."[44] Rathbun takes a similar view, maintaining that some individuals "deliberate more and try harder to develop objective understandings. They 'tend to seek, acquire, think about, and reflect back on information. . . . [They] are characterized generally by active, exploring minds and, through their sense and intellect, reach and draw out information from their environment.'"[45] David Edelstein, meanwhile, focuses not on decision makers but on the environment, arguing that subjective probability judgments become possible as more information becomes available: "Key to my argument is that uncertainty can become risk. States go from a condition of being unable to assess how best to respond to an unknowable future to being able to assign probabilities to whether a state is a threat or not. In particular, it is knowledge about a state's intentions that allows the transformation from uncertainty to risk."[46]

Resorting to subjective probabilities does not solve the problem. To identify the rational choice in a given situation, expected utility maximization requires abundant, dependable information that can be used to generate objective probabilities by statistical means, which can then be run through the formula. That is only possible in an information-rich, small world. International relations, however, is an information-deficient, large world where one cannot use statistics to establish true probabilities. Employing subjective probabilities does not rescue the enterprise because it merely involves guessing probabilities by thinking statistically about scarce and unreliable data. The outcome is as unreliable as the inputs. As a way to make decisions in world politics, actual subjective expected utility maximization is thus no more rational than actual objective expected utility maximization.

Yet to make decisions, policymakers need some sense of probabilities.[47] Among other things, they need to reckon the attitudes of other states – their objectives, intentions, and resolve – and the likely consequences of various actions. Decision-making is impossible without such judgments. The best, though by no means perfect, way to estimate likelihoods in international politics is by employing credible theories: logically consistent, empirically verified, probabilistic statements about the way the world works. This theory-driven approach to decision-making is fundamentally different from expected utility maximization, which is data-driven at its core. Indeed, proponents of a data-driven approach tend to view theory as an obstacle to sound statistical thinking, contrasting "'top-down,' 'theory-driven'" analysis "in which we apply preexisting beliefs to make sense of the world" unfavorably with "'data-driven' analysis," which "allow[s] the world to reveal itself to us."[48]

In sum, expected utility maximization is a non-definition or a flawed definition of individual rationality in world politics. Taken on its own terms, it does not describe a mental process by which rational policymakers either make sense of the world or decide how to move forward. The fallback version – which does describe a mental process—does not provide a rational way to make decisions in the uncertain world of international relations.

A Non-Definition of State Rationality

As for collective rationality, rational choice scholars are largely silent about how rational states aggregate—that is, discuss and decide among—the views of individual policymakers. Given their overwhelming emphasis on individual choice, this is hardly surprising. Nevertheless, the workings of expected utility theory at the individual level make it necessary to talk about strategic rationality at the state level. Once rational choice theorists argue that individuals employ subjective probabilities—and even subjective utilities—they must acknowledge that different policymakers may reach different conclusions about what course of action best achieves their goals and is therefore rational. Those individuals are likely to disagree on what values to assign to the relevant probabilities that go into the expected utility formula. This can lead to significant variation among policymakers regarding which strategy has the highest expected utility.

Consider our stylized case of early Cold War U.S. policy toward the Soviet Union. We assigned a 60 percent chance to the likelihood that the Soviet Union was expansionist and a 40 percent chance to the likelihood it was status quo. The result, according to expected utility maximization, was that the United States should remain in Europe. But had we changed the probabilities and assumed that there was a 40 percent chance Moscow was expansionist and a 60 percent chance it was status quo—hardly a farfetched move given the difficulty of estimating another state's goals—the optimal American policy would have been to withdraw from Europe. Slight changes in the utilities assigned to outcomes can have equally dramatic effects. For instance, we assigned a utility of .25 to super-power war and 0 to Soviet hegemony, which meant that the optimal U.S. policy was to remain in Europe. It is not unreasonable to think, however, that war would have been so devastating that the utilities should be flipped. Were we to do this, the optimal American policy would change to withdrawal from Europe.

Expected utility theorists acknowledge this point. Morrow explains that "under uncertainty, actors form subjective probability estimates that reflect their degree of belief about the underlying state of the world. . . . Under uncertainty, different deciders may hold different probability distributions because they hold different beliefs about the underlying state of the world."[49] This being the case, different decision makers may also reach different judgments about what course of action maximizes utility. Similarly, Bueno de Mesquita notes that a "[common] misconception about rationality is that in any given situation there is an objectively best, rational choice that all rational decision makers would choose. This is not true. Different individuals have different tastes or preference orderings, which will lead them to make different decisions, even though each of the decisions is rational. This will be as true of individuals' preference for policy outcomes as for strategy or risks."[50] Robert Jervis summarizes the problem: "One should not equate expected utility arguments with the claim that all people will behave the same way in the same situation, that is, with arguments that ignore the individual level of analysis. If each person is rational, but has different values and means-ends beliefs, then behavior will be idiosyncratic."[51]

Given this variation, expected utility theorists need a story that explains what a rational collective decision-making process looks like. There is, of course, no need for such an account if policy is made by a leader acting alone; but it is essential when, as is much more common, foreign policy is a collective enterprise involving multiple individuals, each armed with personal opinions. But expected utility theorists provide no such account. Instead, they ignore the collective decision-making process and assume either that policy is made by a single powerful individual or that states can be treated as unitary actors. Both alternatives are consistent with these scholars' emphasis on decision-making at the individual level.

Political Psychology

Like rational choice theorists, political psychologists are principally concerned with individual decision-making. They maintain that policymakers are routinely nonrational because they do not think in terms of expected utility maximization when making choices about the best strategy for moving forward.

Arguing that nonrationality "generally refers to the deviation from some standard model of rational information processing," Janice Gross Stein concludes that "research has now cumulated to show that people rarely conform to the expectations of the abstract rational model. Cognitive psychology has demonstrated important differences between the expectations of rational decision models and the processes of attribution and estimation that people frequently use."[52] Dominic Johnson also recognizes that "as a model within many areas of social science, rational choice (theory) remains central" and finds that "empirically, as a description of human behavior, it is fatally flawed." Moreover, he argues, "Recent scholarship suggests that in international politics, rational choice is in fact empirically rare, even at the top of the decision-making elite where one might—if anywhere—expect it to occur." Indeed, "leaders engage in all sorts of non-rational behavior."[53]

Other political psychologists echo these views. Rathbun writes that "central to the rational choice framework is the notion of instrumental rationality — actors making decisions that maximize their expected utility in light of structural constraints." Yet "while rational choice work has been enormously influential in political science, critics both inside and outside the discipline claim that in practice, individuals generally do not live up to the standard of strategic, calculating, and purposive decision-making implied in the approach."[54] Keren Yarhi-Milo notes that there is "a substantial and diverse literature in international relations establishing that leaders rarely act rationally."[55] Finally, in a review of decisions for war, Richard Ned Lebow comments on "the frequent irrationality of the leaders and the shoddy nature of the policy-making process in countries that draw the sword. Leaders and their advisors do not collect good intelligence, evaluate what information they have on hand, or make careful assessments of the likely short- and longer-term costs and gains of their proposed initiative." For him, "substantive and instrumental irrationality . . . is the norm, not the exception."[56]

The core intuition here — that individuals frequently think in nonrational ways — is central to behavioral economics. Richard Thaler documents "the myriad ways in which people depart from the fictional creatures that populate economic models. . . . The problem is with the model being used by economists, a model that replaces homo sapiens with a fictional creature called homo economicus, which I like to call Econ for short. Compared to this fictional world of Econs, Humans do a lot of misbehaving. . . . You know, and I know, that we do not live in a world of Econs. We live in a world of Humans."[57] Daniel Kahneman, arguably the founding father of behavioral economics along with Amos Tversky, notes that these arguments have gained significant traction over the past half-century: "Social scientists in the 1970s broadly accepted . . . [that] people are generally rational, and their thinking is normally sound. . . . By and large, though, the idea that our minds are susceptible to systematic errors is now generally accepted. . . . Humans are not well described by the rational-agent model."[58]

Political psychologists have proposed a common explanation for the purported prevalence of nonrationality in international politics. Their starting point is that policymakers have significant cognitive limits and cannot carry out the calculations required by the expected utility maximization formula. This being the case, they resort to mental shortcuts — analogies and heuristics — to decide how to move forward. Those rules of thumb in turn lead to biases, which is another word for conclusions that are at odds with expected utility maximization.[59] Commenting on a seminal article by Kahneman and Tversky, Thaler writes: "Humans have limited time and brainpower. As a result, they use simple rules of thumb — heuristics — to help them make judgments. . . . Using these heuristics causes people to make predictable errors. Thus the title of the paper: heuristics and biases."[60]

Analogies are mental shortcuts that are based on the observation of historical events. Reasoning by analogy involves assuming that if there is some similarity between a past event and a current event, then the earlier case is relevant to the present case and prescribes a course of action. Yuen Khong suggests that this phenomenon is commonplace among policymakers: "Statesmen have consistently turned to the past in dealing with the present. . . . They have invoked historical parallels when confronted with a domestic or foreign policy problem." The canonical example is the Munich analogy, which holds that appeasing Hitler led to war in the late 1930s, and thus appeasement always leads to war. Images, schemas, and scripts are similar "intellectual devices."[61] Jervis effectively equates analogies with images, arguing that "international history is a powerful source of beliefs about international relations and images of other countries."[62] Meanwhile, Deborah Larson maintains that schemas and scripts are the products of "a 'matching' process" based on "analogical reasoning."[63]

Heuristics are mental shortcuts that are hardwired into the human brain. They enable individuals to rapidly sort through the facts before them and choose a way forward. Three heuristics have figured most prominently in the politics and economics fields since Kahneman and Tversky first identified them. They are the availability heuristic, the tendency to focus on information that is most easily available; the representativeness heuristic, the tendency to exaggerate the similarity between current and past events; and the anchoring heuristic, the tendency to allow initial judgments to inhibit updating when new information becomes available. Scholars have also found numerous other heuristics that are said to influence policymakers, including fundamental attribution, loss aversion, negativity, overconfidence, risk aversion, and satisficing.[64]

Policymakers use analogies and heuristics to process information because of their cognitive limits. The notion that people have limited cognitive capacities is widespread. As Kenneth Arrow argues, the "extremely severe strain on information-gathering and computing abilities" inherent in making political and economic decisions exceeds "the limits of the human being, even augmented with artificial aids."[65] Likewise, Simon's description of "bounded rationality" emphasizes that "human rational behavior . . . is shaped by a scissors whose two blades are the structure of task environments and the computational capabilities of the actor."[66] All human beings, he says, have "psychological limitations" and constrained "computational capacities."[67] Robert Keohane makes a similar point about international politics: "Decisionmakers are in practice subject to limitations on their own cognitive abilities, quite apart from the uncertainties inherent in their environments."[68]

Political psychologists also argue that the limits of human cognition are what lead policymakers to rely on mental shortcuts. Janice Gross Stein writes: "Situated at the apex of these complex strategic and multilayered games, political leaders, like everyone else, are limited in their capacity to process information. Their rationality is bounded. Because their rationality is bounded, people use a number of cognitive shortcuts . . . to simplify complexity and manage uncertainty, handle information, make inferences, and generate threat perceptions."[69] Likewise, Johnson notes the "widespread idea across the social sciences that rationality is the normative ideal . . . and human brains are prevented from achieving this ideal because of cognitive limitations." At the same time, he argues, "Every day, all of us are able to navigate a stream of complex social and physical challenges without knowing how, thanks to a suite of evolved heuristics."[70]

It is important to emphasize that cognitive shortcuts are different from theories. Rathbun equates the concepts, arguing that "heuristics are simplifying devices that ease the process of thinking, acting as 'theories' that serve as one-size-fits-all decision-making rules."[71] This is wrong. To be sure, analogies and heuristics, on the one hand, and theories, on the other hand, perform similar functions: both are simplifying devices that can be deployed to ease information processing and facilitate choice. But they do so in fundamentally different ways. Theories are explanatory statements that revolve around a causal logic that tells us why the world works the way it does. Analogies and heuristics have no causal story. As Jervis notes, when individuals reason by analogy, they "pay more attention to *what* has happened than to *why* it has happened. Thus learning is superficial, overgeneralized. . . . The search for causes is usually quick and oversimplified. . . . No careful examination is made of the links that are supposed to be present. Few attempts are made to make the comparisons that are necessary to render a judgment on the causal efficacy of the variables."[72]

Individuals who employ analogies or heuristics are nonrational or biased, which is to say their decisions deviate from what expected utility maximization prescribes. "Biases," Tversky and Kahneman write, "stem from the reliance on judgmental heuristics," which are "highly economical and usually effective" but can also "lead to systematic and predictable errors."[73] Janice Gross Stein makes a similar point, noting that individuals who reason by analogy "unconsciously strip the nuance, the context, the subtleties out of the problems they face" and can reach "very oversimplified judgments."[74] According to Tetlock, leaders are just as prone to this kind of thinking as anyone else: "Policymakers often oversimplify. Evidence has accumulated that the price of cognitive economy in world politics is — as in other domains of life — susceptibility to error and bias."[75]

Although political psychologists focus mainly on how policymakers make choices, they also pay much attention to the outcomes — successes and failures — that result from those choices. In particular, there is a long-standing tradition of identifying mental shortcuts with bad outcomes. Jervis observes that "there is an almost inescapable tendency to look at cases of conflict, surprise, and error."[76] Johnson points out: "Cognitive biases are thus seen as liabilities of the human brain that must be guarded against if we are to avoid costly misjudgments, misperceptions, mistakes, crises, policy failures, disasters, and wars. Cognitive biases are bad, and their consequences are bad."[77] Jonathan Mercer makes the same point,

describing "the ubiquitous . . . belief in international relations scholarship that cognitive biases and emotion cause only mistakes."[78]

More recently, however, some political psychologists have
pointed to cases in which analogies and heuristics are associated
with good outcomes.[79] Arguing that "cognitive biases" can be "a
source of success as well as a source of failure," Johnson identifies
specific instances in which they "cause or promote success in the
realm of international relations."[80] Rathbun likewise maintains
that nonrational thinkers "have achieved great things in history, perhaps because of — rather than despite — their less rational cognitive
style. . . . Rational thinking and nonrational thinking both have
their own advantages and disadvantages."[81]

A Flawed Definition of Nonrationality

Any claim about individual nonrationality in international politics
depends on having a definition of that concept. Political psychologists must describe what it means to say that policymakers are nonrational in making sense of the world and making policy decisions.
Much like rational choice scholars, political psychologists who rivet
on analogies and heuristics pay little attention to how individuals
comprehend the world around them and instead explore how they
make choices.

Political psychologists have a straightforward definition of
nonrational choices: biased decisions that result from the employment of analogies or heuristics. One virtue of this definition is that it
depicts decision-making as a mental process, which makes it possible to establish whether a particular choice is rational or nonrational.
Another virtue is that decisions made through shortcuts or rules of
thumb are indeed nonrational. After all, analogies and heuristics are
not theories, let alone credible theories. Yet there are other forms of

nonrational choice in international politics, including decisions based on noncredible theories or expected utility calculations, as well as decisions where individuals are overwhelmed by their emotions.

Still, the fundamental problem with the political psychologists' definition of nonrational choice is that it implies that policymakers are routinely nonrational, a claim that defies common sense. Because political psychologists equate nonrational decision-making with a failure to employ the expected utility maximization formula and because they find no evidence that leaders actually do that, they effectively end up saying that leaders are nonrational all the time. This line of argument is untenable. The idea that human beings are axiomatically nonrational is starkly at odds with the understanding built into the very name of our species, *homo sapiens,* or wise man. It also flies in the face of the widely held belief that we are not simply animals but rather, as Aristotle emphasizes, rational animals.[82] And if humans never behave rationally, who or what does?

Turning to state nonrationality, political psychologists acknowledge that states are the key actors in international politics, but because they focus on the individual, they have little to say about policymaking at that higher level. Janice Gross Stein describes the problem: "Psychologists—and behavioral economists—are methodological individualists; in cognitive psychology and micro-economics, explanations generally remain at the level of the individual and the problem of inference goes away. But theoretical propositions drawn from individual-level analysis do not move easily to 'higher-level' units such as states." More simply, "psychological theories" confront "the challenge of aggregation."[83]

This issue is widely recognized. As Elizabeth Saunders observes, "Studies of individual preferences and beliefs rarely address how biases aggregate, but foreign policy decision making often happens in groups. Many theories of group decision making that could help bridge this gap, such as 'groupthink' or the bureaucratic politics model, do not adequately address how politics can affect groups themselves."[84] Powell is even more critical, arguing that political psychologists "never got around the aggregation problem" and will likely "find it very difficult to get around this problem" in the future.[85] In short, political psychologists do not have a definition of state nonrationality.

Analogies and Heuristics

In light of this discussion of definitions, it makes sense to examine the role that analogies and heuristics play in international relations. This is important not only for understanding rationality, but also for determining whether states are rational actors. There are four problems with the way political psychologists view mental shortcuts and foreign policy.

First, it makes little sense to argue that policymakers rely on analogies and heuristics when formulating grand strategy or managing a crisis. Although individuals surely employ cognitive shortcuts in their daily lives, this is not true of leaders in the domain of international politics. Human beings constantly rely on rules of thumb to deal with the mundane or routine matters they confront every day. We cannot function effectively without an inventory of mental shortcuts. But international politics is a fundamentally different realm: the stakes are much higher, and the decisions are not routine. Major foreign policy decisions can have enormous implications for national security and prosperity. Leaders therefore understand that they cannot employ analogies and heuristics in such situations but must think carefully about their circumstances and how best to pursue their goals.[86]

Second, there are serious theoretical and methodological flaws in the arguments political psychologists make about mental shortcuts. For starters, their account is undertheorized. Scholars in the literature point to a wide variety of analogies and heuristics to account for biased decisions. This is not a problem by itself, but it means that it is essential to provide sound answers to the following questions: Which shortcuts are the key drivers of individual thinking in international politics? Why are they the most important? When do they apply? What is their effect? To which biases do they give rise? Political psychologists fail to answer these questions in a meaningful way and instead invoke analogies and heuristics in an ad hoc manner.

Mercer highlights this theoretical problem, noting that political psychologists "can attribute bad decisions to the need for cognitive consistency, improper assimilation of new data to old beliefs, the desire to avoid value trade-offs, groupthink, idiosyncratic schemas, motivated or emotional bias, reliance on heuristics because of cognitive limitations, incorrect use of analogies, the framing of information, feelings of shame and humiliation, or a miserable childhood."[87] Kenneth Shultz goes further, arguing that political psychologists must develop a theory rather than a mere laundry list of mental shortcuts and rules of thumb. Instead of asserting that leaders are influenced by "myriad different" cognitive factors, political psychologists need to "sort this out" and establish whether these factors "work additively" or whether some are "causally prior to others." He continues: "As this research agenda progresses, it will no longer be enough to show that 'individuals matter' when controlling for domestic and international factors; we also need some guidance on which of the many ways people differ from one another matter most."[88]

Regarding methodology, heuristics-based arguments have an external validity problem. It is not clear that the experiments at the heart of the enterprise accurately reflect how leaders make decisions in the real world. It is one thing to say that subjects confronted with hypothetical scenarios in a laboratory use certain heuristics but quite another to say that experienced policymakers use them when formulating grand strategy or managing a crisis. This is hardly a controversial point, as Janice Gross Stein makes clear: "The internal validity of the results from well-designed experiments tends to be high, but their external validity . . . is much more challenging. . . . The challenge comes in drawing inferences from these kinds of experiments to the behavior of leaders. Just as psychologists have had to be careful not to claim too much from experiments with undergraduate students, scholars of international politics must be careful about the claims they make about leaders' behavior based on experiments with students or undifferentiated publics."[89]

Third, as noted, many political psychologists focus on outcomes, especially disastrous ones, and then reason backward, claiming that mental shortcuts must have been responsible for what happened.[90] This emphasis on outcomes may be intuitively attractive since it appears to link nonrationality with failure, but it is wrongheaded. Whether a state is rational cannot be determined by looking at outcomes. Rational states can fail to achieve their desired outcomes because of exogenous constraints or unforeseen circumstances. Hence, it does not make sense to judge a state that tries and fails to reach some objective as nonrational. The converse is also true: a state that achieves its preferred outcome is not necessarily rational. Nonrational states can succeed for many reasons, including material superiority and dumb luck.

Fourth, political psychologists provide little empirical support for the specific claim that leaders use cognitive shortcuts when devising grand strategies or formulating policy during crises and are therefore nonrational. Consider that they do not provide systematic evidence that analogies or heuristics were at work in their four signal cases of great-power nonrationality: German decision-making during the July Crisis of 1914; the British decision to appease Nazi Germany at Munich in 1938; German decision-making leading up to and following the invasion of the Soviet Union in 1941; and the Japanese decision to attack the United States at Pearl Harbor in 1941. In fact, as will become clear, neither analogies nor heuristics mattered much in these decisions, which were instead underpinned by credible theories.

This is not to say that political psychologists have performed no detailed studies. Indeed, they have carefully examined the role played by analogies and heuristics in a number of cases, including the U.S. decision to implement containment at the beginning of the Cold War, to escalate in Vietnam in 1965, and to confront Britain and France during the 1956 Suez Crisis.[91] But these are exceptions to the rule, and scholars do not cite them as canonical cases of nonrationality.

Deficient Definitions

In sum, the definitions of "rationality" and "nonrationality" found in the rational choice and political psychology literatures are wanting. But what about the common claim that rationality is rare in world politics?

Chapter 5

RATIONALITY AND GRAND STRATEGY

Are states rational in their conduct of foreign policy and especially in their grand strategic and crisis decision-making? This is
ultimately an empirical question: does an examination of the
historical record reveal that states routinely based their policies
on credible theories and that their policy decisions were the results
of a deliberative process? We find that most states are rational
most of the time, a result that should not surprise us. Given that international politics is a dangerous business, states think seriously
about the strategies they adopt, which is to say they are powerfully
inclined to rely on credible theories and deliberate about their every
move.

Assessing Rationality

What does a rational state policy look like? For starters, the views of
the decision makers in the room must be aggregated through a deliberative process that involves robust and uninhibited debate, followed by an ultimate decider making a choice. As we described

———

above, this process can take one of three forms. First, the key policymakers — including the ultimate decider — come to the table with the same credible theories in mind and after discussing the situation, easily reach a consensus on the best way forward. Second, the relevant decision makers arrive with different theories but after engaging in vigorous and unconstrained discussion agree on a guiding strategy based on a credible theory, which is then ratified by the ultimate decider. Third, following robust and uninhibited debate, the principal policymakers fail to agree, at which point the ultimate decider chooses the way forward. Moreover, the policy that the state adopts at the end of the deliberative process must be based on a credible theory or combination of credible theories. To be clear, this does not mean that every policymaker participating in the debate must have a credible theory in mind. Individual decision makers may sometimes bring noncredible theories into the room. For a state to be rational, however, the deliberations must weed out those theories.

There are limits to the evidence we can muster to show that states have routinely met these benchmarks. Because the universe of foreign policy decisions is enormous, it is impossible to provide detailed accounts of even a significant fraction of them. We therefore settle for a second-best strategy, which is to zero in on a few hard cases. We examine ten cases — five grand strategy decisions and five crisis decisions — that have been identified as instances of nonrational decision-making. In each case, we show that the relevant state in fact acted rationally. Thus there is good reason to believe that such a pattern of rational behavior obtained in many other cases as well.[1]

Table 1 lists the five grand strategy cases we discuss in this chapter and the five crisis cases we discuss in the next.

Table 1. Rational Great Power Decision-Making

Grand Strategic Decisions	Crisis Decisions
Germany decides how to deal with the Triple Entente before World War I	Germany decides to start World War I
Japan decides how to deal with the Soviet Union before World War II	Japan decides to attack the United States at Pearl Harbor
France decides how to meet the Nazi threat before World War II	Germany decides to invade the Soviet Union
The United States decides to expand NATO after the Cold War	The United States decides to settle the Cuban Missile Crisis
The United States decides to pursue liberal hegemony after the Cold War	The Soviet Union decides to invade Czechoslovakia

Germany Decides How to Deal with the Triple Entente before World War I

Political scientists commonly describe imperial Germany as nonrational in the run-up to World War I. Jack Snyder maintains that German behavior was "a synonym for self-destructive aggression." Its extreme "belligerence" needlessly provoked an overwhelming coalition, which then imposed "a decisive defeat on the German nation." Asserting that the country "engaged in quixotic folly," Snyder dismisses "rationalistic explanations for German behavior," including the familiar argument that "international circumstances made expansionism a rational gamble."[2] Stephen Van Evera also judges the Kaiserreich's foreign policy nonrational, arguing that it was based on "illusions – the fake news of the time." Worse still, it emerged from a nondeliberative decision-making process. "The

German foreign policy debate before World War I saw frivolous arguments pass unchallenged to become the basis for policy," Van Evera writes. "Fatuous . . . arguments for empire" went "unanswered," while policymakers who spoke out against such "nonsense" were "suppressed."[3]

Historians make similar arguments about Germany's nonrationality before World War I. Ludwig Dehio, for example, claims that the Kaiserreich was overwhelmed by "the daemonic nature of power," which caused it to develop "an exaggerated desire for self-assertion and . . . an amoral lust for battle." He claims that Germany's prominent position in the European balance of power meant that it faced "daemonic temptations of a special kind."[4]

This perspective is at odds with the historical record. Germany's policy for dealing with its great power rivals from July 1909 — when Theobald von Bethmann Hollweg became chancellor — to June 1914, the eve of the July Crisis, was based on credible theories. It was also the product of a deliberative process characterized by broad consensus. Contrary to the conventional wisdom, then, imperial Germany was a rational actor in the run-up to World War I.[5]

Germany was in a fairly favorable strategic position in July 1909. Most important, it was both militarily and economically the mightiest state in Europe. Furthermore, its principal ally, Austria-Hungary, had emerged strengthened from the Bosnian Crisis of 1908–9, although it still had its share of problems at home and abroad. To be sure, Germany faced a balancing coalition composed of three great powers — Britain, France, and Russia — but the Triple Entente was no more than a loose alliance. Moreover, Russia was militarily impotent, having suffered a devastating defeat in the Russo-Japanese War of 1904–5.

In the five years after Bethmann assumed the chancellorship, Germany's threat environment deteriorated in two stages. In the first stage, which ran from July 1909 to June 1912, both the military and diplomatic balances shifted against Berlin in important ways. The trouble started with France's artillery law—passed in July 1909 and fully implemented by late 1910—which significantly improved French military capabilities. This was followed by the Russian military reorganization of 1910, which profoundly affected the balance of power by markedly improving the effectiveness of Russia's fighting forces. Then came the Agadir Crisis of 1911, which pushed Britain and France closer together, leading German policymakers to conclude that any future war would likely be a world war that pitted Germany against all three members of the Entente.

In the second stage, from July 1912 to June 1914, the military and diplomatic balances shifted against Berlin even more. During the summer of 1912, the members of the Entente continued to strengthen their militaries and tighten their alliance. The key event, however, was the Balkan War of 1912–13, which featured two crises: the Mobilization Crisis of November–December 1912 and the Scutari Crisis of April–May 1913. In the course of that war, the Ottoman Empire suffered a major defeat at the hands of Serbia and the other members of the Balkan League, with important strategic consequences. Russia could now move troops from its border with the Ottoman Empire to its borders with Austria-Hungary and Germany. Austria-Hungary also now faced a growing threat from Serbia. To make matters worse, France and Russia both moved to strengthen their armies, introducing the "Three-Year Law" and the "Great Program" respectively in March 1913. These measures further swung the military balance against Germany. The Balkan War also had significant diplomatic consequences. In particular, France and Russia moved even closer together in the course of the conflict, further strengthening the Entente and convincing German policy-makers that they would have to fight a future great-power war on two fronts.

Germany responded to each of these shifts in the military and diplomatic balance with slightly different grand strategies. In the first stage, German decision makers quickly agreed that they should maintain the balance of power and act to deter a great-power war. The centerpiece of their balancing strategy was the army bill of 1912, which modestly increased the size of the German Army from 612,557 to 646,321 men. As for war, they focused their efforts on deterring a French or Russian attack but also prepared to fight in the event deterrence failed. In the second stage, German leaders were again on the same page, though they now wanted to shift rather than merely maintain the balance of power and were prepared to countenance a preventive war against Russia, which would inevitably mean a war with France and probably Britain. Accordingly, the army bill of 1913 provided for a major increase in the size of the German Army, which grew from 646,321 to 782,344 men. In addition, military planners stepped up their preparations for a hegemonic war.

Both of Germany's grand strategic decisions between 1909 and 1914 relied on credible realist theories and were the result of a deliberative process. The decision to build up the German Army in 1912 was clearly based on balance-of-power logic, specifically on the belief that the Kaiserreich must improve its military capability to prevent potential adversaries from gaining a power advantage. As General Franz von Wandel, the director of the General War Department in the War Ministry, put it, "At present few Germans would deny that we are surrounded by enemies . . . and that

Germany's position in the world is therefore at stake. In recognition of this, numerous voices have already spoken out loudly from various parties for a strengthening of the army; people are generally resolved for such a proposition."[6] In an address to the Bundesrat in March 1912, Prussian war minister Josias von Heeringen argued that the hostility and strength of the Entente made military improvements "an absolute state necessity."[7]

As for German thinking about war, Wandel feared that Germany was not strong enough to deter the Entente powers from attacking in the aftermath of Agadir. In November 1911, he warned that "at no time are we safe against war" and argued that increasing Berlin's capabilities was essential to enhance deterrence.[8] Heeringen was even more explicit, arguing that because Germany's enemies were looking for an excuse for war, "a reinforcement of the army in a measure calculated to insure peace must take place." General Helmuth von Moltke, the chief of the German General Staff, worried that deterrence might fail even if Germany built up its army. "Everyone," he wrote, "is preparing for the great war, which they all expect sooner or later." A buildup was essential not only for deterrence, but also as preparation for a war that was growing more and more likely: "It always remains the duty of every state not only to look the future calmly in the eye, but also to prepare itself for the day of decision. . . . Germany must arm for this decision. I consider . . . a greater drawing upon its able-bodied manpower, that is to say a raising of the peacetime strength, as an imperative of self-preservation."[9]

There was hardly any disagreement among German decision makers on Berlin's grand strategy of balancing and deterrence. Nevertheless, they discussed that policy in a robust and uninhibited manner before moving to execute it in 1912. Bethmann set the ball rolling in a series of meetings with Heeringen and Treasury Secretary

Adolf Wermuth in September and October 1911. After Heeringen endorsed the idea of a new army bill on 9 October, Bethmann approached Kaiser Wilhelm II, who needed little convincing that Germany must increase its military capabilities. Wilhelm, Bethmann, and Wermuth then agreed that the military buildup would involve a costly increase in the budget. Detailed planning began soon after. On 19 November, Heeringen produced a memorandum—which he had previously cleared with Moltke—making the case for a new army law. Ten days later, Wandel, who had been tasked with drafting the law, described the shape it should take, and much like Heeringen, he stressed that increasing the size of the German Army was crucial to maintaining the balance of power and deterring great-power war. Then, on 2 December, Moltke sent Bethmann a long memorandum endorsing the proposed army law and essentially reiterating Heeringen's and Wandel's justifications for it. A little more than a week later, Bethmann acknowledged Moltke's memorandum, confirming that all the key policymakers were on the same page.[10]

Balance-of-power logic was again central in the second stage, when policymakers in Berlin decided to initiate a major increase in the size of the German Army. During the Mobilization Crisis in early December 1912, Moltke told Heeringen that he was satisfied with the existing balance of power but feared that it might shift against Germany: "The military-political situation is therefore a favorable one for us at present. But it can change." Were this to happen, "Germany must be strong enough to rely on its own power." The country could "not undertake the development of its military strength soon enough."[11] Heeringen agreed, adding in a conversation with Bethmann that "the development of German military potential on land could absolutely not be extensive enough."[12] In

February 1913, the imperial proclamation introducing the new army law explained that it was necessary because the balance of power was moving against Germany: "As a result of the events that are unfolding in the Balkans, the relationship of power in Europe has been altered." Two months later, Heeringen expanded on this logic in a closed committee session with parliamentary leaders. The government, he said, was "surprised that development had gone so fast" in Russia and worried that "the situation of Germany in comparison with 1912 had become much more difficult." Worse, Russia would be even more powerful "in a few years." It was imperative that the Reichstag pass the army bill. Germany's adversaries understood full well the balancing logic behind the new army law. As General Vladimir Sukhomlinov, the Russian war minister, told the French military attaché in St. Petersburg, "Germany is in a very critical position. It is encircled by enemy forces: to the west France, to the east Russia — and it fears them. It is therefore up to Germany to play a large role on its own."[13]

Meanwhile, German thinking about war began to change. In a speech to the Reichstag in March 1913, Bethmann reiterated the prevailing view. The Kaiserreich wanted to deter an attack and prevail in the event deterrence failed: "We propose to you this bill, not because we want war but because we want peace, and because if war comes we want to be the victors."[14] German policymakers, however, were becoming convinced that deterrence was likely to fail, leading to war with the Entente. As Moltke put it to the Austro-Hungarian military attaché, "The start of a world war was probably to be considered." Given this state of affairs, he preferred to fight now rather than later, when Germany's adversaries would enjoy a military advantage. At the "War Council" meeting on 8 December 1912, Moltke proclaimed, "I consider a war to be inevitable, and the sooner the better."[15] Again, Germany's adversaries recognized the underlying logic. As Major-General Henry Wilson noted in a memorandum outlining Russian military improvements, "It is easy to understand now why Germany is cautious about the future and why she may think that it is a case of 'now or never.'" Russia's stunning growth meant that German policymakers, especially in the military, began to countenance a preventive war against St. Petersburg. French president Raymond Poincaré described their thinking: "They know that this great body gains each day in cohesion; they want to attack and destroy it before it has attained the plenitude of its power."[16] And because France was bound to come to Russia's defense, a preventive war would effectively be a war for European hegemony.

As they had done in the first stage, German decision makers agreed from the start about the best grand strategy. To be sure, when the kaiser first proposed another army bill in a meeting with Bethmann, Heeringen, Moltke, and Foreign Minister Alfred von Kiderlen-Wächter on 13 October 1912, his subordinates responded that another increase in the army was unnecessary even though they shared his concern that the balance was shifting against Germany. Yet they quickly moved to support the kaiser's position as matters worsened in the Balkans. At a meeting on 19 November, Bethmann and Heeringen agreed that a major army increase was essential. Four days later, Bethmann met with Wilhelm, Moltke, and Admiral Alfred von Tirpitz and agreed to introduce a new army bill to the Reichstag in 1913. Then, in early December, following a series of meetings and exchanges of memoranda among the key players, Wilhelm met with Bethmann and Heeringen, and authorized the latter to begin preparing the bill. At that point, a robust debate broke out between the War Ministry and the General Staff about the future size of the army, with the latter advocating an even greater increase than the former. Eventually, Wilhelm and Bethmann stepped in to support the War Ministry position, and the bill was presented to the Reichstag on 1 March 1913.[17]

Japan Decides How to Deal with the Soviet Union before World War II

Japanese grand strategy in the decade before World War II is often described as nonrational. Snyder, for instance, asserts that "Japan's bid for empire and autarky was not a rational strategic gamble." Tokyo's "imperialist binge" was not "a rational grab for autarky, compelled by the necessities of survival in international anarchy." Rather, autarky was a "chimerical goal."[18] Charles Kupchan argues that after 1937, Japan's "strategy was no longer based on hard-headed strategic calculations." Given the "depth of their cognitive and emotional commitment to the extension of empire," decision makers in Tokyo "adopted an image-based notion of security, one that identified Japanese hegemony throughout East Asia as 'an article of faith,' not just a goal of national policy." Worse still, they "failed to respond to clear information indicating that their behavior was producing a dangerous gap between resources and strategic objectives."[19]

Some scholars also emphasize that the Japanese policymaking process was nondeliberative. Robert Butow writes: "Their decision-making was cut to the pattern set by tradition: conformity, not independence; acquiescence, not protest; obedience, not questioning. What the mind thought was kept within the confines of the mind. Conclusions seem to have been based more on intuition than on reason. . . . As a general rule, no one said anything even when assailed by doubts. And because no one said anything, Japan was eventually brought to the verge of ruin."[20] Saburō Ienaga notes that "the Imperial Army and Navy enjoyed virtually unlimited freedom of action" to make policy, "and their modes of action reflected the remarkably irrational and undemocratic character of the military."[21] Van Evera goes even further, arguing that "in Japan fatuous analogies instead of analysis governed policy. . . . Evaluation became so dangerous that it almost never happened. Fatuous policies — and national ruin — were the result."[22]

These claims do not square with the facts. Japan's grand strategy in East Asia — especially its policy toward the Soviet Union — from September 1931 to June 1941 was rational. Not only was it based on credible theories, but it also emerged from a deliberative decision-making process that was marked by consensus from the get-go.[23]

Japan was in a relatively favorable strategic position for most of the 1920s. The Soviet Union — the only other great power in Asia, and a constant rival since the early twentieth century — was especially weak because it had been defeated in World War I and then endured a brutal civil war. At the same time, Tokyo had reasonably good relations with Washington — both countries were members of the Washington Treaty System — and had little to fear from China, which was consumed by civil strife and in no position to challenge Japanese interests on the continent.

Japan's situation began to deteriorate in the late 1920s. Most important, the Soviet Union instituted its first five-year plan in 1928, a move that promised to significantly increase its economic and military power over time. The following year, the Soviets displayed their improved military prowess by defeating China in a major conflict in Manchuria. As the Soviet Union's position in the balance of power improved, Japan's worsened. The Chinese

Nationalists, led by Chiang Kai-shek, began to consolidate their power on the mainland and to resist Tokyo's influence in northern China and Manchuria, an area that was of tremendous economic and strategic importance to Japan. The onset of the Great Depression and the beggar-thy-neighbor policies that accompanied it — especially America's Smoot-Hawley Tariff of 1930 — only made matters worse since Japanese prosperity was heavily dependent on an open international trading system.

Japan's strategic situation in East Asia worsened further from 1931 to 1937. It did establish control over Manchuria, invading in September 1931 and establishing the puppet state of Manchukuo in 1932. But the Soviet Union continued to grow more powerful, introducing a second five-year plan in 1933, and its influence in the neighborhood increased after it turned Mongolia, which bordered Manchuria, into a Soviet satellite state. Meanwhile, the Chinese Nationalists grew in strength and resisted Japanese efforts to control northern China, ultimately starting a war with Japan in September 1937 over control of that region.

From mid-1938 to mid-1941, Japan's threat environment became even more ominous. The increasingly powerful Soviet Union was also increasingly belligerent, initiating provocative actions on Manchuria's borders that led to brief wars with Japan in 1938 and 1939. At the same time, Tokyo's war in China became a quagmire. Moreover, the United States, which had not used its immense power to influence events in East Asia for most of the 1930s, now began imposing ever more stringent economic sanctions on Tokyo, building up its navy, and redeploying the Pacific Fleet from San Diego to Pearl Harbor.

Japanese decision makers were committed to establishing a favorable balance of power in East Asia throughout the interwar period. Before 1931, their strategy emphasized cooperation and engagement with the other great powers and China. Tokyo recognized the Soviet Union in 1925, went to great lengths to foster good relations with Britain and the United States, and adopted a policy of nonintervention in China. This strategy, known as "Shidehara diplomacy" after Foreign Minister Shidehara Kijūrō, proceeded from the assumption that Japan could maximize its economic and military power by promoting and participating in an open international economic order.

In the fall of 1931, however, Japan abandoned cooperation and engagement in favor of a grand strategy of creating an extensive autarkic empire on the Asian mainland. Manchukuo, which was rich in natural resources, especially coal and iron, was to be the centerpiece of that empire, though Japanese leaders realized they would also have to wield significant political influence in northern China as it abutted Japan's new puppet state. This grand strategy was reaffirmed in 1936 and remained in place through June 1941, after which Japan became embroiled in a crisis with the United States.

Japan's grand strategy from 1931 to 1941 relied on credible realist theories and resulted from a deliberative process. The initial decision to establish an autarkic empire relied on self-help logic, specifically the belief that Japan could best address the threatening changes in the balance of power by building up its economic and military strength. In January 1931, Hiranuma Kiichirō, a privy councilor and confidant of Emperor Hirohito, warned that the other "Great Powers . . . steadily expand their military armaments. We cannot simply dismiss as the foolish talk of idiots those who predict the outbreak, after 1936, of a second world war." Therefore, he argued, "our nation must be prepared to serve bravely in the event of an emergency." For Japan not to build up its economic and military power would be "to ignore the emperor's will. . . . To hide the reality and pretend that everything is peaceful would be the height of disloyalty."[24] That same month, in a speech to the Diet, future foreign minister Matsuoka Yōsuke stressed that "economic warfare" in the midst of the Great Depression was leading to the creation of "large economic blocs" and that to survive, Japan must establish its own area of control. If necessary, Tokyo must use force to assert "its rights to a bare existence."[25]

Ishiwara Kanji, an influential general in the Imperial Army, captured the common view that the creation of an autarkic empire centered on Manchuria would strengthen Japan and ensure its survival. With Manchuria and Mongolia, he argued, "we shall have nearly all the resources necessary for national defense, and they are absolutely necessary for the self-sufficiency of the empire." To his mind, "the natural resources of Manchuria and Mongolia . . . are sufficient to stave off the immediate crisis and build the foundations for a great leap forward."[26] Privy Councilor Ishii Kikujirō wrote in *Foreign Affairs* in 1933, "I shall not invoke statistics and marshal figures to prove how vital Manchuria is to us economically. . . . It is enough to say that the increase of our population, the congestion of our country, and our lack of raw materials, are such that Manchuria, with its virgin soil and its immense natural resources, has come to be looked upon as our vital protection. . . . In Manchuria our question is not merely one of prestige, it is one of life or death. . . . Today, as thirty years ago, Manchuria is the key to our security."[27]

Although they had not authorized it, there was broad support among civilian and military leaders in Toyko for the Kwantung Army's move to take control of Manchuria. The Wakatsuki Reijirō cabinet, which included Shidehara, quickly backed the operation. So did senior officers in the General Staff and Army Ministry. This support reflected a consensus that had emerged from a robust and uninhibited debate about Japanese grand strategy. Since the mid-1920s, "activists" and "moderates" had debated how best to address the "Manchuria problem," ultimately agreeing that Japan must exert "greater control over Manchuria, through force if necessary." As Rustin Gates puts it, "by 1931 the line between moderates and activists, if ever a strong distinction existed between the two, had been erased. What had brought the two groups together was the long-running and seemingly worsening Manchurian problem. Far from abandoning Manchuria, the moderates embraced the armed conflict that so quickly secured Japan's position on the mainland." He adds, "The civilian leadership's support for the Kwantung Army's plan, then, was . . . indicative of their enduring desire to protect Imperial interests in Manchuria."[28]

When they revisited their grand strategy in 1936, as the threat environment deteriorated, Japan's decision makers unanimously reaffirmed their commitment to autarkic empire. As in 1931, they invoked the logic of self-help, concluding that the best way to shift the balance of power in Japan's favor and thus enhance its security was to increase its economic and military might. The widely held belief that Japan's survival depended on balancing against the other great powers was reflected in an important army memorandum entitled "General Principles of National Defence Policy." Its authors declared that Japan's "national policy is to establish our status as protector and leader of East Asia. To do this, we must have the power to expunge the pressure of the white races in East Asia." Effective balancing, in turn, continued to depend on the creation of a functioning self-sufficient empire. The underlying logic was spelled out in "Fundamentals of National Policy," the key government document outlining Japan's grand strategy. Given "the situation of Japan domestically and externally, the basic policy Japan should establish is to secure the position of Japan on the East Asiatic continent in both diplomacy and national defence." Manchukuo remained the top priority: "With the development of Manchukuo we expect to strengthen our national power." At the same time, they planned "to develop nationally and economically *vis-à-vis* the Southern area, especially the outer Southern area," meaning the Dutch East Indies. Clearly understanding that its actions would prompt its rivals to respond with their own military measures, Tokyo planned to proceed cautiously. On the advice of the navy, which laid out its views in "General Principles of National Policy," decision makers aimed at "avoiding stimulation of other countries as much as possible" and expanding "[Japanese] power by gradual peaceful means."[29]

Japan's decision to reaffirm its grand strategy of autarky was the product of a deliberative process. The navy's "General Principles of National Policy" and the army's "General Principles of National Defence Policy," produced in April and June 1936 respectively, were discussed at Five Ministers' Conferences attended by Prime Minister Hirota Kōki, Foreign Minister Arita Hachirō, Finance Minister Baba Eiichi, Army Minister Terauchi Hisaichi, and Navy Minister Nagano Osami. Based on these discussions, the five ministers produced "Fundamentals of National Policy" on 7 August. This consensus document was sanctioned by the entire cabinet four days later, and its contents were reported to the emperor on 15 August.[30]

Although many scholars would concede that Japan was a rational actor through 1936, some maintain that its behavior became nonrational after that. As Snyder puts it, Japan engaged in "reckless, self-defeating overexpansion after 1937."[31] This claim is wrong. That Tokyo's grand strategy did not change is shown by a memorandum of February 1938 addressed to Britain and the United States.

Describing a continental empire as "the only chance left for Japan's survival," its authors asked London and Washington to abandon their spheres of influence in the region. "The British possess a great self-sufficient empire, the Americans have an equally self-sufficient position in the two American continents," the memorandum argued. "They ought to be generous enough to concede to Japan a place in the Orient that will meet her dire needs."[32]

Moreover, Japan acted with restraint from 1937 to 1941. Consider the major events of that period that are said to demonstrate its mindless aggression. The war against China, which began in 1937, was initiated by Chiang, not by the Japanese, who wanted to avoid armed conflict. The 1938 and 1939 wars were likewise not started by Japan, which recognized that it was in no position to defeat the Red Army, but by the Soviet Union. As for Tokyo's advances into northern Indochina in 1940 and southern Indochina in 1941, both operations were undertaken because Indochina was the main conduit of arms to Chiang's forces, and in both instances, Japan secured Vichy France's consent before moving in.[33]

France Decides How to Meet the Nazi Threat before World War II

"The popular conception of . . . France" in the 1930s, writes Robert Young, "has been rendered indelible: directionless and defeatist, paralyzed by indecision." French decision-making is said to have suffered "from the 'ineffectiveness of well-intentioned men,' from 'so many accumulated mistakes' . . . 'mediocrity of vision . . . mediocrity of leaders.'"[34]

Randall Schweller reflects this common view, describing French policy toward Germany as an instance of "folly, where threatened countries have failed to recognize a clear and present danger or, more typically, have simply not reacted to it or, more typically still, have responded in paltry and imprudent ways." France's "response to the German challenge was an incoherent series of half measures and indecisive muddling through. French grand strategy, if it can be called that, rested on a combination of contradictory policies that included elements of balancing, buck-passing, bandwagoning, and appeasement—a grand strategy best described by the foolhardy maxim that 'half a Maginot line is better than none.'"[35]

Ernest May also views France's policy in this era as nonrational. French policymakers "adopted and adhered to the suppositions about reality that suited their individual convenience," never asking, "What is the theory of the case?" Instead, they based their decisions "on those pieces of information most consistent with their preconceptions. They did not test or even identify critical presumptions. They believed what they needed to believe in order to do what they thought either desirable or expedient." Moreover, "they made choices and they either blinkered themselves against questions or invented answers to the question 'What is going on?' in order to fortify their preferred answers to the question 'What is to be done?'" Turning to the state level, May suggests that French policymakers hardly deliberated at all but "were consistently reticent; they hoarded information and opinions. . . . Leaders did not state their presumptions or expose them to debate."[36]

This conventional wisdom does not square with the evidence. Not only did French policymakers rely on credible theories to make sense of their threat environment and how to address it, but they also engaged in a robust and uninhibited debate before finally agreeing on a policy for dealing with Nazi Germany. In short, France in the late 1930s was a rational actor.[37]

RATIONALITY AND GRAND STRATEGY

French leaders lived in fear of Germany from the moment the ink dried on the Versailles Treaty, signed in June 1919. Although their level of fear increased significantly in the mid-1930s as the Third Reich started rearming, withdrew from the League of Nations, and reoccupied the Rhineland, it was Germany's annexation of Austria—the Anschluss—in March 1938 that really set off alarm bells in Paris. Many people believed that Germany, having expanded beyond its borders for the first time since the Great War, would move against Czechoslovakia at any moment.

The principal task confronting the Édouard Daladier government, which took power on 10 April 1938, was to design a grand strategy to cope with the new threat environment. There was little debate among key policymakers about what France should do. They immediately decided to ramp up the country's impressive efforts to build powerful military forces that could deal with the Wehrmacht. There was also little debate regarding relations with Eastern Europe, Italy, and especially Britain. Virtually every French policymaker saw Britain as an indispensable ally for dealing with Germany, a position that gave London great leverage over Paris right up to the outbreak of war in Europe.

French leaders disagreed, however, about how to manage relations with Germany and the Soviet Union in the aftermath of the Anschluss. For most of 1938, the debate revolved around two questions: whether to conciliate or contain Germany and whether to make an alliance with the Soviet Union. But after the Munich Agreement was signed, on 30 September 1938, and especially after Germany moved to conquer the rest of Czechoslovakia on 15 March 1939, the opposing camps resolved their differences, agreeing to both contain Germany and seek an alliance with Moscow.

French thinking about how to deal with Germany and the Soviet Union was based mainly on different realist theories. Virtually everyone thought Germany was determined to increase its power through expansion. But policymakers disagreed on how much power Adolf Hitler wanted — that is, whether he wanted Germany to be the leading or the only great power in Europe. The view that he was bent on hegemony is reflected in Daladier's comments to the British in April 1938, in which he warned that Hitler wanted "nothing less than total domination of the European continent." Émile Charvériat, the political director of the Foreign Ministry, concurred: "Hitler appears more concerned with hegemony in Europe than with improving . . . relations with France." Most Quai d'Orsay officials judged that "the idea that Germany will be permanently satisfied if given a free hand in the east is an illusion. . . . The east is only a means to acquire the resources which will permit her to turn against France." The führer had "hegemonic ambition."[38] The alternative perspective — that Germany would be satisfied with dominating Eastern Europe and was therefore not a direct threat to France — was equally widespread. Robert Coulondre, the French ambassador to the Soviet Union, summarized this line of thinking in December 1938, cabling Paris that Germany's "determination to expand in the east seems to me as certain as her renunciation, at least for the present, of any conquests in the west." There was, he reported, a "general desire for the establishment of good relations with France."[39]

There was also substantial disagreement about whether to contain or conciliate Nazi Germany. Minister of the Colonies Georges Mandel believed France must opt for containment, arguing that "rotten compromises" would never satisfy Germany and that "with each new crisis it will be ever more difficult to avoid war and that finally war will be imposed on France in the worst possible conditions."[40] Foreign Minister Georges Bonnet, however, thought France must "restructure" and "renegotiate" its obligations to its East European allies since "French security is not directly threatened."[41] These contrasting policy prescriptions were at play as early as April 1938, when Daladier chose his foreign minister. Noting that Joseph Paul-Boncour was determined to stand by the small states of Eastern Europe and contain Hitler, the new prime minister told him, "The policy you outlined to me is a very fine policy, thoroughly worthy of France: I do not think we are in a position to undertake it." He had decided, he said, "to have Bonnet," a leading advocate of conciliation.[42]

As for France's relations with the Soviet Union, policymakers disagreed about whether Paris should ally with Moscow or buck-pass and let the Soviets deal with Germany largely by themselves. Daladier favored the first option, maintaining that with a Franco-Soviet alliance, "we would have no need to fear the shadow of war in Europe."[43] Bonnet, however, wanted to distance France from the Soviet Union: "I have made a thorough study of the Franco-Russian pact and I discover that we are not tied by it. We do not have to repudiate it, because we are not committed by it to automatically join Russia."[44] Other key players thought neither balancing nor buck-passing was a viable strategy because the Red Army was too weak to stand up to the Wehrmacht. In the fall of 1938, intelligence officials concluded that "militarily" the Soviet Union was "entirely impotent."[45] General Maurice Gamelin, the chief of the Army Staff, judged that the Soviet Union was "incapable of effective intervention in Europe," much like "the little countries . . . who no longer have much military value."[46]

Although French leaders viewed their threat environment predominantly through a realist lens, they also saw the world in ideological terms. Many leaders resisted close relations, not to mention an alliance, with the Soviet Union because they feared the Soviets were committed to world revolution and would take every opportunity to spread communism across the continent. At the time of the Munich conference, Daladier worried that "Soviet Russia would not let the opportunity pass of bringing world revolution to our lands."[47] Bonnet harbored similar concerns even after Germany started World War II. As the British ambassador to France, Sir Eric Phipps, noted, the French foreign minister was "absolutely convinced that [Josef] Stalin's aim is still to bring about world revolution. . . . Germany, as Russia's nearest neighbour, will be the first victim. . . . He wonders whether it will be possible to prevent the disease from spreading."[48] In short, French strategic thinking was influenced by both realist and ideological theories.

Key decision makers clearly thought in terms of these competing theories, taking one of three different positions on how to deal with the Third Reich and, by extension, the Soviet Union. One faction believed it was possible to conciliate Germany and avoid a major European war. Proponents of this view included Bonnet and his supporters in the cabinet, Vice President of the Council of Ministers Camille Chautemps, Minister of Public Works Anatole de Monzie, Minister of Labor Charles Pomaret, and Minister of Finance Paul Marchandeau. Their desire to conciliate Germany usually went hand in hand with a commitment to resisting Moscow's efforts to forge a close alliance with Paris. Bonnet in particular consistently rebuffed Soviet foreign minister Maxim Litvinov's attempts to begin joint staff talks and fashion a concrete military agreement.

An opposing faction concluded that Germany wanted nothing less than hegemony in Europe and had to be contained. Cabinet members of this persuasion included Mandel, Minister of Justice

Paul Reynaud, and Minister of Veterans and Pensioners Auguste Champetier de Ribes. They were supported by Coulondre, Paul-Boncour, and the president of the Chamber of Deputies, Édouard Herriot, all of whom also favored an alliance with the Soviet Union.

Finally, a third group, including Daladier (who was not only prime minister, but also minister of defense), Minister of Military Marine César Campinchi, Minister of Air Guy La Chambre, and Minister of the Interior Albert-Pierre Sarraut, floated between these two positions. So did General Gamelin, though he played only a minor role in formulating French grand strategy.

French policymakers converged on a decision to contain Germany and seek a formal alliance with the Soviet Union via a deliberative process. As Young notes, France's defeat in 1940 should not obscure the fact that French leaders exhibited "a seriousness of purpose toward the perils at hand, a determination to resist German attempts at hegemony, a willingness to devote enormous care and effort to the cause of national defense." France, he continues, "was under the command of competent if not outstanding civil and military leaders, men who went further than some believed was warranted to avert war, men who did more than was subsequently admitted to prepare for it."[49]

In the period between the Anschluss and the Munich Agreement, there was little agreement among French decision makers on policy toward either Germany or the Soviet Union. To be sure, they all believed that having annexed Austria, Hitler was now likely to move against Czechoslovakia. This is why Daladier and Gamelin met frequently with Colonel Louis Rivet, the head of French intelligence. There was substantial disagreement, however, on whether Germany's territorial ambitions extended beyond Czechoslovakia and therefore about whether France should conciliate or contain the Third Reich. As noted, this cleavage was present when Daladier formed his cabinet, and it remained in place through the Munich Crisis.

Given that France did not definitively decide how to deal with Germany until October 1938, it is unsurprising that there was also little consensus on how to deal with the Soviet Union. While Coulondre and others pushed hard for staff talks with the Soviets, Bonnet and the military leadership opposed these talks for both practical and ideological reasons. They believed that a close relationship with the Red Army would spread communism in the ranks of the French Army while tying France's fortunes to a fighting force that had been badly weakened by Stalin's purges.

In the wake of the Munich Crisis, French policymakers across the board came to believe that Germany was bent on dominating all of Europe and thus slowly began converging on a two-pronged policy of containing Germany and allying with the Soviet Union. Perhaps the most important evidence of this convergence was Daladier's decision to come off the fence and embrace a hard-line policy toward the Third Reich. As evidence mounted that Germany had its gunsights on the rest of Czechoslovakia and might even be contemplating an attack on the Low Countries or France itself, the prime minister pushed the British to participate in staff talks and commit to fighting alongside France if Germany attacked in Western Europe. General Gamelin and other military leaders experienced a similar conversion. This shift toward a strategy of containment had important consequences for how Daladier and his generals thought about relations with Moscow. They began seriously contemplating a Franco-Soviet military alliance, even as they worried that Stalin might forge an alliance with Nazi Germany, leaving France dangerously vulnerable to a German attack.

Germany's conquest of all of Czechoslovakia in March 1939 finally led the contending factions in the French national security community — containers, conciliators, and floaters — to embrace a common position on dealing with both Germany and the Soviet Union. Daladier and Gamelin became more committed than ever to containing the Third Reich and allying with the Soviet Union. The more consequential shift occurred among the conciliators, who switched positions and staunchly supported containment. Bonnet was the most important and striking convert to the new strategy, which was already embraced by his deputies at the Quai d'Orsay. As he put it, "the peace and appeasement policy of the 'men of Munich' had suffered a lamentable disaster. . . . In every country warmongers who would lead Europe toward catastrophe were bound to gain the upper hand."[50]

As French thinking about the threat environment crystallized around a single realist position, ideological considerations, which had played some role prior to Munich, faded into the background. General Maxime Weygand, who like many military leaders had feared Communist subversion before the fall of Czechoslovakia, now abandoned these concerns: "Communism should be fought on the internal plane. . . . On the external plane, ideology must not interfere with strategic needs."[51]

Having reached a consensus early in the spring of 1939, French policymakers went to great lengths over the next five months to forge an uncompromising deterrence policy against Nazi Germany, including security guarantees to Poland, Romania, and Greece, as well as a tripartite anti-German alliance with Britain and the Soviet Union. Despite France's best efforts, however, both initiatives failed, in large part because Britain refused to consider the possibility that the Red Army might traverse Poland and Romania in the event of a war with Germany and because the Soviets doubted the Western powers' reliability. On 23 August, Berlin and Moscow formed an alliance, which meant that there would be no great-power balancing coalition against Nazi Germany as there had been against imperial Germany before World War I. Then, on 1 September, Hitler invaded Poland, forcing Britain and France to declare war against the Third Reich.

The United States Decides to Expand NATO after the Cold War

The expansion of NATO following the collapse of the Soviet Union has long been criticized as a nonrational policy. In June 1997, fifty former senators, cabinet secretaries, ambassadors, and foreign policy specialists sent an open letter to President Bill Clinton, declaring that "the current US-led effort to expand NATO . . . is a policy error of historic importance."[52] This thinking was even more prevalent in academic circles. Later the same year, Michael Mandelbaum wrote, "The Clinton plan is therefore perfectly non-sensical. NATO expansion isn't just pointless. It's also dangerous." Describing enlargement as "the administration's folly," he called on the Senate to reject "a scheme that is at best pointless, at worst extremely dangerous."[53]

Similarly, Michael MccGwire described the Clinton administration's plan to move NATO eastward as "a logical and political inconsistency of major proportions," an "illogical" decision he found "hardly surprising." It "was not the outcome of an objective analysis of the long-term requirements for security in Europe"; instead, "US policy has been characterized by a combination of arrogance and wishful thinking."[54] Kenneth Waltz made the point more briefly, calling enlargement a policy "that only an overwhelmingly powerful country could afford, and only a foolish one be tempted, to follow."[55]

Whatever one thinks of the merits of NATO expansion, the decision to enlarge the alliance was rational. Both proponents and opponents of the policy relied on credible theories and engaged in a vigorous and unconstrained debate before President Clinton finally opted for expansion.

After the Cold War ended, almost everyone in the U.S. national security community believed that NATO should remain intact and retain its importance on the world stage. The only question that concerned American decision makers was what shape the alliance should take and, in particular, whether it should maintain its existing membership — to include a reunified Germany — or be expanded eastward. The debate began in 1991, during George H. W. Bush's presidency, but it picked up steam in the first year of the Clinton administration. It was finally settled in December 1994, when NATO announced that it would begin enlargement negotiations with Poland, Hungary, and the Czech Republic.

The Bush administration paid little attention to the issue of NATO enlargement before 1991, save for ensuring that a unified Germany would be a member of the alliance. Once the Soviet Union started to unravel, however, Bush and his advisers seriously considered expanding NATO eastward for largely realist reasons. To be clear, they did not view the alliance primarily as a means to contain Moscow, though there was initially some concern that the Soviet Union might make a comeback. Rather, they viewed it as a vehicle for maintaining and enhancing America's dominant position in Europe. As Soviet forces withdrew from Eastern Europe, National Security Adviser Brent Scowcroft argued that expanding the alliance into the region's "power vacuum" would facilitate "a much more robust and a constructive U.S. role in the center of Europe."[56] Yet despite this enthusiasm for enlargement, no decision was taken on the matter before Bush lost to Clinton in November 1992.[57]

Senior policymakers in the Clinton administration were divided into two factions on NATO expansion. Although both factions were committed to liberal hegemony, they had different views about how Russia would respond to a move eastward by the alliance and thus about the appropriate strategy for dealing with Eastern Europe. The disagreement revolved around realist and liberal theories of state behavior.[58]

One faction argued that Russia would see NATO enlargement as a serious threat and respond aggressively, as realism predicts. The likely consequences would be profound. Not only might Russia's democratic experiment fail, but there was also the possibility that Europe would once again be divided, this time between an expanded NATO and a hostile Russia. As a State Department paper warned in July 1993, putting "expanded membership on NATO's immediate agenda" would have "divisive and potentially destabilizing consequences in the East."[59] This thinking was especially popular in the Pentagon, where there was great fear of antagonizing Russia. General John Shalikashvili, the chairman of the Joint Chiefs of Staff, was concerned that NATO enlargement would be "destabilizing" because it would draw "a new line of division" in Europe. He wanted "to avoid at all costs the establishment of a new line, a new division that in turn, then, would create new tensions and fuel new conflicts."[60]

The other faction recognized these risks but believed that if the West reassured Russia of its benign intentions, Moscow would see the world in liberal and not realist terms, embrace democracy, and ultimately become a responsible member of the liberal international order. According to Deputy Secretary of State Strobe Talbott, "We must ensure that what we eventually propose is seen by key countries of the former Soviet Union as enhancing their security and their sense of belonging in Europe. . . . The key here is to present our expansion plan in a way that stresses eventual inclusion rather than near-term exclusion of Russia—and that is seen to enhance regional stability and security for all states in the area." Clinton believed the United States must tread carefully but that he could reassure the Russians. NATO should expand, he said, "in a careful way, so as to leave open the possibility that the future will be different, rather than recreating the certainty of the past." As Secretary of Defense William Perry—a staunch opponent of expansion— remarked, both Clinton and Vice President Al Gore were confident that "the Russians could be convinced that expansion was not directed against them."[61]

These two theoretical perspectives led to two competing policy options. Opponents of expansion favored the Partnership for Peace (PfP), a program for fostering cooperative relationships between NATO and states across Europe, to include Eastern Europe and even Russia. The initiative, which was aimed at delaying if not precluding enlargement, would allow partners "to build up an individual relationship with NATO, choosing their own priorities for cooperation."[62] Proponents of expansion, on the other hand, wanted to quickly admit a handful of former Warsaw Pact members to NATO while going to great lengths to reassure the Russians that the expanding alliance was not aimed at their country. Some advocates of this two-track policy even believed that Russia might eventually join NATO. As Talbott put it, "Our strategic goal . . . was to integrate both Central Europe and the former Soviet Union into the major institutions of the Euro-Atlantic community."[63]

The Clinton administration began seriously debating NATO enlargement in the wake of Secretary of State Warren Christopher's Athens speech of June 1993 about strengthening the North Atlantic Cooperation Council. Over the next eighteen months, U.S. policy-makers extensively discussed the relative merits of PfP and expansion but without agreement. It was therefore left to the president to make the ultimate decision on how to proceed, and it resulted in NATO's December 1994 announcement that enlargement would begin soon.

Although proponents and opponents of expansion began debating NATO's future soon after the Athens speech — Christopher, Secretary of Defense Les Aspin, and National Security Adviser Anthony Lake discussed the matter throughout the late summer and early fall — the first formal meeting on the issue involving Clinton's principal advisers was held on 19 October, in preparation for the upcoming NATO summit in Brussels. Despite a thoughtful back and forth, both sides remained committed to their different views, making it impossible to agree on the best way forward. Lake forcefully advocated expansion, Aspin and Shalikashvili were strongly opposed and favored PfP, and Christopher leaned toward the Pentagon position. The result was "an ambiguous compromise, a decision not to decide that had kicked the can down the road."[64] According to the National Security Council memorandum that summarized the meeting, the president's comments at the Brussels summit should emphasize the PfP but leave the door open for enlargement.

As the debate over the future of NATO was playing out among his subordinates, Clinton inched toward a pro-expansion position, though he refrained from making a definitive decision. Speaking in Brussels on 9 and 10 January, he strongly endorsed the PfP but also went somewhat beyond the advice he was given, arguing that the

———

PfP "sets in motion a process that leads to the enlargement of NATO." Two days later in Prague, he said in a prepared statement, "While the Partnership is not NATO membership, neither is it a permanent holding room. It changes the entire NATO dialog so that now the question is no longer whether NATO will take on new members but when and how." Next the president traveled to Moscow, where he delivered a different message. His focus, he told Russian president Boris Yeltsin, was on PfP, and NATO expansion was something that would happen only in the distant future.[65]

Given Clinton's failure to make a decision about where NATO was headed, both sides in the debate continued pushing their agendas. Lake took the lead in advocating NATO expansion, instructing his staff to draw up a detailed policy memorandum that he could circulate to the president and senior officials in the Defense and State departments. At the same time, he had serious discussions with key policymakers, the most important of whom was Talbott. In the course of those conversations, Talbott, who had initially been a skeptic on enlargement, became a firm supporter of the idea and even helped Lake persuade Christopher to back NATO expansion and bring Richard Holbrooke into the State Department to help push the plan through the bureaucracy.[66]

Meanwhile, the opponents of enlargement in the Pentagon continued to champion PfP. General Shalikashvili and one of his deputies, General Wesley Clark, went to great lengths to incorporate their thinking into a major speech on the future of NATO that Vice President Gore was scheduled to deliver in Berlin. Although Gore generally supported expansion, his speech did not suggest that the Clinton administration had made a firm decision on the matter.[67]

Clinton finally decided in favor of NATO expansion in late June 1994, after receiving Lake's memorandum.[68] But his commitment was not immediately apparent. In a press conference with Polish president Lech Walesa in July, Clinton remarked that while he had always considered PfP a first step toward enlargement, "now what we have to do is to get the NATO partners together and discuss what the next steps should be." Andrzej Olechowski, the Polish foreign minister, noted, "I would have liked our dialogue on NATO to have gone much further than it did. Today, I feel we have come an inch or maybe half an inch closer toward entry."[69]

More important, the president failed to communicate his decision to all parts of his administration, especially the Pentagon, which remained the center of opposition to his policy. This failure is reflected in two further meetings that took place in the fall of 1994, at which some of the major policymakers continued to vigorously challenge enlargement. At the first of these meetings, held in the State Department on 22 September, Holbrooke clashed with General Clark and Deputy Assistant Secretary of Defense Joseph Kruzel. Challenging their resistance to expansion, he said in no uncertain terms, "It is policy." Finally, on 21 December, three weeks after NATO's announcement that it would expand, Perry met with other key decision makers in the White House and made clear his opposition to enlargement. Although Perry was supported by Shalikashvili, Clinton confirmed that he favored Lake's plan to expand NATO while making this policy palatable to the Russians.[70]

The United States Decides to Pursue Liberal Hegemony after the Cold War

Policymakers and academics alike have described America's post–Cold War grand strategy of liberal hegemony as nonrational. Donald Trump frequently made this argument while running for president in 2016. "Unfortunately, after the Cold War our foreign policy veered badly off course," he said during a major foreign policy address. "We failed to develop a new vision for a new time. In fact, as time went on, our foreign policy began to make less and less sense. Logic was replaced with foolishness and arrogance, which led to one foreign policy disaster after another." Then, for emphasis, he added, "Our foreign policy is a complete and total disaster. No vision. No purpose. No direction. No strategy."[71]

Several prominent academics have made the same point in more measured language. According to Stephen Walt, U.S. grand strategy "failed because its leaders pursued a series of unwise and unrealistic objectives and refused to learn from their mistakes. In particular, the deeper cause of America's recurring foreign policy failures was the combination of overwhelming U.S. primacy, a misguided grand strategy, and an increasingly dysfunctional foreign policy community."[72] Andrew Bacevich places less emphasis on nondeliberation and more on the ideas underpinning liberal hegemony, arguing that "the United States wasted little time in squandering the advantages it had gained by winning the Cold War. Events at home and abroad put this post–Cold War consensus to the test, unmasking its contradictions and exposing its premises as delusional."[73] David Hendrickson contends that "the ideas of the security establishment . . . reflect a sort of 'distilled frenzy' . . . that continues to exert profound influence."[74] Meanwhile, Patrick Porter argues that the U.S.-led international order is "impossible, ahistorical, and hubristic" and rests on "a theology of restoration that frames foreign policy as a morality play" riddled with "conceits."[75]

Yet while there are good reasons to conclude that liberal hegemony was a failure, it was a rational grand strategy. The policy was based on a set of credible liberal theories and was the result of a deliberative decision-making process.[76]

With the end of the Cold War and the subsequent collapse of the Soviet Union, the world became unipolar — a profound transformation in the architecture of the international system that had enormous consequences. For one thing, now that the United States was the only great power on the planet, great-power politics was off the table. Moreover, its Cold War grand strategy of containment was irrelevant because there was no other great power to contain. The question now was: What policy should replace it? The Bush administration, which played the central role in bringing the Cold War to an end, began to seriously address this issue in 1992, soon after the Soviet Union broke apart, but had made no definitive decision by the time it left office in January 1993. It fell to President Clinton and his advisers to formulate a grand strategy for a unipolar world, and they quickly embraced liberal hegemony as the replacement for containment.

Through the end of 1991, Bush and his senior officials viewed international politics mainly through a realist lens. This thinking informed how they handled the end of the Cold War and the dissolution of the Soviet Union. In particular, they went to great lengths to consolidate America's position as the world's only superpower while giving Moscow little reason to reverse course and reignite the Cold War.[77]

By 1992, however, it was clear that the United States needed a new grand strategy. There were two views on this matter inside the Bush administration. The first, championed by Secretary of Defense Dick Cheney and his subordinates in the Pentagon, emphasized the importance of maintaining unipolarity by preventing the emergence of a peer competitor. According to the famous leaked version of the

1992 Defense Planning Guidance (DPG), "Our first objective is to prevent the re-emergence of a new rival. . . . We must maintain the mechanisms for deterring potential competitors from even aspiring to a larger regional or global role."[78] But this realist perspective was also tinged with liberal thinking. The authors of the DPG stressed the importance of international law and "the spread of democratic forms of government and open economic systems."[79]

The second view, advocated by Secretary of State Lawrence Eagleburger, called for the United States to use its preeminent position to establish a liberal world order. Washington, he argued, must be "a provider of reassurance and architect of new security arrangements; an aggressive proponent of economic openness; an exemplar and advocate of democratic values; [and] a builder and leader of coalitions to deal with problems in the chaotic post–Cold War world."[80] Even as these competing approaches were being worked out, however, electoral politics intervened. The future direction of U.S. grand strategy was left to the incoming Clinton administration.

In principle, the Clinton team had three grand strategic options: retreat from the world, maintain the status quo, or transform the international system.[81] The administration's key policymakers quickly and unanimously agreed that the United States must take the lead role in transforming the international system to remake it in America's image. This new grand strategy—commonly referred to as liberal hegemony—rested explicitly on a combination of U.S. leadership and the core liberal theories of international politics: democratic peace theory, economic interdependence theory, and liberal institutionalism.

The centrality of the big three liberal theories in the Clinton team's thinking about grand strategy is reflected in almost every official foreign policy pronouncement these decision makers made.

Consider the foundational statements issued by the president and two of his senior advisers in the fall of 1993, when they first turned their attention from domestic to foreign affairs.[82] In the first major address laying out the administration's grand strategy, Lake declared that "the successor to a doctrine of containment must be a strategy of enlargement—enlargement of the world's free community of market democracies." The United States, he said, must commit to "engagement abroad on behalf of democracy and expanded trade" and promote "habits of multilateralism," which would "one day enable the rule of law to play a far more civilizing role in the conduct of nations."[83]

Speaking at the United Nations the following week, Clinton declared, "In a new era of peril and opportunity, our overriding purpose must be to expand and strengthen the world's community of marketbased democracies. . . . Now we seek to enlarge the circle of nations that live under those free institutions. For our dream is of a day when the opinions and energies of every person in the world will be given full expression, in a world of thriving democracies that cooperate with each other and live in peace."[84] Madeleine Albright, the U.S. ambassador to the United Nations, delivered the same message in a speech at the National War College, emphasizing that "our strategy looks to the enlargement of democracy and markets abroad" and noting that "no one understands the potential advantages of multilateralism better than the United States."[85]

Having declared early on that the United States would pursue liberal hegemony, the Clinton administration remained firmly committed to it throughout its tenure. Decision makers still occasionally disagreed about specific policy issues and about how best to establish a liberal international order. For example, there were different views and repeated discussions about how to deal with Russia and handle NATO expansion. Yet the president and his advisers never wavered in their belief that the United States was the "indispensable nation" and that it should spread democracy, foster economic interdependence, and strengthen multilateral institutions around the world.[86]

Given that there was a powerful consensus among the Clinton administration's leaders in favor of liberal hegemony, they had little need to come together and debate the fundamental elements of the emerging grand strategy.[87] Clinton, Lake, and Albright did not have a major meeting to coordinate their speeches of September 1993, which rolled out the administration's policy. They knew they were operating from the same playbook. They did, however, debate how best to sell liberal hegemony to the American public, which they viewed as a difficult but essential task. At an important meeting in October 1994, before Clinton was scheduled to speak at the United Nations, the president and his foreign policy team had a wide-ranging discussion devoted to finding a simple concept that would capture the essence of their policy the way containment had encapsulated U.S. grand strategy during the Cold War.[88] Despite their best efforts, however, they never agreed on a term they found compelling.

Rational Grand Strategies

All of the states examined in this chapter were rational in the sense that policymakers were guided by credible theories and that their policies emerged from a deliberative decision-making process. German decision makers before World War I, as well as Japanese and French decision makers before World War II, thought in terms of realist logic, whereas American decision makers after the Cold War thought in terms of liberal logic. There is a straightforward structural explanation for these different patterns of thinking. Germany, Japan, and France lived in a competitive multipolar world that was best explained by realist theories. The United States, on the other hand, faced no great-power competitors—it operated in a unipolar world in the 1990s—and therefore could think in liberal terms without risking its security.

The evidence also shows that although the manner in which the final decision was reached varied from state to state, it was always marked by deliberation. When there was consensus on the appropriate strategy from the start, agreement was not mindless but rather based on the informed application of a credible theory that happened to enjoy widespread influence. German decision-making before World War I, Japanese decision-making before World War II, and American decision-making regarding liberal hegemony are cases in point.

When policymakers first disagreed but then found agreement on the best strategy moving forward, as French officials did before World War II, they reached that common understanding through robust and uninhibited debate. Finally, when policymakers were deadlocked and the ultimate decider chose the strategy—as President Clinton had to do regarding NATO expansion—he did not impose his views arbitrarily but instead acted only after encouraging debate among his advisers and considering their different views.

Yet decisions about grand strategy can be made at relative leisure. Crises, on the other hand, are pressure-laden events where time is short, a fact that may prevent policymakers from evaluating the situation carefully and dispassionately and from engaging in robust and uninhibited debate. One could argue that states are likely to be rational in making grand strategy but abandon that rationality during crises. But this, it turns out, is not true either.

——

Chapter 6

RATIONALITY AND CRISIS MANAGEMENT

This chapter considers five prominent crisis decisions that have been identified as instances of nonrational behavior: Germany's decision to start World War I in 1914; Japan's decision to attack the United States at Pearl Harbor in 1941; Adolf Hitler's decision to invade the Soviet Union in 1941; the United States' decision to settle the Cuban Missile Crisis in 1962; and Moscow's decision to invade Czechoslovakia in 1968. In each case, we find that the relevant state was a rational actor: its policy was based on a credible theory and emerged from a deliberative process. Finally, although this book focuses on grand strategy and crisis decisions, we briefly examine two decisions to escalate ongoing wars that have been cited as prominent examples of nonrationality: the U.S. decisions to cross the 38th parallel during the Korean War and to markedly increase American involvement in the Vietnam War.

Germany Decides to Start World War I

A number of scholars hold out German decision-making before World War I as a classic case of nonrationality. According to Richard Ned Lebow, German behavior during the July Crisis, which led up to the conflict, was "a particularly telling example of the causal relationship between cognitive impairment, miscalculation, and war." German leaders relied on false analogies that caused them to believe – wrongly and with catastrophic consequences – that the 1914 crisis would be a repeat of the 1909 Bosnian Crisis, in which Germany and Austria-Hungary forced Russia and Serbia to acquiesce to Vienna's annexation of Bosnia-Herzegovina without a fight.[1] Lebow and Janice Gross Stein make a different argument, claiming that German decision makers in the July Crisis were overcome by their emotions. German chancellor Theobald von Bethmann Hollweg and his advisers, Lebow and Stein argue, realized they were committed to a risky military policy in the shape of the Schlieffen Plan, and the "resulting stress" engendered "anxiety and fear" that blinded them to "repeated warnings of impending disaster."[2]

Defensive realists Jack Snyder and Stephen Van Evera offer a different argument about German nonrationality that zeroes in on military strategy. They maintain that although it was manifestly clear that defense had a marked advantage over offense, German leaders nevertheless believed that offense was superior to defense and that Germany could employ the Schlieffen Plan to win a quick and decisive victory over its rivals. This "wildly over-ambitious offensive strategy" was based on "false ideas" and "political and military myths that obscured the defender's advantages."[3] Although most Europeans at the time were "mesmerized" by this "cult of the offensive," it was most potent in Germany, the most "myth-ridden European power."[4]

Not only are policymakers in Berlin said to have thought non-rationally about strategy, but they have also been accused of failing to deliberate during the crisis. The key obstacle to deliberation was the German military, which kept civilian leaders in the dark about the details of the Schlieffen Plan and ultimately pushed them into war. As Snyder puts it, war happened largely because "civilian authorities had at best partial control over and knowledge of military strategy."[5] Lebow goes further, asserting that civilian decision makers were "stampeded into war."[6] In his analysis of Kaiser Wilhelm II's role in the July Crisis, John Röhl argues that nondeliberation involved more than military dominance of the decision-making process. By 1914, Wilhelm "presided over an often-dysfunctional governmental machine that has aptly been characterized as verging on 'polycratic chaos.'"[7]

These claims do not withstand scrutiny. Both Germany's decision to go to war in 1914 and its strategy for waging that war were based on credible theories from the start. Moreover, German civilian and military policymakers, who broadly agreed on all the key issues confronting them, engaged in deliberative decision-making. In short, Germany was a rational actor during the July Crisis.[8]

As we have seen, when the July Crisis broke out, Germany was confronted by a worsening threat environment. The German Army Law of 1913, which was designed to shift the balance of power in the Kaiserreich's favor, had prompted the members of the Triple Entente—Britain, France, and Russia—to tighten their relations and enhance their own fighting power, leaving Berlin in an even weaker position. Russia, given its large population and industrializing economy, was a particular concern. At the same time, Germany's chief ally, Austria-Hungary, was growing steadily weaker, and German policymakers feared that it might soon cease to be a great power. To resolve its strategic predicament, the Kaiserreich initiated a war against the Triple Entente in the belief that Germany would prevail, emerge as the dominant power in Europe, and eliminate the looming Russian threat once and for all.

Germany's determination to provoke a great-power war in July 1914 was based on credible realist theorizing. The key German leaders adopted the logic of preventive war with a view to establishing hegemony in Europe while they still could. They had some minor internal disagreements, but as Röhl notes, "It is vital to stress . . . that the differences between these decision makers were minimal. All of them . . . believed they could see a golden opportunity that was too good to miss."[9]

Just before the crisis began, Wilhelm declared, "Whoever in Germany still does not believe that Russo-Gaul is working with urgency towards an imminent war against us, and that we must take countermeasures accordingly, deserves to be sent straightaway to the madhouse."[10] Bethmann also feared the Russian threat that was "looming above us as an increasingly terrifying nightmare" and concluded that Germany would do well to start a war sooner rather than later. As he remarked after the war, "Lord yes, in a certain sense it was a preventive war . . . [motivated by] the constant threat of attack, the greater likelihood of its inevitability in the future, and by the military's claim: today war is still possible without defeat, but not in two years!"[11]

Foreign Minister Gottlieb von Jagow took a similar view, arguing on the eve of the July Crisis that "Russia will be ready to fight in a few years. Then she will crush us by the number of her soldiers; then she will have built her Baltic fleet and her strategic railways. Our group in the meantime will have become steadily weaker. . . . I do not desire preventive war, but if the conflict should offer itself, we ought not to shirk it."[12] At the same time, Jagow reported that according to General Helmuth von Moltke, the chief of the German General Staff, "there was no alternative but to fight a preventive war so as to beat the enemy while we could still emerge fairly well from the struggle." Therefore, "our policy should be geared to bringing about an early war."[13] Moltke was more emphatic on this point as the crisis neared its conclusion: "We shall never hit it again so well as we do now with France's and Russia's expansion of their armies incomplete."[14]

German decision makers had also developed a credible theory of victory should the opportunity to launch a preventive war present itself. At the heart of that theory was the recognition that Germany would have to fight a two-front war: a campaign in the west against France and probably Britain and another in the east against Russia. German strategists had long believed that the best chance of prevailing in such a conflict would be to score a quick and decisive victory on one front while defending on the other and then taking the offensive on the second front. By 1905, they had concluded that Russia's vast territory made it difficult to win quickly and decisively in the east. Moreover, France could mobilize its offensively oriented army in short order and attack Germany in the rear while most of its forces were engaged on its eastern front. Logic therefore dictated that France should be the initial target, and Germany would have to start the conflict on the defensive against Russia.[15]

Hence the broad outline of the Schlieffen Plan: German forces would deal France a knockout blow and then turn eastward to defeat the slow-mobilizing Russian Army. The details of the plan were debated at length by Moltke and his subordinates between 1905 and

1914, and over time they modified it in important respects so as to increase the likelihood of success in the western campaign.[16]

German decision makers were confident that the Schlieffen Plan would succeed. Wilhelm reflected the prevailing view in an address to departing German troops in August 1914: "You will be home before the leaves have fallen from the trees." The military thought in similar terms. General Arthur von Loebell maintained, "In two weeks we shall defeat France, then we shall turn round, defeat Russia and then we shall march to the Balkans and establish order there." The British military attaché in Berlin noted that this "supreme confidence" was widespread in German military circles. At the same time, a German observer claimed that the General Staff "looks ahead to war with France with great confidence, expects to defeat France within four weeks."[17]

Nevertheless, leaders in Berlin were well aware that success was by no means guaranteed. They understood that the increasing lethality of contemporary weaponry meant that an assaulting force would face enormous resistance and that it was easier to defend than to attack. Battles would involve major casualties for offensive and defensive forces alike. "Nobody was under any illusion," writes Michael Howard, "that frontal attack would be anything but very difficult and that success could be purchased with anything short of very heavy casualties."[18] Still, German strategists believed that their chances of success were good but would only decrease as the balance of power shifted even further against Germany. In a few years, they thought, "the striking power of Russia would be sufficient to nullify the calculations embodied in the Schlieffen Plan."[19]

Not only was German decision-making based on credible theories, but it was also marked by deliberation. Policy was made by a "tiny" and tight-knit group of individuals who remained in constant contact throughout the crisis, discussing the unfolding situation in a considered fashion.[20] The key players were Wilhelm, Bethmann, Jagow, and Moltke, though they also consulted with Under Secretary of State Arthur Zimmermann, General Georg von Waldersee, Prussian minister of war Erich von Falkenhayn, and Admiral Alfred von Tirpitz, secretary of state of the Imperial Naval Office. Their extensive discussions were characterized by consensus, both on German goals and on how best to achieve them. As Annika Mombauer observes, "Berchtold's famous question 'Who governs in Berlin — Moltke or Bethmann?' is perhaps best answered in the light of these similarities, for, in the end, it was almost immaterial who was in charge. The two men at the summit of military and political decision-making in those crucial months essentially shared the same aims and were motivated by the same desires, not only in July 1914, but also in the months preceding and following the outbreak of war. Post-war attempts by the military leaders to blame civilians and vice versa have confused the issue by suggesting that differences of opinion existed where there was in fact a great resemblance."[21]

Popular arguments to the effect that German decision-making was nondeliberative are wrong. Marc Trachtenberg lists them, asking whether policymakers were "kept in the dark" about military planning, "overwhelmed by forces they could not control . . . carried into war by the rigidity of . . . military plans, and by the premium they placed on preemption," and "stampeded into war by the generals and by the system the military had created." His "answer in every case is essentially no." Both civilian and military leaders understood the political and strategic dynamics of the situation, and the civilians remained firmly in control of the policy process throughout the July Crisis.[22]

Japan Decides to Attack the United States at Pearl Harbor

The Japanese decision to attack the United States at Pearl Harbor is often described as a product of nonrational thinking and nondeliberation. Lebow and Stein argue that Japanese decision makers engaged in "wishful thinking," going to war because they "deluded themselves that their foe would accept . . . defeat instead of fighting to regain the initiative."[23] Snyder also concludes that policymakers in Tokyo were nonrational and that the reason they "failed to retreat from the precipice is that years of strategic mythmaking had so skewed Japanese perceptions that a clear-sighted appraisal of alternatives had become impossible."[24] Charles Kupchan claims that "the image equating Japanese security with the establishment of the Co-Prosperity Sphere so imbued the mindset and values of elites that it overrode logic indicating that efforts to realize this notion of security would likely bring ruin to the metropole." By the time it attacked the United States, Japan "was not simply seeking resources; it was carrying out a spiritual mission." Japanese decision makers were driven by "their cognitive and emotional commitment to realizing their imperial aspirations."[25] Meanwhile, Jeffrey Record argues that Japan's choice of war "owed much to Japanese racism, fatalism, imperial arrogance, and cultural ignorance." Policymakers in Toyko allowed "their imperial ambitions to run hopelessly far ahead of their military capacity . . . displayed a remarkable incapacity for sound strategic thinking [and] were simultaneously mesmerized by short-term operational opportunities and blind to their likely disastrous long-term strategic consequences."[26]

Dale Copeland summarizes this conventional wisdom concerning why Japan decided to attack the United States: "For most

RATIONALITY AND CRISIS MANAGEMENT

international relations scholars who have delved into this question, the answer is straightforward: Japanese leaders and officials by 1941 were no longer operating in a rational manner. They were filled with a host of irrational beliefs, including the argument that to sustain their vision of empire, they had no other choice but to fight the United States."[27]

As for nondeliberation, Robert Jervis emphasizes the shoddy quality of the Japanese decision-making process, quoting Robert Scalapino to make his point: "Instead of examining carefully the likelihood that the war would in fact be a short, decisive one, fought under optimum conditions for Japan, contingency plans increasingly took on a strangely irrational, desperate quality, in which the central issue, 'Can we win?,' was shunted aside."[28] Snyder also concludes that the Japanese policy process was nondeliberative, suggesting that "one way this myopia may have arisen was that elites confused each other about the costs and risks of various alternatives by systematically falsifying or withholding information."[29] Van Evera asserts that the Japanese government "never seriously studied Japan's chances of winning a war against the United States. It made no overall estimate of Japan's power and had no master plan for the conduct of the war. It failed to analyze the likely effect of attacking Pearl Harbor on American will to defeat Japan. The Japanese Navy never seriously discussed the implications of its proposed advance into Southeast Asia. . . . The Japanese army made no real effort to assess the military strength of the United States, and suppressed whatever assessment was done."[30]

These arguments are wrong. Japan's decision to attack the United States in 1941 and its strategy for waging the ensuing war were based on credible theories. Furthermore, both civilian and military leaders, from the start, engaged in a deliberative decision-

148

making process characterized by substantial consensus. All of this is to say that Japan was rational in the run-up to Pearl Harbor.[31]

By early July 1941, Japan was in a grim and deteriorating strategic situation. It was not only embroiled in a quagmire in China, but was also being strangled by the United States. The Export Control Act of 2 July 1940 had cut off Japan's supply of many goods and raw materials, especially iron and steel scrap, which were essential to the continued functioning of the Japanese civilian and military economy. Then, on 25 July 1941, Washington froze all Japanese assets in the United States and imposed a de facto oil embargo on Tokyo, a move that promised to wreck Japan's economy. In response, Japan sought a diplomatic solution — discussions with the United States ran from 17 August to 4 September and from 17 to 26 November — offering major concessions in return for a lifting of the U.S. trade embargo, only to have Washington kill both sets of negotiations. Faced with this dire situation, Japanese leaders reluctantly chose to attack the United States, knowing their chances of victory were slim but reasoning that a risky war was preferable to a crippled economy and elimination from the ranks of the great powers.

This decision was based on credible realist theorizing. Japanese leaders were intent on maintaining Japan's position in the balance of power so as to maximize its prospects for survival. In a high-level meeting on 3 September, Navy Chief of Staff Nagano Osami explained: "In various respects the Empire is losing materials: that is, we are getting weaker. By contrast, the enemy is getting stronger. With the passage of time, we will get increasingly weaker, and we won't be able to survive. Moreover, we will endure what can be endured in carrying on diplomacy, but at the opportune moment we must make some estimates. Ultimately, when there is no hope for diplomacy, and when war cannot be avoided, it is essential that we make up our minds quickly." Three days later, Prime Minister Konoe Fumimaro made an almost identical argument, noting that "if we allow this situation to continue, it is inevitable that our Empire will gradually lose the ability to maintain its national power, and that our national power will lag behind that of the United States." To resolve the problem, Japan should "try to prevent the disaster of war by resorting to all possible diplomatic measures. If the diplomatic measures should fail to bring about favorable results within a certain period, I believe we cannot help but take the ultimate step in order to defend ourselves."[32]

These arguments took on increasing force as the situation worsened. At an important meeting with Emperor Hirohito on 5 November, Tōjō Hideki, who had recently become prime minister, warned that Japan could not "let the United States continue to do as she pleases, even though there is some uneasiness. . . . Two years from now we will have no petroleum for military use. Ships will stop moving. When I think about the strengthening of American defenses in the Southwest Pacific, the expansion of the American fleet, the unfinished China Incident, and so on, I see no end to difficulties. We can talk about austerity and suffering, but can our people endure such a life for a long time? . . . I fear that we would become a third-class nation after two or three years if we just sat tight." At the same meeting, Hara Yoshimichi, who spoke for the emperor, agreed that it was "impossible, from the standpoint of our domestic political situation and of our self-preservation, to accept all of the American demands. We must hold fast to our position. . . . We cannot let the present situation continue. If we miss the present opportunity to go to war, we will have to submit to American dictation."[33]

Having decided on war, Japanese leaders developed what they understood to be a highly risky and yet credible theory of victory. No one believed that Japan could win a long war against the mighty United States. Nagano, who was tasked with war planning, was pessimistic about Japan's prospects. "I think it will probably be a long war," he remarked in September, adding that in all likelihood "it will not be possible to carry on a long war." He warned that "even if our Empire should win a decisive naval victory, we will not thereby be able to bring the war to a conclusion. We can anticipate that America will attempt to prolong the war, utilizing her impregnable position, her superior industrial power, and her abundant resources." This view was widely shared. Summarizing the discussions of a key meeting on 1 November, the official note taker observed, "In general, the prospects if we go to war are not bright. We all wonder if there isn't some way to proceed peacefully. There is no one who is willing to say: 'Don't worry, even if the war is prolonged, I will assume responsibility.' On the other hand, it is not possible to maintain the status quo." Therefore, if diplomacy were to fail, "one unavoidably reaches the conclusion that we must go to war."[34]

Nevertheless, decision makers in Tokyo thought that if they dealt the U.S. military a series of disastrous defeats early in the war and established a robust defensive perimeter in the Pacific, the Americans might lose their will to fight—especially if they were simultaneously embroiled in a European war—and agree to a negotiated peace that would leave Japan as one of the most powerful states in East Asia. In early September, Nagano outlined the common view: Japan must "seize the enemy's important military areas and sources of materials quickly at the beginning of the war, making our operational position tenable and at the same time obtaining vital materials from the areas now under hostile influence." To his mind, "if this first stage in our operations is carried out successfully, our Empire will have secured strategic areas in the Southwest Pacific [and] established an impregnable position." At that point, the outcome would "depend to a great extent on overall national power — including various elements, tangible and intangible — and on developments in the world situation."[35]

Japanese policymakers not only selected strategies based on credible theories, but they also engaged in deliberation from the start of the crisis to the start of the war. They met frequently, vigorously debated all the issues relevant to their predicament and how to deal with it, and quickly reached general agreement. From 1 July to 1 December there were thirty-eight liaison conferences, which included the prime minister, the foreign minister, the war minister, the navy minister, the army and navy chiefs and vice chiefs of staff, and sometimes other ministers, such as the finance minister and the director of the planning board. In addition, the key decision makers met with the emperor at four imperial conferences, on 2 July, 6 September, 5 November, and 1 December, when the final decision for war was made.

There was remarkable consensus at these meetings about the situation facing Japan and how to think about dealing with it. Japanese leaders agreed that their country was being strangled by the United States and was in imminent danger of falling out of the ranks of the great powers. Based on his examination of the minutes of the liaison and imperial conferences, Nobutaka Ike concludes that "the decision makers all had the same basic values. . . . All saw the American position as threatening to Japan's deepest interests. Their disagreements were exclusively over methods and timing." At the same time, given Washington's refusal to negotiate in good faith, everyone agreed that Japan had little option but to embark on a highly risky war. "By the fall of 1941," Ike writes, "Japanese leaders, rightly or wrongly, had come to believe that they were being pushed into a corner by the United States and her allies. To make matters worse, time was running out for them: As the notes of these Conferences demonstrate, the status quo seemed intolerable to them. The consequences of this sense of crisis were, perhaps, inevitable — no course but war seemed possible to the Japanese."[36]

This consensus notwithstanding, Japanese decision makers engaged in a robust and uninhibited debate about all the key issues on the table, including the relative merits of further negotiation versus war and how best to wage a war against the United States. According to Copeland, "the discussion [at the conferences] was open and wide ranging, revolving around what would be best for the Japanese state instead of what was best for some organizational group or individual."[37] Scott Sagan concludes that "if one examines the decisions made in Tokyo in 1941 more closely, one finds not a thoughtless rush to national suicide, but rather a prolonged, agonizing debate between two repugnant alternatives."[38] Finally, Bruce Russett finds that "whatever the nature of the decision to go to war, it was arrived at and reinforced over a long period of time, and was not the result of anyone's possibly 'irrational' impulse."[39]

Germany Decides to Invade the Soviet Union

Nazi Germany's decision to launch Operation Barbarossa, on 22 June 1941, is often cited as a paradigmatic case of nonrationality. German policymaking is usually depicted as a chaotic process in which Hitler ran roughshod over his generals — who disagreed with him about whether to attack the Soviet Union and how to wage the war — and made all the key decisions himself. As Rolf-Dieter Müller notes, "The theory that Hitler alone was responsible for the attack on the USSR . . . has become an important pillar in the historical edifice."[40]

Nondeliberation is said to have gone hand in hand with non-credible thinking. Hitler is routinely described as a nonrational actor, a line of argument that dates back to the early postwar period, when German generals sought to absolve themselves of responsibility for the war and for Germany's defeat by purveying a "narrative of the strategically incompetent Führer, divorced from all reality." Hitler, they argued, "had repeatedly disregarded the limits of what was possible militarily and caused the German catastrophe."[41]

The claim that Hitler was not a rational actor and that he dragged Germany into a disastrous war is also commonplace among political scientists. According to Norrin Ripsman, Jeffrey Taliaferro, and Steven Lobell, Hitler "had megalomaniacal tendencies" that caused him to "dominate foreign policy decision-making, overrule political and military experts, and deny opinions and information at odds with [his views]." This led him to "undertake irrational decisions."[42] Alex Schulman, in an analysis of the planning for Barbarossa, argues that Hitler "drove both his nation and himself to absolute ruin to fulfill what seems to be a blatantly irrational worldview."[43] Daniel Byman and Kenneth Pollack conclude that "Hitler's unique pathologies were the single most important factor in causing both World War II in Europe (at least in the sense of the continent-wide total war that ensued) and Germany's eventual defeat."[44]

Historians make similar arguments. Klaus Hildebrand maintains that "by 1941 at the latest," well before Barbarossa, "the irrational measures . . . came to dominate over the rational, calculated methods of power politics within the system. In the final analysis, the irrational elements . . . brought about their own and the system's downfall."[45] Michael Geyer writes that "the course of German strategy during the Third Reich was not determined by a set of rationally formulated grand objectives. Instead it was shaped by a series of gambles." Consequently, "strategy was no longer a rational means of achieving specific goals, nor was it guided, in this process, by rational concepts of the use of force." The invasion of the Soviet Union was a "flight into military fancy."[46] Finally, Alan Bullock contends that Hitler's "remarkable powers were combined with an ugly and strident egotism, a moral and intellectual cretinism. The passions which ruled Hitler's mind were ignoble: hatred, resentment, the lust to dominate, and, where he could not dominate, to destroy."[47]

This view is wrong. The Nazi decision to conquer the Soviet Union and its plan for doing so rested on widely accepted credible theories. Moreover, the German policymaking process was deliberative from start to finish, and there was little disagreement between Hitler and his generals regarding both goals and strategies. In short, Germany's decision to launch Operation Barbarossa was rational.[48]

In mid-July 1940, Nazi Germany was in a precarious strategic position. Although the Wehrmacht had just won a stunning victory against France, Berlin had no obvious way to knock Britain out of the war. At the same time, German decision makers feared that the Soviet Union, which was growing more powerful and threatening, would eventually attack Germany. To make matters worse, an eventual war with the United States loomed in the background. To resolve this crisis, Germany invaded the Soviet Union in the summer of 1941, confident it would win a quick and decisive victory that would not only eliminate the Soviet threat, but would also cause Britain to capitulate, giving the Third Reich a significant advantage in any war with the United States.

—

Germany's decision to attack the Soviet Union was based on straightforward realist theory. From the moment they took power in 1933, Nazi leaders were bent on guaranteeing Germany's survival by establishing hegemony in Europe. To do that, it was essential that the Third Reich conquer the Soviet Union, its most dangerous competitor on the continent. The urgency of this task was compounded by the fact that while the Red Army was weaker than the Wehrmacht, it had enormous potential. Thus the Germans were motivated by a desire to at least preserve the balance of power and at best overturn it. In essence, the logics of both preventive war and hegemonic war had been at play for some time when the crisis over how to deal with Germany's threat environment broke out in the summer of 1940.

It is clear that the German leadership relied on realist theories. At the height of the crisis, in December 1940, Hitler informed his generals that "the fight against Russia will decide European hegemony."[49] The following month, he described his reason for waging war, noting that if Germany defeated the Soviet Union, "nobody will then be able to defeat her anymore."[50] His generals, unsurprisingly, were also committed to making Germany supreme in Europe. On 2 July 1940, even before Hitler announced his decision to attack in the east, General Walther von Brauchitsch, the commander in chief of the German Army High Command, directed the chief of the Army General Staff, Lieutenant-General Franz Halder, to determine "how a military blow against Russia is to be executed to induce her to recognize the dominant role of Germany in Europe."[51] Halder in turn informed the chiefs of staff of the army groups and armies that the Third Reich was bent on hegemony, which could only be achieved through "war against Russia."[52] Throughout the planning process for Barbarossa, in which the generals played the central role, it was

———

156

clear that the goal was to eliminate the Soviet Union from the balance of power and make Germany the hegemon in Europe.

The salience of preventive war logic in German thinking is equally apparent. In a memorandum of August 1936, which described Moscow's "rapidly increasing" military capabilities, Hitler argued that Germany could not afford to wait much longer to attack the Soviet Union because "otherwise, time will be lost, and the hour of peril will take us all by surprise."[53] In August 1940, with the situation becoming more urgent, he told Lieutenant Colonel Bernhard von Lossberg that "the Soviets were getting stronger every day, but he thought they would collapse within six weeks both militarily and politically if he hit them soon enough and hard enough."[54] Similarly, Halder's predecessor, General Ludwig Beck, warned that the Soviet Union might become "a serious or, under certain circumstances, a deadly danger." As one historian of the German army notes, Beck's view that the Soviet Union "posed a threat to the Reich's supremacy in Europe" was widely shared among German military leaders.[55] In July 1940, the head of the Wehrmacht Operations Department, General Alfred Jodl, declared that "it was better . . . to have this campaign now, when we were at the height of our military power."[56] After the war, Halder described the German attack on the Soviet Union as a way to eliminate a "long but steadily rising political danger."[57]

Once planning for the invasion was set in motion, German leaders deliberated carefully and readily agreed on a credible theory of victory. Hitler's meeting with his generals on 31 July 1940, at which he announced his intention to attack the Soviet Union, was the first of many high-level planning sessions over the course of the next eleven months.[58] The discussions at these meetings covered all the key issues related to the proposed operation in the east. German planners paid careful attention to Soviet military capabilities.[59] They concluded that the Red Army, which was equipped with outdated weaponry and had been badly damaged by Josef Stalin's purges, was hardly a formidable opponent, as it had demonstrated by its poor performance in its 1939–40 war with Finland. Nevertheless, the Germans recognized they might be underestimating Soviet strength. In a meeting with Foreign Minister Joachim von Ribbentrop and his military commanders on 9 January 1941, Hitler described the Red Army as "a headless clay colossus" but warned that Germany must not be complacent and that the Soviet Union should not be underestimated. The following month, Halder acknowledged the Red Army's quantitative superiority but emphasized that that advantage was more than nullified by the Wehrmacht's qualitative edge. Even so, he warned, "surprises [are] not impossible." Concerns about numerical inferiority prompted Hitler to reverse his earlier decision to shrink the German Army and instead order an increase in its size from 120 to 180 divisions.[60]

At the same time, German decision makers worked hard to develop a military plan for defeating the Red Army. Shortly after the decision was made to invade the Soviet Union, serious work began on the Marcks Plan — which was being drafted even before Hitler's announcement — and the Lossberg Plan. These drafts were then combined under the supervision of General Friedrich Paulus, who in late 1940 directed a series of war games designed to test various aspects of the evolving operational plan. The final version was submitted to Halder on 31 January 1941, and he discussed it with Hitler a few days later. Following that conference, Hitler ordered further studies of potential problems with the plan, though its basic features were now well established. The Wehrmacht would employ the blitzkrieg strategy that had worked so well against France in 1940 to rapidly defeat the Red Army—which was forward deployed and vulnerable to the initial German onslaught—west of the Dvina-Dnieper line. With its army destroyed, the Soviet Union would be relatively easy to conquer.[61]

The consensus among Hitler and his generals was that the strategy they had developed was the right one and would work as intended. This confidence was apparent as early as 31 July 1940, when they first discussed the plan's operational details. David Stahel notes that Hitler's announcement that he intended to conquer the Soviet Union was greeted by his "most senior commanders . . . without protest or dispute, and stands in sharp contrast to the impassioned disputes arising from the timing and operational plans for the western campaign." Stahel notes that this pervasive optimism remained firmly in place throughout the planning process. As the details of the invasion were being finalized in early January 1941, he writes, "the operational objectives, the rationale for a second front and premise for victory were all accepted without the slightest utterance of disapproval."[62] This assessment of what was likely to happen when the Red Army and the Wehrmacht clashed was widely shared by policymakers in Washington, London, and even Moscow.[63]

This powerful consensus notwithstanding, some German leaders disagreed about how the operation should proceed in the event the Red Army was not defeated west of the Dvina and Dnieper rivers. Specifically, Hitler and his generals did not reach agreement regarding what should be the main axis of attack as German forces moved further east into the depths of the Soviet Union, mainly because they were confident that the Wehrmacht would crush the Red Army in the initial stage of the operation. If it did not, they were content to resolve the issue when the time came.[64]

The German desire to conquer the Soviet Union and the subsequent operational planning are sometimes described as being driven primarily by ideological and racial considerations rather than by realist logic and battlefield calculations. There is little question that Nazi decision makers were motivated by ideology and saw the upcoming conflict as an apocalyptic struggle between fascism and Bolshevism. They also viewed their Communist adversary in racist terms, describing Slavs and especially Jews as racially inferior peoples who should be murdered on a massive scale to give Germans "living space" in the east. Yet ideological factors, which were based on a credible theory, and racial factors, which were noncredible and abhorrent, were of secondary importance in the decision to go to war and hardly affected military planning.[65] German leaders wanted to conquer the Soviet Union above all for geopolitical reasons. The ideological dimension of the German-Soviet relationship simply reinforced those balance-of-power calculations. And in the planning of Barbarossa, ideological and racial considerations did not come into play until the military blueprint was well developed. Even then, they did not rob the proposed operation of critical resources or meaningfully interfere with the Wehrmacht's strategy for defeating the Red Army.

Two further decisions related to the German invasion of the Soviet Union — one involving Hitler, the other involving Stalin — are also said to be nonrational. The first is Hitler's declaration of war against the United States on 11 December 1941, just after the Wehrmacht's offensive stalled outside Moscow, a decision that historians Brendan Simms and Charlie Laderman note is commonly described as "an inexplicable strategic blunder" and that Ripsman, Taliaferro, and Lobell describe as "irrational."[66]

On close inspection, however, Hitler's decision to declare war against the United States was the product of a credible theory for defeating Germany's great power rivals. With France defeated, Britain on the ropes, and the Soviet Union badly wounded, Hitler feared that the United States would bring its massive power to bear against Germany as it had done in World War I. This being the case, the Japanese attack on Pearl Harbor presented him with an opportunity to get in the first blow against the United States before it mobilized its full resources for war and while it was engaged in what would surely be a protracted conflict with Japan. Besides, a formal declaration of war on the United States was hardly a radical step, as it was clear even before December 1941 that the Roosevelt administration was determined to enter the European war against Germany.[67]

The second supposed example of nonrationality is Stalin's failure to anticipate the German invasion of the Soviet Union in June 1941. Stein argues that cognitive biases caused the Soviet leader to ignore "evidence that was inconsistent with his belief that Adolf Hitler would not turn away from the western front and attack the Soviet Union."[68] Ripsman, Taliaferro, and Lobell portray Stalin as "especially susceptible to failures of rationality" because of his "unique temperament . . . cognitive flaws, eccentricities, or historical experience." These flaws, they argue, made him unwilling "to prepare for an impending German attack in June 1941 despite overwhelming military intelligence of such an attack."[69]

This interpretation of Stalin's behavior on the eve of Operation Barbarossa is mistaken. He was under no illusion about Hitler's intention to attack the Soviet Union at some point and was assiduously preparing his military to meet that eventuality. With respect to what happened in June 1941, the Soviets did not have clear intelligence that a German attack was imminent, in good part because of a sophisticated German disinformation campaign. In addition, deterrence theory told Stalin that Germany was unlikely to attack in the east before defeating Britain in the west. One of the principal reasons imperial Germany had lost World War I was that it was forced to fight on two fronts, and Stalin knew that Hitler knew this. He also knew that Germany was dependent on Soviet supplies, which would obviously disappear if the two countries went to war. Finally, deterrence theory also led him to reject calls to move the Soviet military to its front-line combat positions for fear that such a step might provoke the very attack he wanted to deter.[70]

The United States Decides to Settle the Cuban Missile Crisis

Although some scholars cite the John F. Kennedy administration's handling of the Cuban Missile Crisis in October 1962 as a paradigmatic case of rationality, others argue that it was not, and they even find substantial evidence of nonrationality.[71] Kennedy, in particular, is said not to have acted rationally. According to Mark Haas, "Theories based on the maximization of expected value have difficulty explaining Kennedy's actions from the time the blockade was implemented to when Khrushchev announced he was removing the missiles from the island and returning them to Soviet soil." The case "calls into question the key assumption that grounds most theories of deterrence — that people will behave 'rationally' in terms of basing their decisions on expected value calculations." In fact, he writes, the evidence suggests that "individuals may be inclined to engage in 'irrational,' risk-acceptant behavior."[72] James Nathan is more direct, noting that Kennedy's "private anxiety is well recorded, and a case can be made that dispassionate analysis or problem-solving was all but precluded by the psychology of the situation."[73] Noam Chomsky argues that the president "took stunning risks" and rejected "Russian offers that would seem fair to a rational person" as "unthinkable."[74]

Critics of the U.S. government's rationality during the Cuban crisis have also portrayed the decision-making process as nondeliberative. Lebow contends that "analysts have studiously ignored the 'group think' and other deviations from 'open decision-making' that in fact characterized Kennedy's management of that confrontation" and that a proper review reveals a "strong strain of irrationality" running through the case.[75] David Welch argues that "an ideally rational observer" would identify several "'failings' in the Kennedy administration's handling of the Cuban missile crisis." They would find that the "actual discussions . . . were disorganized, disjointed, sometimes rambling, often ill-informed, largely inarticulate, and seemingly directionless."[76] This line of thinking is also implicit in Graham Allison's *Essence of Decision*, which employs three models—a rational actor model and two alternatives—to analyze U.S. decision-making during the Cuban Missile Crisis and suggests there is abundant evidence for the nonrational alternatives.[77]

Ronald Steel provides a succinct summary of the claim that the Kennedy administration's handling of the Cuban Missile Crisis was marked by both flawed individual thinking and collective nondeliberation: "We see the spectacle of rational minds swayed by passions and the euphoria of power, governmental machinery breaking down into the struggle of individual wills, and decisions affecting the future of humanity made by a handful of men—the best of whom were not always sure they were right."[78]

This view is mistaken. Kennedy and his subordinates relied on credible theories to come up with different strategic options. They also engaged in a robust and uninhibited debate before the president decided the best way forward.

In May 1962, Soviet premier Nikita Khrushchev decided to place nuclear-armed missiles in Cuba. Over the next five months, the Soviet military surreptitiously carried out his plan under the guise of an economic aid mission, but before the deployment was complete, American reconnaissance aircraft spotted some of the missiles and their launch sites. President Kennedy was given the news on the morning of 16 October, the first day of what came to be known as the Cuban Missile Crisis.[79]

From the outset, there was a consensus among American policymakers that the Soviet Union must remove all of its missiles and warheads from Cuba. They disagreed, however, about how to accomplish this overriding goal. Because these differences were never resolved, it fell to the president to make the ultimate decision on how to resolve the crisis, and he did so on Saturday, 27 October, promising that in exchange for Moscow's removing its nuclear arms from the island, the United States would withdraw its Jupiter missiles from Turkey and not invade Cuba. Since removing the Jupiters was certain to be politically unpopular at home and in Europe, only a handful of American and Soviet policymakers were told about that element of the deal.

American thinking about the crisis was informed by two markedly different theories. One theory called for using military force to eliminate the nuclear weapons and their delivery systems, while the other identified subtle coercion as the best strategy for restoring the status quo ante. Proponents of war were confident the United States had strategic nuclear superiority and local conventional superiority and thus could eliminate the Soviet weapons while deterring Moscow from escalating in the Caribbean or Europe.

Proponents of coercion feared that using force might cause the Soviet Union to respond militarily in Cuba; in Berlin, where the

Soviets enjoyed a significant local advantage; and perhaps even against the American mainland. In each case, the specter of nuclear war loomed in the background. At the same time, advocates of coercion believed that the implicit and ever-present threat of force coupled with careful diplomacy could produce a deal acceptable to both sides.

It is widely believed that American decision-making was guided by a third theory: nuclear brinksmanship, which involved explicit military threats and big-stick diplomacy. There is little evidence, however, that aggressive coercion was considered. The debate among American leaders revolved around the use of force versus subtle coercion.[80]

The military theory of victory produced two strategic options. The first called for air strikes, ranging from surgical attacks on the Soviet missile sites to a large-scale bombing campaign against a host of military targets. The second called for invading Cuba to resolve the problem. Although these were distinct options, the hawks in the Kennedy administration favored different military options at different times. CIA director John McCone and General Maxwell Taylor, chairman of the Joint Chiefs of Staff, pressed for both air strikes and invasion at various points during the crisis. The Joint Chiefs were united in supporting air strikes but divided on the wisdom of invasion. Meanwhile, Secretary of the Treasury Douglas Dillon and National Security Adviser McGeorge Bundy were strong proponents of the air strike option throughout the crisis.

The coercive theory called for a naval blockade of Cuba in conjunction with a demand that the Soviet Union withdraw its nuclear-armed missiles from the island. In an ideal world, Moscow would simply capitulate, but the proponents of this approach knew that was unlikely. It would be necessary to work out a deal in which the Soviets complied with Washington's demand in exchange for U.S. concessions on some other issue. Both Secretary of State Dean Rusk and Secretary of Defense Robert McNamara embraced this more dovish position, as did Under Secretary of State George Ball, Ambassador-at-Large Llewellyn Thompson, and special counsel to the president Theodore Sorensen.

The president and his brother, Attorney General Robert Kennedy, embraced a military theory of victory at the start of the crisis but eventually supported coercion, aiming to work out an acceptable deal with Moscow. Both initially favored surgical air strikes against the Soviet missiles, but they soon concluded that only a large-scale air assault could neutralize the threat. Later, as the crisis unfolded, they abandoned their belief in a military solution and instead became advocates of coercion, which ultimately forced the Soviets to put two different deals on the table. One proposal had Moscow removing its missiles in exchange for an American pledge to not invade Cuba, and the second added the further provision that Kennedy would remove the Jupiters from Turkey. The president was prepared to accept either deal, as was his brother, who helped negotiate the final agreement.

American leaders deliberated throughout the crisis, meeting around the clock and seriously debating the various policy options. The key decision-making group — which came to be known as the Executive Committee — met at least once a day for several hours from 16 to 28 October. Those meetings were models of free-wheeling discussion, as the participants vigorously debated the pros and cons of each strategy. On 20 October, for example, facing the need to determine what the president would say in his first public address about the crisis, the Executive Committee debated two rival drafts—one declaring a blockade of Cuba and the other announcing air strikes against the island—and took a vote that yielded a split decision in favor of the blockade. Similarly, after Moscow proposed the Jupiter deal on the morning of 27 October, the key decision makers went back and forth not only on whether the new offer reflected Khrushchev's real thinking, but also on whether to accept it.

The president and his close advisers also went to great lengths to gather relevant information. At various times during the crisis, the Executive Committee sought advice from individuals who were not part of the group, including hawks such as former secretary of state Dean Acheson and Assistant Secretary of Defense Paul Nitze and doves such as arms control czar John McCloy and Ambassador to the United Nations Adlai Stevenson. Kennedy did the same with the British ambassador in Washington, David Ormsby-Gore. The president and his inner circle even turned to some prominent journalists—Charles Bartlett, Frank Holeman, and John Scali—to ferret out information from their Soviet sources.

Yet deliberation did not yield agreement. As late as 27 October, the Executive Committee was still divided between hawks and doves, and the doves disagreed among themselves about which of the two Soviet deals was preferable. At that point, the president, who had been an engaged participant throughout the discussions, decided it was time to break the deadlock and make the ultimate decision. In a late evening meeting with his brother, McNamara, Rusk, and Bundy, he instructed Robert Kennedy to strike a deal with the Soviets, preferably without trading the Jupiters but doing so if necessary. The following morning, Radio Moscow announced that Khrushchev and Kennedy had reached a deal and the crisis was over.

The Soviet Union Decides to Invade Czechoslovakia

The view that the Soviet decision, in August 1968, to intervene in Czechoslovakia was nonrational emerged soon after the event. That November, a key member of the NATO Defense Planning Committee concluded that "the sudden, even reckless manner in which the final decision to invade appears to have been taken causes deep concern for the future. We now perceive, I think, a greater risk of an impulsive, irrational thrust by the Soviets which would have grave consequences for all of us."[81] The following year, Vernon Aspaturian observed that Soviet policy during the Czech Crisis "seemed to veer from one extreme to the other." He thought the Soviet Union suffered from "instability at the top, unpredictability in behavior, and diminished capability for rational control and containment of dangerous situations." The leadership team of Leonid Brezhnev and Aleksey Kosygin "represented not so much a new unified collective rationality as it did a latently explosive marriage of factional convenience." There was, he concluded, significant "continuity in policy between the Brezhnev-Kosygin regime" and the "irrational pattern of behavior during the decade of Nikita Khrushchev's rule."[82]

Other scholars have made similar arguments. In a detailed analysis of the Soviet invasion, Fred Eidlin warns against assuming that "Soviet decisionmakers were much more knowledgeable, prescient, rational, clear in their aims, unified among themselves, and guided by long-range strategy than they actually were." He suggests that "the shifting and unstable aims chosen in a confused manner by the Soviet decisionmaking system will be seen as resulting from an evolving process of response to the changing situation in

---

Czechoslovakia within a decisionmaking system largely paralyzed in its capability to cope with the problems it confronted."[83] Jiri Valenta makes the point more briefly in his own assessment of the case: "Soviet foreign policy actions, like those of other states, do not result from a single actor (the government) rationally maximizing national security or any other value."[84] David Paul finds that the Soviet decision to intervene was "based on rational, calculated motives to an indeterminate degree and on nonrational, often spontaneous, motives to a similarly indeterminate degree."[85]

The fact is that the key Soviet policymakers relied on credible theories and debated each other in a vigorous and unconstrained fashion, finally agreeing that invasion was the best option. In other words, the Soviet decision to invade Czechoslovakia was a rational act.

Alexander Dubček became the first secretary of the Communist Party of Czechoslovakia on 5 January 1968, setting in train a process of liberalization that came to be known as the Prague Spring. At first, Soviet policymakers were not seriously concerned about this development, believing it did not threaten to undermine communism in Czechoslovakia or weaken Prague's close ties with Moscow. Their views changed, however, when the hard-line Communist Antonín Novotný was ousted as Czech president on 21 March. This raised the fear that the Czechs might abandon communism and the Warsaw Pact and, worse, build on their budding relationship with West Germany and eventually join the Western camp.[86]

Soviet thinking about the Czech Crisis and its geopolitical implications was based on a combination of realist and ideological theories. Given that Czechoslovakia was a frontline state in the Cold War, the idea that it might abandon the Warsaw Pact and shift the balance of power on the critically important Central Front was unthinkable. Worse still, Soviet decision makers feared ideological contagion to other East European states, including the Soviet Union itself, that might ultimately cause the pact to unravel, with catastrophic consequences for Moscow's security. Taken together, these considerations left Soviet policymakers little choice but to end the Prague Spring before it ended the Warsaw Pact.

This consensus on the nature of the Czech problem did not extend to the Soviet leaders' plan for solving it. They advocated for one of two broad theories: coercion and overthrow. Proponents of coercion were convinced that the Soviet Union could combine diplomacy with threats of military force to make Dubček reverse course, though they had different views about the ideal balance between those elements. Proponents of overthrow disagreed, believing coercion was bound to fail and that Moscow faced a choice between backing a coup by Czech hardliners to bring down the Dubček government or invading and installing a reliably pro-Soviet regime.

The principal Soviet decision makers, clearly thinking in terms of these competing theories, took three different positions. First, the hawks urged intervention with military force throughout the crisis. They included KGB head Yuri Andropov, Defense Minister Andrey Grechko, Foreign Minister Andrey Gromyko, Chairman of the Presidium of the Supreme Soviet Nikolay Podgorny, and First Secretary of the Communist Party of Ukraine Petro Shelest. Second, the doves favored coercion from the beginning of the crisis until its final stage, when they decided invasion was necessary to deal with the problem. The key figure in this group was Brezhnev, who was supported by his second in command and party ideologue Mikhail Suslov, along with the editor in chief of *Pravda* and former ambassador to Czechoslovakia Mikhail Zimyanin. Finally, there were policymakers who vacillated between coercion and overthrow,

---

including Kosygin; Aleksandr Shelepin, who was a powerful member of the Politburo; and Stepan Chervonenko, the ambassador to Prague.

Although the decision to invade Czechoslovakia was made inside the Soviet Union, the leaders of four other Warsaw Pact countries influenced the choice. Their thinking was informed by the same theories that drove Moscow's views about how to deal with Prague. The most hawkish was East German leader Walter Ulbricht, although both Poland's Wladyslaw Gomulka and Bulgaria's Todor Zhivkov were also strong supporters of overthrowing the Czech reformers. In contrast, Hungarian leader János Kádár urged a combination of diplomacy and the threat of force for most of the crisis, and he was Brezhnev's key supporter in making the case for coercion during meetings of the "Five."

Ultimately it was Czech behavior that persuaded the proponents of coercion to change their minds and make common cause with the proponents of overthrow. A key consideration from the Soviet viewpoint was Dubček's repeated failure to fulfill his commitments to halt or reverse liberalization. Early in the crisis, the Czech leader met with the leaders of the Five at Dresden and promised to rein in the reformers. Yet shortly thereafter, the Czech Communist Party announced an "Action Plan" that envisaged further liberalization, as well as increasing contacts with the West. Later, having assured the Five at Bratislava in early August that he would curtail the reform process, Dubček took no steps to do so.

The Czech leadership also resorted to evasion, refusing several Soviet invitations to meet and discuss key issues between the two sides. For example, Dubček turned down a proposed meeting with Brezhnev in June and with the Five in Warsaw in July. On other occasions, he went so far as to reject Soviet demands. In late July, he

—

refused to allow the Soviets to station forces permanently in Czechoslovakia, a step that Moscow favored as a way of slowing down liberalization.

Perhaps most important, Moscow was increasingly convinced that the Dubček government had lost control and was probably fueling the Prague Spring. Having announced the Action Plan, the Czech Communist Party then endorsed a reformist manifesto known as the "Two Thousand Words," and it twice brought forward the date of the Fourteenth Party Congress, a move that struck fear into the hearts of Soviet leaders because they knew that it would sweep away the old Communist order once and for all.

In response to this unfolding crisis, Soviet policymakers engaged in a deliberative decision-making process from start to finish. They had numerous internal meetings, frequent bilateral exchanges with the Czechs, and several multilateral conferences with the other members of the Five. As noted, the Soviets were concerned enough about developments in Czechoslovakia by late March that they convened a conference at Dresden, where the Five met with the Czech leadership. This meeting was followed in early April by a Soviet Communist Party plenum in Moscow, at which the assembled leaders recognized that events in Czechoslovakia were deeply worrisome and had consequences far outside its borders.

Seeing that liberalization continued apace in Czechoslovakia throughout April and fearing that Dubček was losing control of the situation, Soviet leaders summoned him to Moscow for two days of talks beginning on 4 May. Following those discussions, the Politburo met on 6 May and debated different measures, ranging from persuasion to invasion, for dealing with the evolving crisis. Brezhnev held meetings with the other members of the Five two days later, at which the East European allies' differences about the best way forward came to the fore. There was also continuing disagreement when the Politburo assembled on 15 May. Thus Soviet policymakers decided to hold military maneuvers in Czechoslovakia while also continuing negotiations with Prague. Meanwhile, Moscow continued to gather information about events in Czechoslovakia. Both Grechko and Kosygin visited Prague on fact-finding missions in mid-May.

As the situation in Czechoslovakia deteriorated – over the course of two weeks at the end of May and the beginning of June, the Czechs announced the convocation of the Fourteenth Party Congress and Dubček refused to meet with Brezhnev – Soviet policymakers continued to debate their options. Czechoslovakia was the main topic of discussion at Politburo meetings on 6 and 13 June, where decision makers discussed the merits of continued bilateral diplomacy, enhanced military pressure, and the possibility of overthrowing Dubček and replacing him with Josef Smrkovský, a popular politician who remained committed to communism. Later in June, Brezhnev met with Kádár, and the two leaders resolved to continue exploring all the available options, though Moscow upped the coercive pressure on Prague, deciding to keep Soviet troops in Czechoslovakia when the Šumava military maneuvers ended on 30 June.

Despite this pressure, however, events in Czechoslovakia were spiraling out of control. The last days of June saw the publication of the "Two Thousand Words" manifesto and Czech leaders suggesting they might bring the Fourteenth Party Congress forward from September to August. In early July, Dubček refused to attend the proposed Warsaw meeting with the Five. These developments triggered a slew of meetings among Soviet decision makers and between them and their East European allies. Familiar arguments were rehearsed and debated at a Politburo meeting on 10 July, a Soviet plenum on 17 July, and at the Warsaw conference on 15 July, with no firm resolution. Later in the month, however, the situation began to change. At four Politburo meetings from 19 to 27 July, Soviet policymakers began planning for an invasion in the event Dubček failed to get the situation under control, though they remained committed to combining diplomacy with military pressure for the time being and also continued to explore the coup option.

The Soviets made two further attempts to reach a negotiated settlement with the Czechs, first in a bilateral meeting from 29 July to 1 August at Čierna nad Tisou and then on 3 August, when the Five met with Czech negotiators at Bratislava. Although the various parties reached several understandings at those meetings, it became clear to Moscow that coercion was not working as intended. After an expanded session of the Politburo on 6 August, at which it was decided the time was not yet ripe for invasion but that planning for it should continue, many of the key Soviet policymakers went on vacation to Crimea.

They remained deeply engaged with the crisis, however, mainly because the Czechs had started preparing for the Fourteenth Party Congress. Soviet policymakers held a series of ad hoc Politburo meetings and met to discuss the situation with Kádár. At the same time, Brezhnev wrote letters and made phone calls to Dubček, urging him to follow through on the promises he had made at Čierna nad Tisou and Bratislava. One of those phone calls, on 13 August, was key to persuading Brezhnev that coercion had failed and an invasion was necessary. In that conversation, Dubček broke down, admitted that he had lost control of the situation in Czechoslovakia, and told Brezhnev that he should take whatever measures he deemed necessary. After that, events moved quickly. The Politburo discussed the invasion on 16 August and a day later voted unanimously to invade. The following day, the Soviets told the other members of the Five of their decision, which met with universal agreement.

American Escalation in Korea and Vietnam

Turning from crises to the conduct of war, Irving Janis famously identifies two cases of purported nonrationality: the American decisions to escalate during the Korean and Vietnam wars. Both decisions, he argues, were the product of nondeliberation or what he calls "groupthink," a process in which the entire decision-making circle converges on a policy without meaningful discussion. This collectively nonrational behavior appears to be driven by two logics. The first emphasizes that human beings are social animals who "consider loyalty to the group the highest form of morality." Their instinctive "strivings for unanimity override their motivation to realistically appraise alternative courses of action." The second points to the subtle pressures for conformity that arise when individuals come together in cohesive groups. "Groupthink," writes Janis, "refers to a deterioration of mental efficiency, reality testing, and moral judgment that results from in-group pressures."[87]

Janis offers the American decision to cross the 38th parallel (the dividing line between North and South Korea) and seek to unify Korea in the fall of 1950 as a classic example of nondeliberation. Groupthink blinded U.S. policymakers to the dangers of escalating the Korean War, he maintains, and specifically to the likelihood that China would intervene to prevent an American conquest of North Korea. Because President Harry Truman and his close advisers formed a tight-knit group characterized by pronounced "esprit de corps and mutual admiration," they placed too

---

much value on agreement among themselves, suppressing their doubts about the wisdom of widening the war and ignoring warnings that China would intervene if the United States moved north. The resulting "gross errors of judgment . . . [had] disastrous consequences." On 15 October, having driven the North Korean Army out of South Korea, U.S. forces crossed the 38th parallel and began advancing toward the Chinese border. But in late November, China launched a devastating offensive against the American forces, pushing them back across the 38th parallel.[88]

The American decision to move into North Korea was the product of a deliberative process, not the result of groupthink. For starters, the relevant leaders met frequently throughout the crisis to discuss the appropriate policy. There was widespread consensus in these high-level meetings, but it was not the product of in-group pressures. Janis provides no evidence that it was. Instead, from the start, the key decision makers thought the same way about the situation and the appropriate U.S. strategy. They favored crossing the 38th parallel; thought it unlikely that China would come into the war; and believed that if it did, the United States would easily prevail. Of course, they were wrong—not, however, because the decision-making process was flawed but because they misjudged Chinese intentions and capabilities, which were difficult to estimate both before and after U.S. forces moved into North Korea.[89]

Janis also describes the American decision to escalate in Vietnam beginning in 1964 as an example of nondeliberation caused by groupthink. He argues that President Lyndon Johnson and his "Tuesday lunch group," which made the key decisions regarding the conflict in Vietnam, chose to Americanize the war because they anticipated a U.S. victory despite abundant contrary evidence. The reason, Janis argues, is that "members of the in-group" who expressed doubts about escalation were "effectively 'domesticated' . . . through subtle social pressures." The result of this failure to debate the issues was that Johnson and his advisers "persistently ignored the major consequences of practically all their . . . policy decisions," embroiling the United States in a disas-trous war.[90]

There is, however, hardly any evidence that this consensus came about through groupthink. Janis says as much, noting that his evidence "is far from complete" and that his "conclusions will have to be drawn quite tentatively."[91]

It is clear from the historical record that the Johnson adminis-tration's decision to escalate was the product of a deliberative pro-cess. As Janis himself notes, "A stable group of policy advisers met regularly with President Johnson to deliberate on what to do about the war in Vietnam."[92] Moreover, Leslie Gelb and Richard Betts ex-plain that "virtually all views and recommendations were considered and virtually all important decisions were made without illusions about the odds for success." Proponents of escalation were not de-luded: "Each time they turned the ratchet of escalation up another notch they did not believe that the increase would provide victory in the classic sense of decisive defeat of the enemy. At best they *hoped* they might be lucky, but they did not *expect* to be." Dissenters were neither domesticated nor ignored. Proponents "heard them out and were usually pessimistic themselves. And although the doves within the government agonized and doubted more than their other col-leagues, they were not really overridden. With very few exceptions, even the most reticent of these men, seeing what they did and hag-gling on the margins of options, *supported* the critical decisions on aid, troops, and bombing."[93]

Rational State Behavior

All the states examined in this chapter were rational actors — that is, their decisions during the relevant crises were based on credible theories and were the products of deliberative policymaking processes.

A careful analysis reveals that German decision makers during the July Crisis, Japanese decision makers in the run-up to Pearl Harbor, and German decision makers in the months before Operation Barbarossa based their strategic thinking on credible theories of international politics and of military victory. As for the Americans during the Cuban Missile Crisis, some relied on credible theories of military victory while others relied on credible theories of coercion. The same is true of the Soviets during the Czech Crisis, who also employed credible theories of international politics.

It is also clear that these policymakers engaged in deliberation. When there was a consensus from the start — as in the July Crisis, the Pearl Harbor decision, and Operation Barbarossa — the agreed strategy was nevertheless subjected to extensive and thorough discussion. When policymakers were deadlocked, as happened during the Cuban Missile Crisis, President Kennedy listened to the views of his subordinates and participated in the deliberations before choosing, as the ultimate decider, how to proceed. Finally, when Soviet decision makers first disagreed but then reached a common view on the best strategy for dealing with the Czech Crisis, they did so through robust and uninhibited debate.

The cases of crisis decision-making discussed in this chapter and the cases of grand strategic decision-making discussed in the previous chapter not only support our core claims, but they also shed light on some common misconceptions about rationality in international politics. They confirm that policymakers employ theories to guide their thinking about grand strategy and crisis management rather than employing expected utility maximization or mental shortcuts such as analogies and heuristics. In fact, the extent to which decision makers are *homo theoreticus* rather than *homo economicus* or *homo heuristicus* is striking. In addition, they demonstrate that the decision-making process is largely unaffected by the nature of political institutions, the influence of powerful domestic interest groups, the need to respond to public opinion, or interference by military leaders. Instead, the key policymakers are typically insulated from domestic pressures, and although particular military leaders are consulted, their opinions do not loom large in the final decision.

Finally, rational actors are not always successful. There is a difference between process and outcomes. In nine of the ten cases – the Cuban Missile Crisis is the exception – the relevant state arguably failed to achieve its intended goal.

None of this is to say that all states are rational all the time. There are a handful of important cases in which states adopted strategies based on noncredible theories or emotions and that resulted from a nondeliberative decision-making process. We turn to them now.

Chapter 7

NONRATIONAL STATE BEHAVIOR

It should be apparent by now that most states are rational most of the time, which is to say their policies are based on credible theories and result from a deliberative process. Yet states do occasionally make nonrational decisions. Logically, nonrationality can take one of three forms: decision makers employ a noncredible theory or a nontheoretical argument and fail to deliberate; they rely on a credible theory but the policymaking process is nondeliberative; or they employ a noncredible theory or a nontheoretical argument, but engage in deliberation.

Empirically, however, failures to employ credible theories and failures to deliberate appear to go hand in hand. Of the four cases described in this chapter, two involve the formulation of nonrational grand strategies: imperial Germany's decision to build a powerful navy designed to challenge Britain at the turn of the twentieth century and Britain's choice to not build an army to fight on the European continent in the late 1930s. The other two cases concern nonrational policies during crises: America's decisions to launch the Bay of Pigs invasion in 1961 and to invade Iraq in 2003. In each case, the

Table 2. Nonrational Great Power Decision-Making

Grand Strategic Decisions	Crisis Decisions
Germany decides on the risk strategy before World War I	The United States decides to invade Cuba
Britain decides on a no-liability strategy before World War II	The United States decides to invade Iraq

government's policy relied on noncredible theories or emotion-driven arguments and emerged from a nondeliberative process. Table 2 provides a breakdown of these cases.

Germany Decides on the Risk Strategy before World War I

Under Chancellor Otto von Bismarck, Germany became a first-rate power on land but not at sea. Kaiser Wilhelm II, who fired Bismarck in March 1890, was determined that the Kaiserreich become a great naval power as well. He eventually found the ideal person to accomplish that task in Admiral Alfred von Tirpitz, who was secretary of state of the Imperial Naval Office — the Reichsmarineamt (RMA) — from June 1897 to June 1900, when all the critical decisions about building the German fleet were made.[1]

Tirpitz had his first serious discussion with Wilhelm about the development of the German Navy at a meeting in Kiel in the spring of 1891, where it became clear that the two men shared a commitment to making Germany a dominant sea power. The following year, Tirpitz became chief of staff of the Navy High Command, or Oberkommando der Marine (OK), which along with the RMA was one of the two key German navy offices. There he played a major

181

role in formulating the "Draft Plan for the Renewal and Expansion of Fleet Material," though he resigned in September 1895, just two months before the document was completed and sent to the kaiser. After Wilhelm read the draft plan, he asked Tirpitz to comment on it, and this led to a memorandum outlining Tirpitz's views on the subject. After the two men met at the end of January 1896, it was clear that Tirpitz, once he completed an assignment as commander of the East Asian Cruiser Squadron, would become the head of RMA. It was understood that his principal goal in that capacity would be to expand the navy.

Tirpitz began by pushing forward two naval laws. Germany's First Naval Law, an updated version of the November 1895 draft plan, was presented to Wilhelm in August 1897, approved by the Bundesrat three months later, passed by the Reichstag in March 1898, and signed into law the following month. It provided for the creation of a fleet comprising nineteen battleships organized into two squadrons. Tirpitz raised the prospect of further expansion in a meeting with Wilhelm at Rominten in September 1899 and presented the kaiser with a draft of the Second Naval Law in January 1900. This second bill was quickly approved by the Bundesrat, passed by the Reichstag on 12 June, and signed into law two days later. It called for doubling the size of the fleet to thirty-eight battleships organized into four squadrons. Further naval laws followed — in 1906, 1908, and 1912 — but these Novelles, or amendments, simply modified the basic configuration established by the First and Second Naval Laws of 1898 and 1900.

Germany's naval buildup — especially as specified in the Second Naval Law — was based on the famous "risk theory," or Risikogedanken, which Tirpitz had developed over several years. The theory rested on three novel elements. First, while naval planners had long focused on France and Russia as Germany's primary threats at sea, Tirpitz focused on Britain. Second, in keeping with the kaiser's ambitions, the secretary of state was determined to build the Imperial Navy around battleships rather than cruisers, which many naval officers preferred. In other words, the fleet would be designed to operate in the North Sea, where battleships were considered the decisive instrument, rather than on the world's oceans, where cruisers made more sense. Third, whereas German strategists had envisioned achieving naval superiority over France and Russia, Tirpitz accepted that such an advantage was not possible against Britain. His aim instead was to achieve a 2:3 overall battleship ratio, which he believed would allow the German Navy to match and perhaps even outnumber the British Navy in the North Sea. This belief rested on two assumptions: Britain had worldwide commitments that demanded dispersal of its battleships all over the globe, and Germany, because it did not have to equal Britain, would not end up worse off if Britain decided to engage in a naval arms race.

Tirpitz believed the projected distribution of German and British battleships in the North Sea meant that in a future Anglo-German naval war, the Royal Navy could do no better than win a Pyhrric victory: the crippled British fleet would be left weaker than its French and Russian rivals. This prospect, in turn, would deter Britain from attacking Germany and also give Berlin coercive leverage over London. Fearing that any conflict with Germany could have devastating consequences, the British would refrain from starting a fight. London would thus be forced to acquiesce to Germany's expansion outside Europe, commonly known as Weltpolitik. As Tirpitz put it, "Apart from the battle circumstances, which would by no means be hopeless for us, England would . . . have lost any inclination to attack us; and would in consequence accord to Your

Majesty such a measure of sea power and thus enable Your Majesty to carry out a great overseas policy."[2]

Risk theory, however, was a noncredible theory. It stood in direct contradiction to well-established balance-of-power theory, which maintains that states almost always respond to increases in their rivals' capabilities by increasing their own and sometimes forming countervailing alliances with other states. More specifically, Tirpitz assumed that Britain would not balance against Germany's emerging risk fleet, even though London had a long history of countering similar threats by internal and external means and even though its existing policy—the "two-power" standard, developed in 1889—mandated balancing against Berlin if Germany built a navy that threatened to undermine Britain's supremacy at sea. Similarly, Kaiser Wilhelm remarked that Britain's internal debates about the two-power standard demonstrated that "they respect our firm will, and must bow before the accomplished fact [of the German naval program]! Now further quiet building."[3] Germany's "error," writes Paul Kennedy, was the "expectation that Britain would maintain the same naval dispositions, the same strategy, and the same foreign policy when Germany became a great and powerful threat to British maritime supremacy as when she had no navy worth speaking of at all."[4]

Although our focus is not on outcomes, it is worth noting that Britain responded to Tirpitz's risk strategy in accordance with balance-of-power theory. London quickly moved to redistribute its fleet, placing the bulk of its battleship force in and around the North Sea. Britain also accelerated its battleship construction program and eventually started building super-battleships known as dreadnoughts. Together, these policies ensured that the Royal Navy maintained a significant advantage over the German Imperial Navy in home waters. Britain's first sea lord, Admiral Sir John Fisher, described the underlying logic: "Our only probable enemy is Germany. Germany keeps her whole fleet always concentrated within a few hours of England. We must therefore keep a fleet twice as powerful as that of Germany always concentrated within a few hours of Germany."[5] Britain supplemented these internal balancing measures with external balancing initiatives, drawing closer to both France and Russia.

Germany's decision to build the risk fleet was not only based on a noncredible theory, but it was also the product of nondeliberative policymaking. In developing the theoretical rationale for that navy, Tirpitz had no meaningful consultation with other navalists either inside or outside the government. Almost everyone qualified to hold an opinion had different views from his. Of course, policymakers often formulate their initial thinking on important strategic issues by themselves. But they typically refine their ideas and make policy together with their colleagues in a deliberative fashion. Tirpitz was an exception. He kept his thinking to himself, surrounded himself with individuals who were unlikely to challenge him, and crushed anyone who disagreed with him.

The available evidence indicates that Tirpitz came up with his ideas about naval strategy by himself. His early thoughts about risk theory appeared in two private letters — dated December 1895 and February 1896 — to retired admiral Albrecht von Stosch; in a confidential memorandum of January 1896 for Wilhelm about the OK draft plan; and in a draft of a March 1896 speech that he never delivered. In the first few months after becoming head of the RMA in June 1897, Tirpitz concentrated on the politics of pushing the First Naval Law through the Reichstag rather than on providing a strategic logic for how the navy would be used. But when he

—

needed to justify further naval expansion, he unveiled a full-fledged version of risk theory to Kaiser Wilhelm, first during their September 1899 meeting at Rominten and then in the rationale — or Begründung — attached to the draft of the Second Naval Law. Risk theory was introduced to the public for the first time when the draft law went to the Bundesrat and then to the Reichstag in January and February 1900.[6]

To further grasp the extent to which Tirpitz was alone in his strategic thinking, consider that his views on the kind of navy Germany should build and against which country it should be built were not widely shared. Most naval planners wanted to emphasize cruisers rather than battleships. When Tirpitz took up his position as secretary of state in June 1897, Admiral Eduard von Knorr, the head of OK, and other senior naval officers, including some of Tirpitz's subordinates at RMA, favored a cruiser strategy and opposed the draft naval law's emphasis on battleships. At the same time, there was a powerful consensus that the German Navy should continue to focus on France and Russia as potential adversaries rather than Britain. But Tirpitz was determined to target Britain, a goal he made clear to Wilhelm in their January 1896 meeting. He reiterated the point when he took command of RMA in the summer of 1897, offering a view that stood "in stark contrast to the plans prepared in his absence."[7]

Rather than discuss his strategic ideas and policy proposals openly within the navy, Tirpitz surrounded himself with a tight-knit group of deeply loyal individuals who did not challenge his views and were dedicated to bringing his risk fleet to fruition. Chief among these subordinates were two future admirals, Eduard von Capelle, who worked out the details of the building program, and August von Heeringen, who was tasked with selling the risk fleet to politicians and the public.

———

Finally, Tirpitz went to great lengths to eliminate any opposition to his plans by turning RMA into a super ministry and using his personal power to crush individuals who had or might develop dissenting views. In early 1899, for example, he persuaded Wilhelm to criticize retired vice admiral Victor Valois's endorsement of cruisers, to prohibit publication of a Naval Academy manuscript questioning the use of battleships against a superior sea power, and, more generally, "to silence unauthorized statements from active and retired officers."[8]

Britain Decides on a No-Liability Strategy before World War II

Adolf Hitler became chancellor of Germany in January 1933, bent on restoring his country's military might and altering the map of Europe in its favor. His determination to rearm Germany and make it a formidable great power became clear in March 1935, when he revealed that the Third Reich had begun building an air force and intended to introduce conscription, with a view to creating a five-hundred-thousand-man army. One year later, German troops reoccupied the Rhineland, which had been demilitarized under the terms of the Versailles Treaty. In 1938, Germany annexed Austria and then, during the Munich Crisis, forced Czechoslovakia to cede the Sudetenland, a large area along the Czech border with Germany populated with ethnic Germans. In March 1939, the Wehrmacht conquered the rest of Czechoslovakia. Six months later Hitler invaded Poland, which led Britain and France to declare war against Germany, thus starting World War II.[9]

Britain recognized that Germany might be a serious threat soon after Hitler took control in 1933, though it was not easy to know how to deal with that menace given that Britain was in dire economic straits and that Italy and Japan were also potential adversaries. There was the danger that a powerful Germany could conquer all of Western Europe and threaten Britain's survival. This possibility, in turn, meant that British policymakers had to make a decision about a continental commitment, which would involve sending an army to France to help deter Germany and to fight against it if deterrence failed.

The decision-making process can be divided into three periods that produced three different policies regarding the commitment of British ground forces to the continent. In the first period, from November 1933 to May 1937, Britain opted for a strategy of limited liability. This called for creating a Field Force, composed of five divisions that could be sent to the continent shortly after the outbreak of war, and a reserve force of two Territorial Army (TA) divisions that could follow within four months. This army was designed to aid France in a war with Germany, though it would provide little help if the war was on the scale of World War I.

In the second period, which began when Neville Chamberlain became prime minister, on 28 May 1937, and ended with the Munich Agreement of 30 September 1938, Britain adopted a policy that Michael Howard describes as "no liability at all."[10] The British government decided that France would handle a German invasion by itself. In the third period, from October 1938 to April 1939, London reversed course and embraced a strategy of full liability. If Germany attacked France, Britain would send a five-division Field Force to the continent upon the outbreak of hostilities, to be followed by ten TA divisions within six months and sixteen more within a year.[11]

British leaders had a rich history of thinking about how to deal with a state that might dominate all of Western Europe, and they had developed a credible balance-of-power theory for addressing the problem. At the heart of that theory was the belief that any state that controlled the western half of the continent would be not only especially powerful, but also well positioned to directly threaten the British homeland. Thus it was necessary to deter any state that might make a run at dominating Europe and to defeat it if deterrence failed.

The optimum strategy for checking a potentially dominant power was buck-passing, in which Britain relied on states located on the continent to prevent any adversary from conquering Western Europe. British strategists understood, however, that should they fail to find states capable of countering that threat, Britain would have to join a balancing coalition to deter and defeat it. Both policies required Britain to build an army that could be sent to the continent. In the first instance, that army would not be deployed to the continent but would provide insurance in case the other powers failed to check the threat to Western Europe. In the second instance, the army would be sent to the continent to assist the balancing coalition before or shortly after a war broke out.

An examination of the theoretical bases of Britain's policies and the nature of the decision-making process that led to them reveals that Britain was rational in the first and third periods but nonrational in the second. The strategy of limited liability adopted in the first period relied on balance-of-power theory and emerged from a deliberative policymaking process. So too did the strategy of full liability embraced in the third period. But the strategy chosen in the second period—no liability at all—had no apparent theoretical basis and did not emerge from careful deliberation. Instead, the principal decision makers based their preferred policy largely on wishful thinking and then forced it on their domestic opponents.

In the three years following Hitler's accession to power, British planners began to rethink their policy toward Europe, paying particular attention to the possibility of creating an army to fight on the continent. The evolution of their thinking is reflected in three reports produced by the Defence Requirements Sub-Committee (DRC) and a report by the chiefs of staff. The first two DRC reports — issued in February 1934 and July 1935 — called for the creation of a Field Force composed of five divisions. The third, known as the "Ideal Scheme" because it described the military forces Britain would build absent financial considerations, retained the Field Force but also recommended equipping twelve TA divisions that could be sent to the continent within eight months of the onset of war. Finally, the chiefs of staff report, presented to the Cabinet in January 1937, recommended a virtually identical force structure of five regular and twelve reserve divisions.

The Cabinet, which had monitored and discussed the planning process from the start, began to seriously debate the shape of the British Army in 1936 and split into two factions. Chamberlain, then chancellor of the exchequer, and Prime Minister Stanley Baldwin favored restricting Britain's commitment to the Field Force. Secretary of State for War Duff Cooper and the chiefs of staff thought this was not enough and that Britain needed twelve TA divisions as well.

The two factions engaged in vigorous debate, ultimately reaching a compromise at a Cabinet meeting on 5 May 1937. At a series of high-level meetings in the winter of 1936–37, the two antagonists, Chamberlain and Cooper, forcefully made their respective cases and debated the wisdom of their opposing views. The key to breaking the deadlock was involving Thomas Inskip, the minister for coordination of defense, who produced a paper in February

1937 that underpinned the 5 May decision to opt for a limited liability strategy, entailing a Field Force and two TA divisions.

At the beginning of the second period, Chamberlain, now the prime minister and more influential than ever, reopened the debate about sending troops to the continent. His goal, which he had been unable to pursue as chancellor of the exchequer, was a strategy of no liability at all, which was directly at odds with Britain's traditional reliance on balance-of-power theory. In fact, his preference for abandoning the continental commitment had no apparent theoretical foundation and instead was driven largely by emotional thinking. He was horrified at the prospect of British troops fighting another world war and wanted desperately to avoid it. In other words, he privileged fear and hope above theoretical reasoning, seeking "at almost any cost, to prevent another world war because of the horrors he had witnessed during the first."[12]

To achieve his aim, Chamberlain effectively shut down the deliberative process, using his newfound power to purge advocates of limited liability from the government and replacing them with individuals who he believed shared his views. The first wave of purges involved the War Office. Cooper was replaced in late May 1937 as secretary of state for war by Leslie Hore-Belisha, whom Chamberlain expected to support his position on the British Army. Then, in early December, the chief of the imperial general staff, General Cyril Deverell, and other important members of the Army Council, including Generals Harry Knox and Hugh Elles, all of whom favored committing an army to France, were dismissed in the most significant purge of the military since 1904.[13]

The second wave of purges involved the Foreign Office. In January 1938, the permanent under secretary of state for foreign affairs, Sir Robert Vansittart, Chamberlain's principal opponent in the Foreign Office, was removed from his position. His replacement, Alexander Cadogan, was known to support the prime minister's views regarding a continental commitment. The following month, Foreign Secretary Anthony Eden, who had worked closely with Vansittart and had grown increasingly disenchanted with the direction of British foreign policy, resigned from the Cabinet. His successor, Viscount Halifax, was a close confidant of the prime minister. He and Cadogan worked together to ensure that "the Foreign Office quickly fell into line" with Chamberlain's agenda.[14]

These purges were part of a wider campaign by the prime minister to avoid deliberation and ensure that the British government endorsed a "no-liability" strategy. In the summer of 1937, Chamberlain tasked Inskip with producing another study of the role of the British Army in a European war. Working with the Treasury, which was headed by Chamberlain's staunch ally John Simon, Inskip produced an interim report on 15 December 1937 that called for eliminating the continental commitment. When the report was discussed in the Cabinet a week later, Chamberlain, Simon, and Hore-Belisha endorsed it enthusiastically, even though Inskip warned that if Britain did not have an army and "France were again in danger of being overrun" by Germany, then the British government "would most certainly be criticised for having neglected to provide against so obvious a contingency."[15] Only Eden raised doubts, and without much conviction. This no-liability strategy was detailed in Inskip's final report, which was produced on 8 February 1938 and approved by the Cabinet eight days later.[16] In April, the Chamberlain government reaffirmed the strategy, cutting the army's budget by a further 20 percent.[17]

This nonrational strategic decision had a significant impact on British policy toward Germany in 1938. Because it now lacked an army capable of influencing events on the continent, Britain did virtually nothing when Germany annexed Austria just one month after the decisive February Cabinet meeting. Nor did London take action six weeks after the Anschluss, when Hitler began calling for major political changes in the Sudetenland. In late September, Chamberlain had little choice but to appease Germany at Munich by allowing the Sudetenland's annexation.

Following the Munich Crisis, British decision makers slowly moved away from a strategy of no liability to one of full liability, embracing balance-of-power theory through a deliberative process. The individuals who brought this transformation about were Halifax and Hore-Belisha, who had changed their views about France's ability to defend itself against Germany and what that meant for Britain's strategy toward the continent. The foreign secretary was heavily influenced by a series of memoranda from the ambassador to Paris, Eric Phipps, who warned that France could not stand up to Germany alone and might even bandwagon with it, allowing Hitler to take aim at Britain. Meanwhile, the secretary of state for war was deeply impressed by reports emanating from the chiefs of staff that painted a bleak picture of Belgium's, Holland's, and France's prospects of holding out in a war against Germany, with dire consequences for Britain.

Although Chamberlain and Simon initially held their ground, refusing to countenance a continental commitment of any kind, they allowed their opponents to speak their minds and eventually accepted a strategy of full liability. The first clear evidence that British policy was changing emerged in February 1939. In a series of Cabinet meetings, Chamberlain and Simon reluctantly moved toward the Halifax and Hore-Belisha position, eventually agreeing on 22 February that Britain would have to build some kind of army to send to France. Less than a month later, Germany conquered the rest of Czechoslovakia, an event that had a galvanizing effect on British thinking. In mid-April, the Cabinet approved a plan to create a Field Force of five divisions, to be reinforced by twenty-six TA divisions in the event of war. General Henry Pownall remarked that Britain had decided on a "continental commitment with a vengeance!"[18]

Some scholars agree with us that the Chamberlain government was nonrational in the late 1930s, but they tell a different story from ours, emphasizing Britain's behavior at Munich. They maintain that cognitive flaws caused the prime minister to misread Hitler's intentions and decide to appease Nazi Germany rather than balance against it. Keren Yarhi-Milo argues that Chamberlain's view of Germany was "relatively more benign" than those of his subordinates, and that he continued to hold that view even as evidence mounted of Hitler's malign intentions. "The egocentric bias, the salience-vividness bias, and Chamberlain's motivated defensive avoidance," she writes, "pushed him to adhere to his existing assessment of Hitler's intentions even during late 1938."[19]

We disagree with this interpretation. Chamberlain's policy during the Munich Crisis was rational as it was driven by credible balance-of-power theory. Noting Germany's growing military might and uncertain about Berlin's intentions, the prime minister was acutely aware of the potential for a European war. At the same time, however, he understood that his earlier nonrational decision to adopt a strategy of no liability now left him no choice but to appease Germany. Britain did not have the wherewithal to confront the Wehrmacht, either alone or with France. Had London possessed an army that could fight on the continent, it would likely have pursued a more forceful policy. Chamberlain said as much: "I hope . . . that my colleagues will not think that I am making any attempts to disguise the fact that, if we now possessed a superior force to Germany, we should probably be considering these proposals in a very different spirit. But we must look facts in the face."[20]

The United States Decides to Invade Cuba

The origins of the Bay of Pigs invasion can be traced to January 1960, when the National Security Council authorized CIA director Allen Dulles to engage in contingency planning to overthrow Cuban leader Fidel Castro. The initial plan – Operation Pluto – which President Dwight D. Eisenhower approved on 17 March 1960, called for covertly inserting a guerilla force of three hundred Cuban exiles back into their homeland, where they would meet up with local anti-Castro insurgents and spark a revolution.[21]

American decision makers quickly lost confidence in Operation Pluto, however, and starting that summer developed a new plan that called for a two-day air campaign aimed at destroying the Cuban air force, to be followed by an amphibious invasion by a brigade of U.S.-trained Cuban exiles. The exile force would land near the town of Trinidad, establish a beachhead, and set up a provisional government before linking up with the organized resistance on the island and fomenting a mass insurrection that would eventually topple Castro and install a pro-American government.

President-elect John F. Kennedy was briefed three times on Operation Trinidad between his electoral victory and inauguration. Dulles and CIA deputy director for plans Richard Bissell gave him a comprehensive description of the proposed operation on 18 November 1960. Although Kennedy said little during the meeting, he later told a close aide that he was "staggered" by the scope of the planning. Cuba was also among the subjects discussed during

Kennedy's two transition meetings with Eisenhower, on 6 December 1960 and 19 January 1961. At the latter meeting, the outgoing president told his successor that the plan to oust Castro "was going well, and it was Kennedy's 'responsibility' to do 'whatever is necessary' to follow it through."[22]

Kennedy's advisers were briefed for the first time on Operation Trinidad by Dulles and Bissell, both of whom were retained by the new president, on 22 January 1961 and again six days later with Kennedy in attendance. At the conclusion of the second meeting, the president gave the green light for planning to continue. When Bissell briefed the White House again on 11 March, however, Kennedy expressed reservations. The proposed operation was "too spectacular," he said, and it would make it difficult for the United States to deny its involvement.[23] He directed the CIA to come up with an invasion plan that would better disguise America's role. Bissell responded on 16 March with a new plan — code-named Operation Zapata — that called for moving the landing site from Trinidad to the Bay of Pigs and for attacking at night rather than during the day. This time, Kennedy approved the operation. On 17 April, the anti-Castro forces landed in Cuba, where they immediately ran into trouble before surrendering two days later.

Although the American theory of victory was straightforward — an air campaign followed by an amphibious landing and the instigation of a mass insurrection together with the organized anti-Castro resistance on the island — it was also noncredible, and the Bay of Pigs plan was therefore nonrational.

While there was some chance that the air assault might destroy the Cuban air force, there was a shortage of exile pilots, those available were poorly trained, and they were flying old planes that were in bad shape. There was also hardly any chance that the amphibious operation would succeed. For starters, the landing force was poorly trained and equipped, and only 20 percent of the troops had any military experience. Morale was so bad that 250 of them mutinied at their training camp in Guatemala in January 1961. The amphibious force would have to land at night on an especially challenging landing zone. Most important, the 1,500 invading troops would be heavily outnumbered and outgunned once they arrived on the beaches. The Cuban leadership, which knew an attack was imminent and where it was likely to occur, could draw on a military force of roughly 300,000 militia, 32,000 army regulars, and 9,000 armed police.

All of this was abundantly clear to American planners. A Joint Chiefs of Staff report on the state of the exile forces in February 1961 concluded that "their capability was marginal without resistance, but impossible with it." Defense Department analysts maintained that the imbalance of forces in the conflict zone would be so great that the operation could not possibly succeed without significant American participation, which had been ruled out from the beginning.[24] It is important to note that these assessments concerned Operation Trinidad and that Bissell described Operation Zapata as "more operationally difficult" than its predecessor.[25]

Nor was there any chance of a popular insurrection. Kennedy administration officials agreed that toppling Castro would require a large, well-organized, and competent resistance movement within Cuba. It would be impossible to foment a revolution without a powerful indigenous opposition committed to overthrowing the regime. Operation Zapata relied for its success almost entirely on support from a broad-based resistance movement, as the invasion force could never survive against Castro's forces on its own, let alone form the basis for a mass insurrection. Yet as CIA planners knew, there was no such movement. Bissell realized in the fall of 1960 that "there was no chance to build an effective underground [in Cuba] and that the invasion forces had to succeed on their own." This was still true in March 1961. Bissell was fully aware that "CIA operatives had failed to create an organized resistance on the island, meaning there was no chance for a popular insurrection."[26] In short, the odds that Operation Zapata would succeed were virtually zero.

In addition to Operation Zapata's being based on a noncredible theory of victory, the Kennedy administration's decision to launch the Bay of Pigs invasion was the product of a nondeliberative process. The principal proponent of Operation Zapata was the CIA, which not only planned all aspects of the campaign, but also controlled all the relevant information. Bissell and Dulles took advantage of this situation to deceive Kennedy and his advisers about the most important elements of the plan and persuade them of its feasibility.[27]

The CIA leadership repeatedly painted a rosy picture of the invasion force's effectiveness and morale.[28] On the eve of the invasion, Bissell's chief aide, Colonel Jack Hawkins, reported that the exile brigade was "a truly formidable force" and that he shared its confidence that it "[would] win all engagements against the best Castro has to offer."[29] Robert Kennedy described the report, which Bissell forwarded to the president, as "the most instrumental paper" in the decision-making process.[30]

At the same time, Bissell and Dulles assured the president that Castro's forces were "poorly equipped, poorly trained, riddled with dissension, and unable to cope with even a small-scale invasion," even though experts in the State Department and British intelligence said the opposite.[31] And Bissell failed to tell Kennedy that the CIA had not created an organized resistance in Cuba, a failure that meant there was no prospect of a popular uprising.[32] Hawkins reported that the exiles "know their own people and believe after they have inflicted one serious defeat upon opposing forces, the latter will melt away from Castro, who they have no wish to support." He added, "I share their confidence."[33]

One might have expected the Joint Chiefs of Staff (JCS) to have altered the CIA's plan or persuaded Kennedy to abandon it. The Bay of Pigs invasion was an amphibious operation, which was within the purview of the military rather than the CIA. Yet top military officials, including the chairman of the JCS, General Lyman Lemnitzer, had hardly any influence in the policymaking process. When the CIA told them, "You will not become involved in this; the United States military will be kept out of this; you will not tell anybody in your service," the Joint Chiefs put up virtually no resistance.[34] And even when they were consulted, they invariably fell in line with the CIA, despite doubting the feasibility of its plans. Although they believed Operation Trinidad was deeply flawed, they gave it their lukewarm approval in February.[35] The following month, the Joint Chiefs approved Operation Zapata after it became clear that Kennedy supported the plan, even though they believed it was even worse than Trinidad.[36] The generals' unwillingness to challenge the CIA is reflected in what happened when Bissell briefed Kennedy about a JCS evaluation of Operation Trinidad. General David Gray, the principal author of the study, who was present at the briefing, remained silent when Bissell misrepresented the military's views.[37]

As for Kennedy and his top advisers, they failed to ask serious questions about the CIA's plans, allowing it to steer the decision-making process in such a way as to ensure that the proposed invasion went ahead. The president, who had little enthusiasm for the

CIA's various plans, accepted what Bissell and Dulles told him during their meetings. To make matters worse, he gave the impending invasion little thought, admitting to his aide Arthur Schlesinger, "I think about it as little as possible."[38] Secretary of State Dean Rusk and Secretary of Defense Robert McNamara also failed to ask hard questions even though some of their key subordinates thought the Cuban operation was doomed to fail.

Finally, individuals who challenged the CIA view were ignored. When former secretary of state Dean Acheson told Kennedy that the proposed invasion could not succeed, the president paid his views little attention.[39] The same was true of Senator William Fulbright, who made an impassioned speech against Operation Zapata during a meeting with Kennedy and his advisers in early April.

Doubters within the administration also went unheard. Under Secretary of State Chester Bowles prepared a memorandum for Rusk vigorously opposing the invasion, but Rusk did not pass it on to the White House. Rusk told his director of intelligence and research Roger Hilsman that he was not allowed to scrutinize the CIA's plans.[40] Another high-level State Department official, Thomas Mann, forwarded a dissenting paper to his superiors, but no one followed up.[41] Skeptics in the military — including director of the Joint Staff General Earle Wheeler and Marine Corps commandant General David Shoup — were likewise ignored.[42]

The United States Decides to Invade Iraq

In the immediate aftermath of 11 September 2001, some senior policymakers in the George W. Bush administration made the case for attacking Iraq and removing Saddam Hussein from power, arguing that he posed a significant threat to both the United States and its interests in the greater Middle East. Instead, the president invaded Afghanistan in an effort to topple the Taliban regime and root out Al Qaeda, which was responsible for the 9/11 attacks. By early December 2001, U.S. forces had defeated the Taliban and Washington had installed a pro-American government headed by Hamid Karzai. At that point, Bush officials began to think seriously about dealing with Baghdad. Over the next fifteen months, plans were put in place for launching a war against Iraq, which began on 19 March 2003.[43]

The Bush administration's goal in attacking Iraq was to solve the twin problems of terrorism and nuclear proliferation in the greater Middle East. That region was seen as a breeding ground and safe haven for terrorists; American policymakers believed as well that "rogue states," including Iraq, Iran, and Syria, were bent on developing weapons of mass destruction (WMD), which they would give to terrorist groups such as Al Qaeda. After a fact-finding mission to Washington in July 2002, Richard Dearlove, the head of British foreign intelligence, reported to Prime Minister Tony Blair, "Military action was now seen as inevitable. Bush wanted to remove Saddam, through military action, justified by the conjunction of terrorism and WMD."[44]

The administration's strategy for achieving that goal, commonly known as the Bush Doctrine, was based on democratic peace theory and called for democratizing the greater Middle East. The core version of that theory holds that democracies do not fight each other because they share norms of live-and-let-live and institutions that constrain the recourse to war. Bush and his main advisers, however, emphasized two lesser-known implications of the theory that directly addressed the twin problems that concerned them:

democracies do not sponsor terrorism against fellow democracies, and because they do not fear each other, democratic states do not need nuclear weapons.

In practice, democratizing the greater Middle East was expected to involve three policies, each resting on a different theory. To begin with, American decision makers developed a plan for conquering Iraq and removing Saddam from power. Their innovative theory of victory called for launching sudden and massive air strikes against a wide variety of Iraqi targets before turning the U.S. army loose to destroy the much weaker Iraqi ground forces. As General Tommy Franks, who commanded the invasion, described it just as the war began, "This will be a campaign unlike any other in history, a campaign characterized by shock, by surprise, by flexibility, by the employment of precise munitions on a scale never before seen, and by the application of overwhelming force."[45]

Once Iraq was defeated, Bush and his advisers believed it would be easy to turn the country into a functioning democracy. The United States would need to play only a minimal role in that task. As the president explained, "It's important for the world to see that first of all, Iraq is a sophisticated society. . . . The degree of difficulty compared to Afghanistan in terms of the reconstruction effort, or emerging from dictatorship, is, like, infinitesimal."[46] This belief rested on a version of forcible democracy promotion theory, which holds that tyrants are the principal obstacles to the public yearning for democracy. Deputy Secretary of Defense Paul Wolfowitz laid out the logic in an interview with the *Detroit News:* "Our principal goal is the psychological one, to convince the Iraqi people that they no longer have to be afraid of Saddam . . . and once that happens I think what you're going to find, and this is very important, you're going to find Iraqis out cheering American troops."[47]

American decision makers also expected that once Iraq became democratic, other states in the region would follow suit. Domino theory was at the core of their thinking. They believed that the United States might have to use force to remove one or maybe two more tyrants, but dictators across the region would soon realize that their days were numbered, surrender their positions, and allow democracy to take hold in their states as well. In a memorandum for Secretary of State Colin Powell, one of his principal deputies, William Burns, noted, "We all seek a process of regime change in Iraq that leads to a democratic, representative government and security in the region. It could be a historic turning point in the Middle East, and for U.S. interests." The extent of the Bush administration's belief in domino theory is captured in the president's comments to a group of Iraqi exiles two months before the war: "I truly believe that out of this will come peace with Israel and the Palestinians. Maybe one year from now, we'll be toasting to victory and talking about the transition to freedom."[48]

These three elements at the heart of the Bush Doctrine — conquest, democratization, and dominoes — went hand in hand. One of Powell's subordinates described the combination as "the Beautiful Vision," a set of ideas that said, "We'll overthrow this brutal dictator. We'll create this provisional government of exiles. They'll be welcomed, and we'll leave them to their economic prosperity and representative government. All these other awful regimes in the region will fall like dominoes. The whole place becomes better for Israel. Beautiful picture!"[49] Here is how journalist George Packer describes the Bush administration's strategy: "It would, with one violent push, shove history out of a deep hole. By a chain reaction, a reverse domino effect, war in Iraq would weaken the Middle East's dictatorships and undermine its murderous ideologies and begin to spread the balm of liberal democracy. The road to Jerusalem, Riyadh, Damascus, and Tehran went through Baghdad. . . . With will and imagination, America could strike one great blow at terrorism, tyranny, underdevelopment, and the region's hardest, saddest problem."[50]

The Bush Doctrine was based on a combination of credible and noncredible theories. Democratic peace theory—including the claims that democracies do not sponsor terrorism against each other and have no need to acquire nuclear weapons to defend themselves against other democracies—is credible. So, too, was the Bush administration's "shock and awe" theory of victory. But forcible democracy promotion theory and domino theory are both noncredible. It is clear from the historical record that attempts to force democracy on other states almost always fail. The United States' own dismal track record before the Iraq invasion made this clear. In only one case—Panama after the removal of Manuel Noriega—did American intervention clearly lead to the establishment of a consolidated democracy. Indeed, if anything, the evidence pointed in the other direction.[51]

There is also hardly any evidence that the domino theory works as advertised. The theory was tested in a variety of circumstances during the Cold War and found wanting. The Communist victory in China in 1949, for instance, "did not lead to any new communist revolutions in Asia or prevent the defeat of the already-existing ones in Burma, the Philippines, Malaya, and Indonesia." Nor did communism spread in the Western Hemisphere after the Cuban revolution in 1959, despite Castro's best efforts. During the mid-1970s, the Soviet Union supported successful Marxist revolutions in Angola and Ethiopia, but this did not lead other African states to adopt communism, and "a decade later Ethiopia had proven to be an anti-model for other African countries . . . [while] Angola

had distanced itself from the Soviet Union and was seeking open-
ings to the West." One might argue that events in Southeast Asia
after the Communist victory in Vietnam in 1975 lend support to
domino theory. But apart from Laos and Cambodia, whose futures
were inextricably linked to what happened in Vietnam, no other
states in the region went Communist after the fall of Saigon.[52]

Not only was the decision to invade Iraq based on two noncredible theories, but the policymaking process was also nondeliberative.[53] Although he was determined to go to war to democratize
the greater Middle East, Bush was not deeply involved in the relevant debates inside his administration. Also largely absent from
these discussions were National Security Adviser Condoleezza Rice
and her deputy, Stephen Hadley, even though both were committed
to realizing the president's wishes. Instead, the main battles in the
decision-making process were fought between two factions. The
chief proponents of war were Vice President Richard Cheney and
Secretary of Defense Donald Rumsfeld and their subordinates,
Chief of Staff to the Vice President I. Lewis Libby, Under Secretary
of Defense Douglas Feith, and Deputy Secretary of Defense
Wolfowitz. The doubters were led by Powell and a number of top
army generals who thought it would be difficult to democratize Iraq,
not to mention the entire region.

The proponents prevailed over the doubters by employing
four tactics that undermined deliberation. Most important, they refused to engage in meaningful discussion about what would happen
in Iraq and the surrounding countries after Baghdad fell. In June
2002, Richard Haass, the head of the Policy Planning Staff, met
with Rice and began to lay out the State Department's misgivings
about a war, only to be told, "Save your breath. The president has
already made up his mind."[54] Later in the summer, Rice created the

Executive Steering Group to coordinate postwar planning, but Rumsfeld and his subordinates refused to cooperate with the other relevant agencies.[55] The lack of a plan for dealing with post-Saddam Iraq so concerned Hadley that he convened a meeting of key decision makers two months before the invasion and demanded that they come up with a postwar plan, adding, "You're not leaving the room until it's finished."[56] After Hadley's words had no effect, Rice brought up the matter in two meetings with the president and vice president in February 2003. But Bush had no interest in discussing the issue, and Cheney said to Rice, "You really shouldn't be questioning the Pentagon."[57] The following month, just days before the war began, Lawrence Di Rita, one of Rumsfeld's closest aides, told military leaders tasked with running the occupation not to bother drawing up a strategy: "Within 120 days, we'll win this war and get all U.S. troops out of the country, except 30,000."[58]

As Iraq began to devolve into chaos, a number of people who were close to the policymaking process noted the almost complete absence of planning for the postwar period. General Keith Kellogg, one of the senior members on the staff of the Joint Chiefs of Staff, noted, "There was no real plan. The thought was, you didn't need it. The assumption was that everything would be fine after the war."[59] Another American general remarked that well before March 2003, "concern was raised about what would happen in the postwar period, how you would deal with this decapitated country. It was blown off. Concern about a long-term occupation—that was discounted. The people around the president were so, frankly, intellectually arrogant. They *knew* that postwar Iraq would be easy and would be a catalyst for change in the Middle East. They were making simplistic assumptions and refused to put them to the test. It's the vice president, and the secretary of defense, with the knowledge of the chairman of the Joint Chiefs and the vice chairman. They did it because they already had the answer, and they wouldn't subject their hypothesis to examination."[60] Finally, General Tim Cross, who was responsible for planning Britain's role in the occupation, observed that "the plan is that we do not need a plan. The plan is that once we have moved into Iraq, then the Iraqi people, generally speaking, will welcome us."[61]

The second tactic that proponents of the war employed was to ignore their critics. In late 2002, seventy Middle East scholars met for a two-day conference at the National Defense University and produced a document titled "Iraq: Looking beyond Saddam's Rule," which warned that the occupation would "be the most daunting and complex task the U.S. and the international community will have undertaken since the end of World War II." Colonel Paul Hughes, a major player in the postwar planning process, forwarded a copy of the report to Feith, but "never heard back from him or anyone else." Another meeting dealing with the occupation of Iraq — this one involving two dozen military experts, regional specialists, diplomats, and intelligence officials — was convened by the army staff in December. The group concluded, "The possibility of the United States winning the war and losing the peace is real and serious" and warned that "successful occupation will not occur unless the special circumstances of this unusual country" were understood and taken into account. Although the report was received enthusiastically in the army, the civilian leadership in the Pentagon ignored it. "It was not clear to us until much later," writes army historian Conrad Crane, "how unsuccessful [the army] staff had been in shaping the final plans." Thomas Ricks sums up the situation: "What is remarkable is that again and again during the crucial months before the invasion, such warnings from experts weren't heeded — or even welcomed."[62]

The third tactic for dealing with doubters was suppression. On 25 February 2003, Army Chief of Staff General Eric Shinseki told the Senate Armed Services Committee that the occupation of Iraq would require "something on the order of several hundred thousand soldiers." This directly contradicted the views of Rumsfeld, Feith, and Wolfowitz, who envisaged a force of only around thirty thousand — which they believed would be enough to democratize Iraq and indeed spread democracy across the greater Middle East. Wolfowitz humiliated Shinseki by openly contradicting him in testimony to the House Budget Committee, asserting that the chief of staff's "notion that it will take several hundred thousand U.S. troops to provide stability in post-Saddam Iraq, are wildly off the mark." This public slap in the face made it clear that criticism of the Bush Doctrine by government officials was unacceptable. At the same time, Rumsfeld was engaging in suppression behind closed doors, ordering General Jay Garner, the individual in charge of planning for the occupation, to fire two of his leading advisers, Tom Warrick and Meghan O'Sullivan. Their offense, notes Powell's deputy Richard Armitage, was that they were "inconvenient . . . wanted the facts to get into the equation. These were not people who stood up for the party line, that we'd be welcomed with garlands."[63]

Finally, proponents of the war used coercion to get their way. It is well known, for example, that Rumsfeld would not tolerate disagreement with his views. Robert Draper observes that "the secretary's bullying propensity for kicking down and disempowering subordinates meant that dissent on critical issues was close to nonexistent in the Pentagon."[64] Cheney and Libby made it clear to the intelligence community that they would not accept any assessments that did not match what they wanted to hear. In the fall of 2002, the vice president and his deputy repeatedly told the CIA that they wanted it to find a link between Saddam and Al Qaeda and were dis-satisfied with the agency's conclusion that there was no evidence of such a connection. Their relentless pressure paid off. In testimony to the Senate Select Committee on Intelligence in October, CIA direc-tor George Tenet, who had previously denied links between the Iraqi government and terrorist groups, reversed himself, telling Senator Bob Graham: "We have solid reporting of senior-level contacts be-tween Iraq and al-Qa'ida going back a decade. . . . We have credible reporting that al-Qa'ida leaders sought contacts in Iraq who could help them acquire WMD capabilities. The reporting also stated that Iraq has provided training to al-Qa'ida. . . . Baghdad's links to ter-rorists will increase, even absent U.S. military action."[65]

Dominators and Nonrationality

In sum, although states are routinely rational, these four cases dem-onstrate that they can, on occasion, adopt nonrational policies based on noncredible theories or emotion-laden thinking.

Because nonrationality is uncommon in international politics, it is difficult to generalize about its causes. Nevertheless, our sense is that if noncredible theories or emotions are in play, their impact on policy largely depends on the nature of the decision-making groups. Those groups are invariably structured hierarchically to ensure that a final decision will be made and enable the state to deal with the is-sue at hand. The key issue is whether the ultimate decider is a facili-tator or a dominator. When a facilitator is in charge, different theories are debated in a vigorous and unconstrained fashion; the process is deliberative. But when a dominator is in charge, delibera-tion fails. There is little debate about the appropriate theory; in-stead, subordinates are forced to accept the dominator's views.

Tirpitz, Chamberlain, Bissell, and Cheney were all dominators who played the central role in causing their respective states' nonrational decisions.

To this point, we have focused on the issue of strategic rationality, explaining that it involves credible theories and deliberation. There is, however, another important aspect of state rationality: whether states are rational with respect to their goals.

Chapter 8

GOAL RATIONALITY

Some scholars maintain that there is little point in discussing goal rationality because there is no such thing as a rational or nonrational goal. For them, there is only one kind of rationality, what we call strategic rationality. Bertrand Russell, for example, asserts that rationality has a "clear and precise meaning. It signifies the choice of the right means to an end that you wish to achieve. It has nothing whatever to do with the choice of ends." Herbert Simon declares, "Reason is wholly instrumental. It cannot tell us where to go; at best it can tell us how to get there. It is a gun for hire that can be employed in the service of whatever goals we have, good or bad."[1] According to this view, goal rationality is an unimportant concept.

We disagree. If rationality means making sense of the world for purposes of navigating it in pursuit of particular goals, then an understanding of the concept must involve how states think about their goals as well as how they pursue them. We begin by noting that although rational states invariably have many goals, they rank survival as the most important. This observation enjoys widespread but not unanimous support among international relations theorists, some of whom argue that prioritizing survival is not the hallmark of goal rationality. We examine this alternative perspective and explain its shortcomings.

Next we turn to the empirical record and show that states have routinely thought and acted rationally with respect to their goals. Some scholars claim to have identified a handful of instances in which states either ignored the survival imperative or pursued policies that recklessly put their survival at risk. But as we make clear, these alleged cases of goal nonrationality do not withstand scrutiny. In international politics, goal rationality is ubiquitous.

Defining Goal Rationality

Recall that rational actors employ credible theories: logically consistent explanations derived from realistic assumptions and supported by substantial empirical evidence. They do so not only to formulate strategies, but also to establish goals.

Individual goals stem from various root sources, including biological needs, innate sentiments, personal experiences, and socialization.[2] Different people thus have different sets of goals. Almost all of those goals are likely to be rational, provided there are no obvious logical contradictions or empirical disconnects between them and the root sources from which they derive. Individuals with different goals may sometimes view each other as nonrational—because their respective goals rest on different sources—but virtually any goal that is logically and empirically connected to its root sources is rational. As Max Weber notes, "Something is not of itself 'irrational,' but rather becomes so when examined from a specific 'rational' *standpoint*. Every religious person is 'irrational' for every irreligious person, and every hedonist likewise views every ascetic way of life as 'irrational,' even if, measured in terms of *its* ultimate values, a 'rationalization' has taken place."[3]

Although rational individuals have many goals, some stand out as important to almost everyone. Most obviously, people want to survive. Thomas Hobbes maintains that "reason" tells us that "a man is forbidden to do that which is destructive of his life, or takes away the means of preserving the same."[4] People also typically want the freedom to lead their lives as they see fit, to increase their personal prosperity, to spread their values, to foster their favored policies, and to promote their versions of the good life.

States are also likely to have many goals, some of which are readily apparent. Survival is particularly important. States aim to preserve the integrity of their physical base and maintain their ability to determine their own political fate.[5] A state's physical base includes its territory, its population, and the resources within its borders. It can run its own domestic and international affairs if it retains control over its domestic institutions, especially its executive, legislative, judicial, and administrative bodies.[6] States have other prominent goals as well, including maximizing their prosperity and spreading their ideology.

Given that states have many goals, there is the ever-present possibility that goals will clash, and this raises the question: what is the rational way to discriminate among them? There is only one inviolable rule. Survival is primary, and all other objectives must be subordinated to it. It is a matter of incontrovertible logic and evidence that a state cannot achieve any other goal if it does not first survive as a state. As Kenneth Waltz observes, "In anarchy, security is the highest end. Only if survival is assured can states safely seek such other goals as tranquility, profit, and power."[7] Rational states can, of course, have all manner of secondary goals besides survival and can rank them however they want, but they cannot rank any goal above survival.[8] It follows that actors who do not want to survive, or who rank survival below other goals, are nonrational.

Our claim that rational states rank survival as their primary goal is not universally accepted. James Fearon, for example, says the notion that states "put a high premium on survival" is "doubtful" and the claim that survival is a prerequisite for other goals is "incorrect."[9] He argues that prosperity may be more important than survival for states, in which case they might surrender sovereignty—be willing to die—so as to maximize their prosperity.[10] "Imagine two states," he writes, "each with the goal of maximizing the per capita income of its citizens. If this were best served by merger into a single state, they would merge; they need not try to survive as independent entities to achieve this end." To illustrate the point, he likens states to firms, arguing that "firms just want to maximize profits, and if a merger would increase owner profits, a neoclassical firm will gladly go out of business as that firm."[11]

This argument rests on a misunderstanding of the nature of states and the social groups that underpin them. Human beings—who prize survival above all other goals—are social animals. They are born into and operate in tight-knit social groups, which also rank survival as their number one goal. To function effectively and protect their constituents, these groups construct political institutions. The form of the resulting political entities has varied over time, but those "states," in Charles Tilly's lexicon, have existed throughout human history.[12] Survival is their primary goal.

To be sure, states care greatly about their prosperity. But that goal always takes a back seat to survival. It makes little sense to argue that in order to maximize their wealth, states would voluntarily go out of existence by merging with other states since this would put an end to the state whose wealth is supposedly being maximized. Fearon's mistake is to equate states and neoclassical firms when they are in fact fundamentally different entities. Unlike business firms, which exist to make money for their owners, political entities exist in order to exist. Amalgamation into a new entity, which can be an attractive option for a firm, is thus off the table for states.

Goal Rationality in Practice

Throughout history, states have almost invariably exhibited goal rationality. To make this case, we first show that although states have pursued many objectives in addition to survival, those other goals have been subordinated to self-preservation. We then turn to the handful of cases where scholars claim states were goal-nonrational — pursuing strategies that recklessly put their survival at risk or ignoring the survival imperative — and show that these states were in fact goal-rational.

Privileging Survival

There are many examples of states ranking survival above other important goals. Consider the Thirty Years' War (1618–48). There is little doubt that the major protagonists in that conflict were animated by religious goals. Catholic and Protestant states fought each other in the hope of converting their adversaries. Still, the desire to ensure survival by maintaining a favorable balance of power was more important, and decision-making among the five major combatants was dominated by power considerations rather than religious ones. For instance, there is substantial evidence that Austrian-Spanish cooperation had little to do with Austria's and Spain's shared Catholicism and much to do with balance-of-power considerations. Religion was also subordinate to concerns about survival in the Danish, French, and Swedish decisions to enter the war.[13]

Germany's decision to go to war in 1914 provides further evidence that states privilege survival over other goals. Before World War I, Europe's major economies were highly interdependent. A great-power war was thus expected to do significant damage to German prosperity, which Berlin considered an important goal. At the same time, victory over the Triple Entente would have shifted the balance of power decisively in Germany's favor, all but assuring its survival. German leaders subordinated prosperity to survival and chose war.[14] A similar logic applies to China's relationship with Taiwan today. Chinese leaders have emphasized that they view an independent Taiwan as a threat to China's survival because it would represent the permanent loss of national territory, something that virtually no Chinese is willing to countenance. Beijing has said it will go to war if Taipei declares independence, despite economic consequences that Thomas Friedman has described as "mutual assured economic destruction."[15]

Another example concerns British foreign policy during World War II. Throughout the 1930s, ideological considerations—a deep-seated aversion to communism—played an important role in Britain's decision to reject an alliance with the Soviet Union to contain Nazi Germany. But the fall of France in 1940 changed British thinking. Now that Germany controlled the western half of the European continent and Britain's survival was under threat, London set aside its anti-communism and tried to form a balancing coalition with Moscow against Berlin. Winston Churchill captured the logic in his famous statement, "If [Adolf] Hitler invaded Hell, I should at least make a favorable reference to the Devil in the House of Commons."[16] Survival trumped ideology.

The same principle applies to liberal democracies' foreign policy behavior generally. Some scholars argue that the leaders of such states are strongly inclined to avoid war because they are accountable to domestic constituencies that may oppose the use of force. In other words, democratic governments view peace and its benefits as a particularly important objective. These liberal theorists acknowledge, however, that when the goal of survival conflicts with the goal of peace, the former dominates. As Bruce Russett and Zeev Maoz note, "If states come to believe that their application of . . . democratic norms would endanger their survival, they will act in accordance with the [violent] norms established by their rival."[17]

States also subordinate their international institutional and legal commitments whenever they are at odds with survival. Most of the time, member states aim to abide by the rules embodied in international institutions since they believe they can benefit from doing so; this is why they create or join institutions in the first place. The same is true of international law: compliance is the goal because it is beneficial. But sometimes states conclude that rule-following is at odds with survival, and when that happens, the latter invariably wins out. Consider the Iranian, Iraqi, and North Korean nuclear programs. All three countries signed the Treaty on the Non-Proliferation of Nuclear Weapons (NPT), which explicitly prohibited them from developing a nuclear weapons program. In all three cases, however, fears that they faced threats to their survival led them to violate the NPT and begin developing a nuclear weapons capability.[18]

In wartime, survival is clearly the paramount goal. The best evidence of this concerns the targeting of civilians for military advantage. A rich tradition, with both philosophical and religious roots, mandates that states should aim to avoid killing civilians while waging war. This line of thinking is especially powerful in liberal democracies, where it is widely believed that human rights are inalienable and directly targeting noncombatants is therefore an atrocity. Yet the historical record shows that when states believe their survival is at stake, they do not hesitate to kill large numbers of civilians if such murderous behavior will help them avoid defeat or massive casualties on the battlefield. Britain and the United States blockaded Germany during World War I in an attempt to starve its civilian population and force the Kaiserreich to surrender. The United States also relentlessly firebombed Japanese cities beginning in March 1945 before dropping atomic weapons on Hiroshima and Nagasaki in August, to bring World War II to an end and minimize American casualties.[19]

Risking Survival

Scholars describe two ways that states have risked their survival. Some claim there are prominent historical instances where states recklessly overexpanded, ultimately suffering decisive defeat at the hands of their adversaries. Jack Snyder contends, "Great powers in the industrial age have shown a striking proclivity for self-inflicted wounds. Highly advanced societies with a great deal to lose have sacrificed blood and treasure, sometimes risking the survival of their states, as a consequence of their overly aggressive foreign policies."[20] The canonical cases are Napoleonic France, Wilhelmine Germany, Nazi Germany, and imperial Japan, all of which launched bids for regional hegemony that ended in catastrophic defeat.

Other scholars maintain that states have sometimes put their survival at risk by underbalancing, meaning they failed to take the necessary measures to deter a dangerous rival. Randall Schweller, for example, claims that this kind of behavior is commonplace in international relations, arguing that states often fail to realize that they face a serious threat, and when they do, they often fail to take the appropriate steps to check that adversary. Instead they resort to foolish policies such as appeasement, bandwagoning, and buck-passing, as Britain and France are said to have done in the late 1930s.[21]

To be clear, claiming that states behave in ways that risk their survival is not the same as saying they subordinate their survival to another goal. At no point do Snyder or Schweller argue that the states they describe failed to treat survival as their number one goal. Rather, they maintain that the relevant states pursued foolish, imprudent, or reckless policies.

In fact, there is good evidence that the overexpanders were deeply concerned about their security and launched bids for domination to maximize their prospects for survival. For Napoleon, continental domination was the prelude to destroying Britain, a rival that had "assumed an ascendancy and temerity which threaten[ed] the existence of all nations in their industry and commerce, the life-blood of states." Similarly, in July 1914, Kurt Riezler, Chancellor Theobald von Bethmann Hollweg's personal secretary, noted that German leaders wanted a general European war in order to defeat Russia before it became too powerful and threatened to overwhelm the Kaiserreich. Preventive war was essential because "the future belongs to Russia, which grows and grows, and thrusts on us a heavier and heavier nightmare." Hitler, thinking along the same lines, noted in 1941 that if Germany defeated the Soviet Union, the Third Reich would establish hegemony in Europe and "nobody will then be able to defeat her anymore."[22] Admiral Nagano Osami defended Japan's decision to start World War II in the Pacific on the grounds that his country "was like a patient suffering from a serious illness. . . .

Should he be let alone without an operation, there was danger of a gradual decline. An operation, while it might be extremely dangerous, would still offer some hope of saving his life."[23]

As for the underbalancers, both Britain and France were deeply concerned about their survival in the face of the growing threat from Nazi Germany. While there are reasons to doubt the wisdom of British prime minister Neville Chamberlain's deterrence strategy — which, as we have seen, was briefly nonrational — there is no question that maintaining British security was his overriding concern. The French case is even clearer. France's leaders not only understood that the Third Reich threatened the European balance of power, but they also pursued a rational strategy aimed at ensuring France's survival.[24]

Ignoring Survival

Occasionally, policymakers or pundits argue that states simply do not care about their survival. This claim is usually made in the context of nuclear proliferation. Chinese leader Mao Zedong made a number of cavalier comments about nuclear war that led American and Soviet observers to conclude that he cared little about China's survival. In 1955, for example, he told the Finnish ambassador in Beijing that "even if the U.S. atom bombs were so powerful that, when dropped on China, they would make a hole right through the earth, or even blow it up, that would hardly mean anything to the universe as a whole, though it might be a major event for the solar system."[25] More recently, commentators have suggested that the "Iranian regime is innately irrational" and that Iran's policy is made by "mad mullahs" unconcerned with the country's survival.[26]

But apart from public posturing, there is no evidence that leaders seeking nuclear weapons have not cared about the survival of their states. In fact, the pursuit of such weapons suggests the opposite. A nuclear weapons capability is the ultimate deterrent; it maximizes a country's prospects of surviving. Consider that Beijing has had a nuclear arsenal for well over fifty years and has never threatened to use it—let alone actually used it—in ways that could risk China's destruction.

Finally, some scholars claim that states "choose to die," voluntarily surrendering sovereignty to international institutions. Dustin Howes, for instance, emphasizes that in ceding "autonomy to international institutions," states have willingly given up their lives since he views autonomy, sovereignty, and survival as interchangeable concepts. The paradigmatic case is the creation of the European Union (EU), a process that Howes and others argue involved the West European states surrendering their sovereignty to a powerful international institution.[27]

There are two problems with this argument. First, states that join institutions like the EU do not surrender sovereignty but instead delegate authority to make decisions on particular issues. Ultimate authority remains in the hands of the member states, which can take it back at any time, as Britain's exit from the EU in 2020 makes clear.[28] Second, states delegate authority to institutions with the express purpose of enhancing their prospects for survival, not abandoning it. The West Europeans created the European Community, the precursor to the EU, in order to maximize their prospects for survival. They joined NATO for the same reason.[29]

The Survival Imperative

There is abundant evidence that states are goal rational, which is to say they have sought to survive and have placed survival above their other goals. To be clear, this does not mean that states always manage to survive. The Soviet Union, Yugoslavia, and Czechoslovakia died after the Cold War ended. But in each case, the leaders preferred to keep their country intact; they were simply unable to do so. In fact, we have found only one example of goal nonrationality in the historical record: Germany's behavior at the end of World War II. Faced with the prospect of certain defeat, the Third Reich continued to fight rather than surrender, ensuring its own destruction. As Michael Geyer notes, the last years of the war were marked by a "progression of mass death" fueled by "Germans soldiering on in the midst of the cataclysm of their own destruction."[30]

Chapter 9

RATIONALITY IN INTERNATIONAL POLITICS

Much of modern international relations theory — especially the liberal and realist theories that dominated academic discourse in the 1970s, 1980s, and 1990s — is based on the notion that states are rational actors, meaning their leaders act in a purposive way when making foreign policy. To be sure, scholars in those traditions did not devote much attention to defining and defending the rational actor assumption, and it is striking that there is no major work on the subject. Yet there was a loose consensus that rational states thought in terms of the pros and cons of different policies when deciding how to navigate the international system.

Criticism of the rational actor assumption has come in two waves. Many early critics drew on the insights of psychology to argue that policymakers, like all human beings, have cognitive limitations that often prevent rational decisions.[1] Other critics, who worked in the rational choice tradition, assumed that states could be treated "as if" they acted rationally for the purposes of explaining their behavior but noted that their leaders were not actually rational if that term meant they thought in terms of maximizing their

---

expected utility.[2] In short, political psychologists and rational choice scholars agreed — for different reasons — that states are not routinely rational in practice.

In the last two decades, challenges to the rational actor assumption have intensified with the coming of a second wave of critics. Drawing on new empirical research about preferences, beliefs, and decision-making, political psychologists, much like behavioral economists, have rejected the claim that state leaders are routinely rational.[3] At the same time, rational choice theorists have focused on explaining how states would make decisions about competition, cooperation, war, and peace if they were rational, suggesting either implicitly or explicitly that they often are not.[4]

If the critics are right, theorists and practitioners of international politics are in trouble. Since most liberal and realist international relations theories rely on a rational actor assumption, a finding that states are frequently nonrational would cripple those theoretical approaches, leaving them with little to say about how the world works. At a practical level, it would be especially difficult for states to formulate strategies if they could not expect other states to think and act rationally. After all, they would have no reliable way of predicting how other states might react to their policies.[5]

In marked contrast to the emerging conventional wisdom, we find that states are routinely rational. To say a state is a rational actor means that it bases its policies on credible theories and makes decisions through a deliberative policymaking process. By this standard, the historical record reveals that most states are rational most of the time. The consequences are profound. Inside the academy, realism and liberalism are alive and well.[6] In the policy world, states have a sound basis for making foreign policy.

One final point is in order. Many scholars associate rationality with interstate peace. Their argument, in brief, is that rationality tells states that security competition and war make little sense and that they have a vested interest in cooperating with each other. Some go so far as to argue that if states routinely employ their powers of reason, war will go the way of other violent "practices that passed from unexceptionable to controversial to immoral to unthinkable to not-thought-about."[7] This perspective confuses rationality with morality. Rational decision makers simply try to figure out the most effective strategy for dealing with other states, and as should be apparent by now, threatening or initiating violence sometimes makes sense. This message is hardly uplifting, but such is the reality of international politics.

NOTES

PREFACE

1. "UK's Johnson Says Russia's Putin May Be 'Irrational' on Ukraine," *Reuters*, 20 February 2022; Mitt Romney, "We Must Prepare for Putin's Worst Weapons," *New York Times*, 21 May 2022.

2. We use the term "nonrational/nonrationality" rather than "irrational/irrationality" to denote actors that are not rational. The reason is that the word "irrational" is often used to criticize – even disparage – someone, but we seek only to assess whether leaders and states meet the criteria for rationality. We are not interested in criticizing or praising the quality of their decisions.

3. Nina L. Khrushcheva, "Putin Joins a Long Line of Irrational Tyrants," *Globe and Mail*, 26 February 2022; Bess Levin, "An 'Increasingly Frustrated' Putin, a Madman with Nuclear Weapons, Is Lashing Out at His Inner Circle," *Vanity Fair*, 1 March 2022; Tony Brenton, "This Isn't the Vladimir Putin That I Once Knew," *Telegraph*, 1 March 2022.

4. Kevin Liptak, "Biden Says Putin 'Totally Miscalculated' by Invading Ukraine but Is a 'Rational Actor,'" CNN, 11 October 2022.

5. "H. R. McMaster on 'Face the Nation,'" *CBS News*, 27 February 2022.

6. Quoted in "Vladimir Putin's Televised Address on Ukraine," *Bloomberg News*, 24 February 2022.

7. Ramzy Mardini, "Course Correcting toward Diplomacy in the Ukraine Crisis," *National Interest*, 12 August 2022.

8. David Ignatius, "Putin's Impending 'March of Folly' in Ukraine," *Washington Post*, 13 February 2022.

9. James Risen and Ken Klippenstein, "The CIA Thought Putin Would Quickly Conquer Ukraine. Why Did They Get It So Wrong?" *Intercept*, 5 October 2022.

10. Warner quoted in "Reading Putin: Unbalanced or Cagily Preying on West's Fears?" *Independent*, 1 March 2022; Michael McFaul, "Putin Is Menacing

---

227

the World. Here's How Biden Should Respond to His Nuclear Threats," *Washington Post*, 3 March 2022.

11. William J. Burns, *The Back Channel: A Memoir of American Diplomacy and the Case for Its Renewal* (New York: Random House, 2019), 233; "Foreign Minister Sergey Lavrov's Interview with the BBC TV Channel, St. Petersburg," Ministry of Foreign Affairs of the Russian Federation, 16 June 2022.

CHAPTER 1. THE RATIONAL ACTOR ASSUMPTION

1. See, for example, Ewen MacAskill, "Irrational, Illogical, Unpredictable — 24 Years On, the World Awaits Saddam's Next Move," *Guardian*, 18 March 2003; Victor Davis Hanson, "The Not-So-Mad Mind of Mahmoud Ahmadinejad," *Chicago Tribune*, 20 January 2006; Phil Gunson, "Is Hugo Chavez Insane?" *Newsweek*, 11 November 2001; Kate Kelland, "No Method in Deciphering Gaddafi's Mind," *Reuters*, 3 March 2011; Mark Bowden, "Understanding Kim Jong Un, the World's Most Enigmatic and Unpredictable Dictator," *Vanity Fair*, 12 February 2015.

2. Emilie M. Hafner-Burton, Stephan Haggard, David A. Lake, and David G. Victor, "The Behavioral Revolution and International Relations," *International Organization* 71, no. S1 (2017): 2.

3. On this point, see Uriel Abulof, "The Malpractice of 'Rationality' in International Relations," *Rationality and Society* 27, no. 3 (2015): 359; Kevin Narizny, "On Systemic Paradigms and Domestic Politics: A Critique of the Newest Realism," *International Security* 42, no. 2 (2017): 160–161; Alexander Wendt, "Anarchy Is What States Make of It: The Social Construction of Power Politics," *International Organization* 45, no. 2 (1992): 391–395. For the claim that the rationality assumption is central to both liberal and realist approaches, see Robert O. Keohane and Joseph S. Nye, Jr., *"Power and Interdependence* Revisited," *International Organization* 41, no. 4 (1987): 728. For the claim that it is central to liberal approaches, see Andrew Moravcsik, "Taking Preferences Seriously: A Liberal Theory of International Politics," *International Organization* 51, no. 4 (1997): 516–521. And for the claim that it is central to realist approaches, see Robert O. Keohane, "Theory of World Politics: Structural Realism and Beyond," in *Neorealism and Its Critics*, ed. Robert O. Keohane (New York: Columbia University Press, 1986), 164–165; Jeffrey W. Legro and Andrew Moravcsik, "Is Anybody Still a Realist?" *International Security* 24, no. 2 (1999): 6, 12; Brian C. Schmidt and Colin Wight, "Rationalism and the 'Rational Actor Assumption' in Realist International Relations Theory," *Journal of International Political Theory* (forthcoming).

4. For the view that one cannot abandon or alter the assumptions of a research program without also abandoning the program itself, see Imre Lakatos, *The Methodology of Scientific Research Programmes: Philosophical Papers*, ed. John Worrall and Gregory Currie (New York: Cambridge University Press, 1978), 1:1–101.

---

5. For a similar definition, see Steven Pinker, *Rationality: What It Is, Why It Seems Scarce, Why It Matters* (New York: Viking, 2021), 36–37. Specifically, Pinker writes: "A definition that is more or less faithful to the way the word is used is 'the ability to use knowledge to attain goals.'"

6. For recent works describing the rational choice and political psychology enterprises, see Andrew H. Kydd, *International Relations Theory: The Game-Theoretic Approach* (New York: Cambridge University Press, 2015); Alex Mintz, Nicholas A. Valentino, and Carly Wayne, *Beyond Rationality: Behavioral Political Science in the 21st Century* (New York: Cambridge University Press, 2022).

7. As should be apparent, we take a scientific realist perspective to theorizing international relations. For us, theories comprise statements that reflect how the world actually works. It follows that the assumptions that underpin those theories must accurately reflect particular aspects of international politics and can be shown to be right or wrong. Those assumptions are not merely useful fictions that help generate interesting theories, as instrumentalists claim. In the case at hand, this means that a sound definition of rationality must reflect how rational leaders actually think. On the difference between scientific realism and instrumentalism, see Paul K. MacDonald, "Useful Fiction or Miracle Maker: The Competing Epistemological Foundations of Rational Choice Theory," *American Political Science Review* 97, no. 4 (2003): 551–565; John J. Mearsheimer and Stephen M. Walt, "Leaving Theory Behind: Why Simplistic Hypothesis Testing Is Bad for International Relations," *European Journal of International Relations* 19, no. 3 (2013): 432–434; and on scientific realism, see Anjan Chakravartty, "Scientific Realism," in *The Stanford Encyclopedia of Philosophy* (Summer 2017 edition), ed. Edward N. Zalta; https://plato.stanford.edu/archives/sum2017/entries/scientific-realism/.

8. To be clear, we use the term "strategic rationality" to denote the rationality of a state's strategy or policy. Rational choice scholars employ the term somewhat differently, emphasizing the interactive nature of decision-making. They focus on how actors must take each other's strategies into account when making choices. See, for example, David A. Lake and Robert Powell, "International Relations: A Strategic-Choice Approach," in *Strategic Choice and International Relations*, ed. David A. Lake and Robert Powell (Princeton, NJ: Princeton University Press, 1999), 3–4.

CHAPTER 2. STRATEGIC RATIONALITY AND UNCERTAINTY

1. Herbert A. Simon, "Rationality as Process and as Product of Thought," *American Economic Review* 68, no. 2 (1978): 1, 9; emphasis in original.

2. Debra Satz and John Ferejohn, "Rational Choice and Social Theory," *Journal of Philosophy* 91, no. 2 (1994): 73; emphasis in original.

---

3. For the claim that individuals have beliefs about the nature of the political world and beliefs about decision-making, see Stephen G. Walker, "Foreign Policy Analysis and Behavioral International Relations," in *Rethinking Foreign Policy Analysis: States, Leaders, and the Microfoundations of Behavioral International Relations,* ed. Stephen G. Walker, Akan Malici, and Mark Schafer (New York: Routledge, 2011), 6.

4. Quoted in Stephen Kalberg, "Max Weber's Types of Rationality: Cornerstones for the Analysis of Rationalization Processes in History," *American Journal of Sociology* 85, no. 5 (1980): 1159–1160.

5. David A. Lake and Robert Powell, "International Relations: A Strategic-Choice Approach," in *Strategic Choice and International Relations,* ed. David A. Lake and Robert Powell (Princeton, NJ: Princeton University Press, 1999), 6–7.

6. Brian C. Rathbun, *Reasoning of State: Realists, Romantics and Rationality in International Relations* (New York: Cambridge University Press, 2019), 18. See also Dan Spokojny and Thomas Scherer, "Foreign Policy Should Be Evidence-Based," *War on the Rocks,* 26 July 2021.

7. Sidney Verba, "Assumptions of Rationality and Non-Rationality in Models of the International System," *World Politics* 14, no. 1 (1961): 93.

8. Norrin M. Ripsman, Jeffrey W. Taliaferro, and Steven E. Lobell, *Neoclassical Realist Theory of International Politics* (New York: Oxford University Press, 2016), 61–62, 123–129; Alexander Wendt, "The State as Person in International Theory," *Review of International Studies* 30, no. 2 (2004): 296–301.

9. Stanley Ingber, "The Marketplace of Ideas: A Legitimizing Myth," *Duke Law Journal* 1984, no. 1 (1984): 3–4.

10. Jon Elster, "Introduction," in *Rational Choice,* ed. Jon Elster (New York: New York University Press, 1986), 5; James D. Morrow, *Game Theory for Political Scientists* (Princeton, NJ: Princeton University Press, 1994), 28.

11. Frank H. Knight, *Risk, Uncertainty and Profit* (Boston: Houghton Mifflin, 1921), 214–216, 224–225, 230; quote on p. 214.

12. Knight, *Risk, Uncertainty and Profit,* 214.

13. John Maynard Keynes, "The General Theory of Employment," *Quarterly Journal of Economics* 51, no. 2 (1937): 213–214. On uncertainty, see also David Dequech: "Fundamental Uncertainty and Ambiguity," *Eastern Economic Journal* 26, no. 1 (2000): 41–60, and "Uncertainty: A Typology and Refinements of Existing Concepts," *Journal of Economic Issues* 45, no. 3 (2011): 621–640; Friedrich A. Hayek, "The Use of Knowledge in Society," *American Economic Review* 35, no. 4 (1945): 519–530; John Kay and Mervyn King, *Radical Uncertainty: Decision-Making beyond the Numbers* (New York: W. W. Norton, 2020), 14–15; Jonathan Kirshner, "The Economic Sins of Modern IR Theory and the Classical Realist Alternative," *World Politics* 67, no. 1 (2015): 168–177; Knight, *Risk, Uncertainty and Profit,* 198–199, 225, 231–233; Jennifer Mitzen and Randall L. Schweller, "Knowing the Unknown Unknowns: Misplaced Certainty and the Onset of War,"

Security Studies 20, no. 1 (2011): 2-35; Brian C. Rathbun, "Uncertain about Uncertainty: Understanding the Multiple Meanings of a Crucial Concept in International Relations Theory," *International Studies Quarterly* 51, no. 3 (2007): 533-557.

14. On "small" and "large" worlds, see Gerd Gigerenzer, "Axiomatic Rationality and Ecological Rationality," *Synthese* 198 (2021): 3548-3550.

15. Kay and King, *Radical Uncertainty*, 12.

16. Carl von Clausewitz, *On War*, ed. and trans. Michael Howard and Peter Paret (Princeton, NJ: Princeton University Press, 1976), 101-102.

17. See, for example, Geoffrey Blainey, *The Causes of War*, 3rd ed. (New York: Free Press, 1988); James D. Fearon, "Rationalist Explanations for War," *International Organization* 49, no. 3 (1995): 379-414; Jack S. Levy, "Misperception and the Causes of War: Theoretical Linkages and Analytical Problems," *World Politics* 36, no. 1 (1983): 76-99; Ernest R. May, "Capabilities and Proclivities," in *Knowing One's Enemies: Intelligence Assessment before the Two World Wars*, ed. Ernest R. May (Princeton, NJ: Princeton University Press, 1984), 504-519.

18. Stephen M. Walt, "The Case for Finite Containment: Analyzing U.S. Grand Strategy," *International Security* 14, no. 1 (1989): 6. See also Barry R. Posen, *Restraint: A New Foundation for U.S. Grand Strategy* (Ithaca, NY: Cornell University Press, 2014), 1; Nina Silove, "Beyond the Buzzword: The Three Meanings of 'Grand Strategy,'" *Security Studies* 27, no. 1 (2018): 34-39.

19. See, for example, Robert Jervis, "Was the Cold War a Security Dilemma?" *Journal of Cold War Studies* 3, no. 1 (2001): 36-60; Marc Trachtenberg: *The Craft of International History: A Guide to Method* (Princeton, NJ: Princeton University Press, 2006), ch. 4, and "The Influence of Nuclear Weapons in the Cuban Missile Crisis," *International Security* 10, no. 1 (1985): 137-163; John J. Mearsheimer, "The Inevitable Rivalry: America, China, and the Tragedy of Great-Power Politics," *Foreign Affairs* 100, no. 6 (2021): 48-58.

CHAPTER 3. DEFINING STRATEGIC RATIONALITY

1. For an insightful analysis linking theories—the authors use the terms "ideas" or "beliefs"—and foreign policy, see Judith Goldstein and Robert O. Keohane, "Ideas and Foreign Policy: An Analytical Framework," in *Ideas and Foreign Policy: Beliefs, Institutions, and Political Change*, ed. Judith Goldstein and Robert O. Keohane (Ithaca, NY: Cornell University Press, 1993), 3-30.

2. On balance of threat theory, see Stephen M. Walt, *The Origins of Alliances* (Ithaca, NY: Cornell University Press, 1987).

3. On democratic peace theory, see Bruce M. Russett, *Grasping the Democratic Peace: Principles for a Post-Cold War World* (Princeton, NJ: Princeton University Press, 1993).

---

4. Steven Pinker, *Rationality: What It Is, Why It Seems Scarce, Why It Matters* (New York: Viking, 2021), 74.

5. Brian C. Rathbun, *Reasoning of State: Realists, Romantics and Rationality in International Relations* (New York: Cambridge University Press, 2019), 18, 20.

6. Robert Jervis, *Perception and Misperception in International Politics* (Princeton, NJ: Princeton University Press, 1976), 158.

7. John Kay and Mervyn King employ a similar framework for thinking about reasoning in different informational contexts, though they refer to "narratives" rather than "theories." They also do not develop their concept of narratives in the way we develop the notion of theories. See Kay and King, *Radical Uncertainty: Decision-Making beyond the Numbers* (New York: W. W. Norton, 2020).

8. Carl von Clausewitz, *On War,* ed. and trans. Michael Howard and Peter Paret (Princeton, NJ: Princeton University Press, 1976), 578.

9. Robert B. Zoellick, *America in the World: A History of U.S. Diplomacy and Foreign Policy* (New York: Hachette, 2020), 8.

10. Quoted in Michael C. Desch, *Cult of the Irrelevant: The Waning Influence of Social Science on National Security* (Princeton, NJ: Princeton University Press, 2019), 240–241.

11. Desch, *Cult of the Irrelevant,* 241.

12. Kay and King, *Radical Uncertainty,* 12–17.

13. John Maynard Keynes, *General Theory of Employment, Interest and Money* (New York: Classic Books America, 2009), 331. See also Immanuel Kant, "Perpetual Peace: A Philosophical Sketch" in *Kant: Political Writings,* ed. H. S. Reiss (New York: Cambridge University Press, 1970), 93, 114–115.

14. Binyamin Applebaum, *The Economists' Hour: False Prophets, Free Markets, and the Fracture of Society* (New York: Little, Brown, 2019), 67, 82. See also Todd G. Buchholz, *New Ideas from Dead Economists: An Introduction to Modern Economic Thought,* rev. and updated ed. (New York: Plume, 2007); Paul Krugman, *Peddling Prosperity: Economic Sense and Nonsense in the Age of Diminished Expectations* (New York: W. W. Norton, 1994); Nicholas Wapshott, *Samuelson Friedman: The Battle over the Free Market* (New York: W. W. Norton, 2021).

15. Strobe Talbott, "Why NATO Should Grow," *New York Review of Books,* 10 August 1995.

16. Quoted in Thomas L. Friedman, "Foreign Affairs; Now a Word from X," *New York Times,* 2 May 1998.

17. Quoted in David Dessler, "Beyond Correlations: Toward a Causal Theory of War," *International Studies Quarterly* 35, no. 3 (1991): 349. On this point, see also Jessica D. Blankshain and Andrew L. Stigler, "Applying Method to Madness: A User's Guide to Causal Inference in Policy Analysis," *Texas National Security Review* 3, no. 3 (2020): 76–89.

18. For a description of the debate between scientific realists and instrumentalists over assumptions and causal logics, see Paul K. MacDonald, "Useful Fiction or Miracle Maker: The Competing Epistemological Foundations of Rational Choice Theory," *American Political Science Review* 97, no. 4 (2003): 551–565.

19. Milton Friedman, "The Methodology of Positive Economics," in Milton Friedman, *Essays in Positive Economics* (Chicago: University of Chicago Press, 1953), 14.

20. Ronald H. Coase, *How Should Economists Choose?* (Washington, DC: American Enterprise Institute for Public Policy Research, 1982), 7. See also Terry Moe, "On the Scientific Status of Rational Models," *American Journal of Political Science* 23, no. 1 (1979): 215–243.

21. On causal logics, see Jon Elster, *Nuts and Bolts for the Social Sciences* (New York: Cambridge University Press, 1989), 3–10; Gary Goertz, *Multimethod Research, Causal Mechanisms, and Case Studies: An Integrated Approach* (Princeton, NJ: Princeton University Press, 2017), ch. 2; Peter Hedström and Petri Ylikoski, "Causal Mechanisms in the Social Sciences," *Annual Review of Sociology* 36 (2010): 49–67.

22. Kenneth J. Arrow, "Mathematical Models in the Social Sciences," in *The Policy Sciences,* ed. Daniel Lerner and Harold D. Lasswell (Stanford, CA: Stanford University Press, 1951), 129.

23. Stephen M. Walt, "Rigor or Rigor Mortis? Rational Choice and Security Studies," *International Security* 23, no. 4 (1999): 12, 14–20.

24. Kenneth N. Waltz, *Theory of International Politics* (New York: McGraw-Hill, 1979), 171–172.

25. Joseph M. Grieco, "Anarchy and the Limits of Cooperation: A Realist Critique of the Newest Liberal Institutionalism," *International Organization* 42, no. 3 (1988): 485–507.

26. Quoted in Walt, "Rigor or Rigor Mortis?" 31–32. Walt quotes George Stigler to similar effect: "Does the new theory help us to understand observable economic life? . . . Until [this] . . . question is answered, a theory has no standing and therefore should not be used as a guide to policy." Ibid., 22.

27. See, for example, Dale C. Copeland, *The Origins of Major War* (Ithaca, NY: Cornell University Press, 2000); John J. Mearsheimer, *The Tragedy of Great Power Politics,* updated ed. (New York: W. W. Norton, 2014); Jack Snyder, *Myths of Empire: Domestic Politics and International Ambition* (Ithaca, NY: Cornell University Press, 1991); Stephen Van Evera, *Causes of War: Power and the Roots of Conflict* (Ithaca, NY: Cornell University Press, 1999).

28. For the liberal view, see Michael W. Doyle, "Kant, Liberal Legacies, and Foreign Affairs," *Philosophy and Public Affairs* 12, no. 3 (1983): 205–235; for the realist view, see Christopher Layne, "Kant or Cant: The Myth of the Democratic Peace," *International Security* 19, no. 2 (1994): 5–49.

29. None of this is to deny that individual scholars often argue that their theory provides the best explanation for how the world works. After all, theorizing is a competitive enterprise and theorists devote considerable time and effort to defending their own theories and criticizing rival theories. In most cases, they conclude that their theory is superior to the alternative, yet still credible, theory. In a handful of cases, however, they maintain that the alternative theory is not merely flawed and inferior, but also in fact noncredible. For examples from our own work where we claim our theory is superior to a rival credible theory, see John J. Mearsheimer, "The False Promise of International Institutions," *International Security* 19, no. 3 (1994/95): 5–49; Sebastian Rosato, "The Flawed Logic of Democratic Peace Theory," *American Political Science Review* 97, no. 4 (2003): 585–602. For an excellent study that recognizes the connection between theory and rationality and provides criteria for identifying the best theory for understanding international politics, see Fred Chernoff, *Theory and Metatheory in International Relations: Concepts and Contending Accounts* (New York: Palgrave Macmillan, 2007).

30. Krugman, *Peddling Prosperity,* xiii.

31. On these techniques, see Derek Beach and Rasmus Brun Pedersen, *Causal Case Study Methods: Foundations and Guidelines for Comparing, Matching, and Tracing* (Ann Arbor: University of Michigan Press, 2016); Andrew Bennett and Jeffrey T. Checkel, *Process Tracing: From Metaphor to Analytic Tool* (New York: Cambridge University Press, 2015); John Gerring, *Social Science Methodology: A Unified Framework,* 2nd ed. (New York: Cambridge University Press, 2012); Kosuke Imai, *Quantitative Social Science: An Introduction* (Princeton, NJ: Princeton University Press, 2017); Paul M. Kellstedt and Guy D. Whitten, *The Fundamentals of Political Science Research,* 3rd ed. (New York: Cambridge University Press, 2018); Gary King, Robert O. Keohane, and Sidney Verba, *Designing Social Inquiry: Scientific Inference in Qualitative Research,* new ed. (Princeton, NJ: Princeton University Press, 2021); Jason Seawright, *Multi-Method Social Science: Combining Qualitative and Quantitative Tools* (New York: Cambridge University Press, 2016); Marc Trachtenberg, *The Craft of International History: A Guide to Method* (Princeton, NJ: Princeton University Press, 2006). For a discussion of various possible criteria for judging whether the evidence supports a theory, see Goertz, *Multimethod Research, Causal Mechanisms, and Case Studies,* 204–208.

32. Jonathan Kirshner, "The Economic Sins of Modern IR Theory and the Classical Realist Alternative," *World Politics* 67, no. 1 (2015): 175.

33. See, for example, Barry Posen, *Inadvertent Escalation: Conventional War and Nuclear Risks* (Ithaca, NY: Cornell University Press, 1991); Caitlin Talmadge, "Would China Go Nuclear? Assessing the Risk of Chinese Nuclear Escalation in a Conventional War with the United States," *International Security* 41, no. 4 (2017): 50–92.

34. For an overview of the realist and liberal schools of thought, see Michael W. Doyle, *Ways of War and Peace: Realism, Liberalism, and Socialism* (New York:

W. W. Norton, 1997); Brian C. Schmidt, *The Political Discourse of Anarchy: A Disciplinary History of International Relations* (Albany: State University of New York Press, 1998).

35. On research traditions, see Alan F. Chalmers, *What Is This Thing Called Science?* 4th ed. (Indianapolis, IN: Hackett, 2013), 97–148; Peter Godfrey-Smith, *Theory and Reality: An Introduction to the Philosophy of Science,* 2nd ed. (Chicago: University of Chicago Press, 2021), 101–150.

36. Kevin Narizny, "On Systemic Paradigms and Domestic Politics: A Critique of the Newest Realism," *International Security* 42, no. 2 (2017): 160.

37. For a succinct discussion of realism, see Sean M. Lynn-Jones and Steven E. Miller, "Preface," in *The Perils of Anarchy: Contemporary Realism and International Security,* ed. Michael E. Brown, Sean M. Lynn-Jones, and Steven E. Miller (Cambridge, MA: MIT Press, 1995), ix–xxi.

38. The following analysis focuses on realist theories that seek to explain how the world actually works and can therefore be used by decision makers to formulate foreign policy. For that reason, we do not include two prominent contributions to the realist canon: James D. Fearon, "Rationalist Explanations for War," *International Organization* 49, no. 3 (1995): 379–414, and Charles L. Glaser, *Rational Theory of International Politics: The Logic of Competition and Cooperation* (Princeton, NJ: Princeton University Press, 2010). Both scholars explicitly say that they are not offering an explanatory theory. Fearon engages in a logical thought experiment, describing reasons why "truly rational" states – and there is no such thing – would go to war (Fearon, "Rationalist Explanations for War," 392). Meanwhile, Glaser notes that his is "a theory of what states should do to achieve their goals, given the constraints they face; in this sense, it is a prescriptive, normative theory" (Glaser, *Rational Theory of International Politics,* 23).

39. David Hume, "Of the Balance of Power," in *Essays: Moral, Political, and Literary,* ed. Eugene F. Miller (Indianapolis, IN: Liberty Fund, 1994); Stanley Hoffmann and David P. Fidler, eds., *Rousseau on International Relations* (Oxford: Clarendon, 1991); Jervis, *Perception and Misperception in International Politics,* and "Cooperation under the Security Dilemma," *World Politics* 30, no. 2 (1978): 167–214; Waltz, *Theory of International Politics;* Barry R. Posen, *The Sources of Military Doctrine: France, Britain, and Germany between the World Wars* (Ithaca, NY: Cornell University Press, 1986); Walt, *The Origins of Alliances;* Robert Powell, "Absolute and Relative Gains in International Relations Theory," *American Political Science Review* 85, no. 4 (1991): 1303–1320; Snyder, *Myths of Empire;* Van Evera, *Causes of War.*

40. Thomas C. Schelling, *The Strategy of Conflict* (Cambridge, MA: Harvard University Press, 1960); Robert Jervis: *The Logic of Images in International Relations* (Princeton, NJ: Princeton University Press, 1970), and "Cooperation under the Security Dilemma"; Randall L. Schweller, "Neorealism's Status-Quo Bias: What Security Dilemma?" *Security Studies* 5, no. 3 (1996): 90–121; Glaser, *Rational*

Theory of International Politics; Andrew H. Kydd, *Trust and Mistrust in International Relations* (Princeton, NJ: Princeton University Press, 2005); Dale C. Copeland, *Economic Interdependence and War* (Princeton, NJ: Princeton University Press, 2015).

41. Thomas Hobbes, *Leviathan,* ed. David Johnston (New York: W. W. Norton, 2021); G. Lowes Dickinson, *The European Anarchy* (New York: Macmillan, 1916); Nicholas J. Spykman, *America's Strategy in World Politics: The United States and the Balance of Power* (New York: Harcourt, Brace, 1942); John H. Herz, *Political Realism and Political Idealism: A Study in Theories and Realities* (Chicago: University of Chicago Press, 1951); Hans J. Morgenthau, *Politics among Nations: The Struggle for Power and Peace,* 5th ed. (New York: Alfred A. Knopf, 1973); Eric J. Labs, "Offensive Realism and Why States Expand Their War Aims," *Security Studies* 6, no. 4 (1997): 1–49; Mearsheimer, *The Tragedy of Great Power Politics;* Keir A. Lieber, *War and the Engineers: The Primacy of Politics over Technology* (Ithaca, NY: Cornell University Press, 2005).

42. Thucydides, *The Landmark Thucydides: A Comprehensive Guide to the Peloponnesian War,* ed. Robert B. Strassler (New York: Free Press, 1996); Robert Gilpin, *War and Change in World Politics* (New York: Cambridge University Press, 1981); Stephen G. Brooks and William C. Wohlforth, *America Abroad: The United States' Global Role in the 21st Century* (New York: Oxford University Press, 2016).

43. George H. Quester, *Offense and Defense in the International System* (New York: John Wiley, 1977); John J. Mearsheimer, *Conventional Deterrence* (Ithaca, NY: Cornell University Press, 1983); T. V. Paul, *Asymmetric Conflicts: War Initiation by Weaker Powers* (New York: Cambridge University Press, 1994); Stephen Van Evera, "Offense, Defense, and the Causes of War," *International Security* 22, no. 4 (1998): 5–43.

44. Robert Jervis, *The Meaning of the Nuclear Revolution: Statecraft and the Prospects of Armageddon* (Ithaca, NY: Cornell University Press, 1990); Brendan Rittenhouse Green, *The Revolution That Failed: Nuclear Competition, Arms Control, and the Cold War* (New York: Cambridge University Press, 2020); Keir A. Lieber and Daryl G. Press, *The Myth of the Nuclear Revolution: Power Politics in the Atomic Age* (Ithaca, NY: Cornell University Press, 2020).

45. Alexander L. George, *Forceful Persuasion: Coercive Diplomacy as an Alternative to War* (Washington, DC: United States Institute of Peace, 1991); Daniel Byman and Matthew Waxman, *The Dynamics of Coercion: American Foreign Policy and the Limits of Military Might* (New York: Cambridge University Press, 2002); Robert J. Art and Patrick M. Cronin, eds., *The United States and Coercive Diplomacy* (Washington, DC: United States Institute of Peace, 2003).

46. Matthew Kroenig, *The Logic of American Nuclear Strategy: Why Strategic Superiority Matters* (New York: Oxford University Press, 2018). Below we show that Kroenig's theory of nuclear coercion in peacetime is noncredible.

47. Clausewitz, *On War*; Alfred T. Mahan, *The Influence of Sea Power upon History, 1660–1783* (Boston: Little, Brown, 1890); Thomas C. Schelling, *Arms and Influence* (New Haven: Yale University Press, 1966); Robert A. Pape, *Bombing to Win: Air Power and Coercion in War* (Ithaca, NY: Cornell University Press, 1996); Ivan Arreguín-Toft, *How the Weak Win Wars: A Theory of Asymmetric Conflict* (New York: Cambridge University Press, 2005); Stephen Biddle, *Military Power: Explaining Victory and Defeat in Modern Battle* (Princeton, NJ: Princeton University Press, 2010).

48. Albert Wohlstetter, "The Delicate Balance of Terror," *Foreign Affairs* 37, no. 2 (1959): 211–234; Paul H. Nitze, "Assuring Strategic Stability in an Era of Détente," *Foreign Affairs* 54, no. 2 (1976): 207–232; Schelling: *Arms and Influence*, and *Strategy of Conflict;* Keir A. Lieber and Daryl G. Press, "The End of MAD? The Nuclear Dimension of U.S. Primacy," *International Security* 30, no. 4 (2006): 7–44.

49. Narizny, "On Systemic Paradigms and Domestic Politics," 161.

50. Andrew Moravcsik, "Taking Preferences Seriously: A Liberal Theory of International Politics," *International Organization* 51, no. 4 (1997): 513–553.

51. Kant, "Perpetual Peace," 93–130; Doyle, "Kant, Liberal Legacies, and Foreign Affairs"; Russett, *Grasping the Democratic Peace;* John M. Owen, IV, *Liberal Peace, Liberal War: American Politics and International Security* (Ithaca, NY: Cornell University Press, 1997); Bruce Bueno de Mesquita et al., "An Institutional Explanation of the Democratic Peace," *American Political Science Review* 93, no. 4 (1999): 791–812; John Rawls, *Law of Peoples*, rev. ed. (Cambridge, MA: Harvard University Press, 2001); Charles Lipson, *Reliable Partners: How Democracies Have Made a Separate Peace* (Princeton, NJ: Princeton University Press, 2003).

52. Norman Angell, *The Great Illusion: A Study of the Relationship of Military Power in Nations to Their Economic and Social Advantage* (London: William Heinemann, 1910); Richard Rosecrance, *The Rise of the Trading State: Commerce and Conquest in the Modern World* (New York: Basic Books, 1986); Stephen G. Brooks, *Producing Security: Multinational Corporations, Globalization, and the Changing Calculus of Conflict* (Princeton, NJ: Princeton University Press, 2005); Eric Gartzke, "The Capitalist Peace," *American Journal of Political Science* 51, no. 1 (2007): 166–191; Patrick J. McDonald, *The Invisible Hand of Peace: Capitalism, the War Machine, and International Relations Theory* (New York: Cambridge University Press, 2009); Copeland, *Economic Interdependence and War.*

53. John Locke, *Two Treatises on Government,* ed. Peter Laslett (New York: Cambridge University Press, 1960); Stephen D. Krasner, ed., *International Regimes* (Ithaca, NY: Cornell University Press, 1983); Robert O. Keohane, *After Hegemony: Cooperation and Discord in the World Political Economy* (Princeton, NJ: Princeton University Press, 1984); Helen Milner, *Interests, Institutions and Information: Domestic Politics and International Relations* (Princeton, NJ: Princeton University Press,

1997); Celeste Wallander, *Mortal Friends, Best Enemies: German-Russian Cooperation after the Cold War* (Ithaca, NY: Cornell University Press, 1999); G. John Ikenberry, *After Victory: Institutions, Strategic Restraint, and the Rebuilding of Order after Major Wars* (Princeton, NJ: Princeton University Press, 2001).

54. Doyle, "Kant, Liberal Legacies, and Foreign Affairs"; Ido Oren and Jude Hays, "Democracies May Rarely Fight One Another, but Developed Socialist States Rarely Fight at All," *Alternatives* 22, no. 4 (1997): 493–521; Owen, *Liberal Peace, Liberal War;* Mark L. Haas, *The Ideological Origins of Great Power Politics, 1789–1989* (Ithaca, NY: Cornell University Press, 2005).

55. John K. Fairbank, "Introduction: Varieties of Chinese Military Experience," in *Chinese Ways in Warfare*, ed. Frank A. Kierman, Jr. and John K. Fairbank (Cambridge, MA: Harvard University Press, 1974), 1–26; Henry Kissinger, *On China* (New York: Penguin, 2011); Yan Xuetong, *Ancient Chinese Thought, Modern Chinese Power*, ed. Daniel A. Bell and Sun Zhe, trans. Edmund Ryden (Princeton, NJ: Princeton University Press, 2011).

56. Martha Finnemore, *National Interests in International Society* (Ithaca, NY: Cornell University Press, 1996); Peter J. Katzenstein, ed., *The Culture of National Security: Norms and Identity in World Politics* (New York: Columbia University Press, 1996); Emanuel Adler and Michael Barnett, eds., *Security Communities* (New York: Cambridge University Press, 1998); Alexander Wendt, *Social Theory of International Politics* (New York: Cambridge University Press, 1999); Ted Hopf, *Social Construction of International Politics: Identities and Foreign Policies, Moscow, 1955 and 1999* (Ithaca, NY: Cornell University Press, 2002); Nina Tannenwald, *The Nuclear Taboo: The United States and the Non-Use of Nuclear Weapons since 1945* (New York: Cambridge University Press, 2007).

57. Bernard Lewis, "The Roots of Muslim Rage," *Atlantic Monthly,* 1 September 1990; Samuel P. Huntington, *The Clash of Civilizations and the Remaking of World Order* (New York: Simon & Schuster, 1996).

58. Stephen M. Walt, "Building Up New Bogeymen: The Clash of Civilizations and the Remaking of World Order," *Foreign Policy* 106 (1997): 176–189.

59. Robert Vitalis, *White World Order, Black Power Politics: The Birth of American International Relations* (Ithaca, NY: Cornell University Press, 2015), 46–54, 88–92; quote on p. 50; Carol M. Taylor, "W. E. B. DuBois's Challenge to Scientific Racism," *Journal of Black Studies* 11, no. 4 (1981): 454.

60. Norrin M. Ripsman, Jeffrey W. Taliaferro, and Steven E. Lobell, *Neoclassical Realist Theory of International Politics* (New York: Oxford University Press, 2016), 69–71, 179.

61. Narizny, "On Systemic Paradigms and Domestic Politics," 184.

62. Edward D. Mansfield and Jack Snyder: "Democratic Transitions, Institutional Strength, and War," *International Organization* 56, no. 2 (2002): 297–337,

and *Electing to Fight: Why Emerging Democracies Go to War* (Cambridge, MA: MIT Press, 2005).

63. Vipin Narang and Rebecca M. Nelson, "Who Are These Belligerent Democratizers? Reassessing the Impact of Democratization on War," *International Organization* 63, no. 2 (2009): 363, 365. See also Goertz, *Multimethod Research, Causal Mechanisms, and Case Studies,* 196–199. For a response that fails to address these criticisms, see Edward D. Mansfield and Jack Snyder, "Pathways to War in Democratic Transitions," *International Organization* 63, no. 2 (2009): 381–390.

64. James D. Fearon, "Domestic Political Audiences and the Escalation of International Disputes," *American Political Science Review* 88, no. 3 (1994): 577–592; Kenneth A. Schultz, *Democracy and Coercive Diplomacy* (New York: Cambridge University Press, 2001); Alastair Smith, "International Crises and Domestic Politics," *American Political Science Review* 92, no. 3 (1998): 623–638.

65. Marc Trachtenberg, "Audience Costs: An Historical Analysis," *Security Studies* 21, no. 1 (2012): 3–42; quote on p. 32. See also Goertz, *Multimethod Research, Causal Mechanisms, and Case Studies,* 199–203.

66. Jack Snyder and Erica D. Borghard, "The Cost of Empty Threats: A Penny, Not a Pound," *American Political Science Review* 105, no. 3 (2011): 455. See also Alexander B. Downes and Todd S. Sechser, "The Illusion of Democratic Credibility," *International Organization* 66, no. 3 (2012): 457–489.

67. Charles Krauthammer, "Democratic Realism: An American Foreign Policy for a Unipolar World," Irving Kristol Lecture, American Enterprise Institute, Washington, DC, 10 February 2004; Joshua Muravchik, *Exporting Democracy: Fulfilling America's Destiny* (Washington, DC: American Enterprise Institute, 1992), ch. 8; Nancy Bermeo, "Armed Conflict and the Durability of Electoral Democracy," in *In War's Wake: International Conflict and the Fate of Liberal Democracy,* ed. Ronald Krebs and Elizabeth Kier (New York: Cambridge University Press, 2010).

68. George W. Downs and Bruce Bueno de Mesquita, "Gun-Barrel Diplomacy Has Failed Time and Again," *Los Angeles Times,* 4 February 2004. For the original study, see Bruce Bueno de Mesquita and George W. Downs, "Intervention and Democracy," *International Organization* 60, no. 3 (2006): 627–649. See also Alexander B. Downes, *Catastrophic Success: Why Foreign-Imposed Regime Change Goes Wrong* (Ithaca, NY: Cornell University Press, 2021); William Easterly, Shanker Satyanath, and Daniel Berger, "Superpower Interventions and Their Consequences for Democracy: An Empirical Inquiry" (Cambridge, MA: National Bureau of Economic Research, Working Paper no. 13992, May 2008); Nils Petter Gleditsch, Lene Siljeholm Christiansen, and Havard Hegre, "Democratic Jihad? Military Intervention and Democracy" (Washington, DC: World Bank Research Policy Paper no. 4242, June 2007); Arthur A. Goldsmith, "Making the World Safe for Partial Democracy? Questioning the Premises of Democracy Promotion," *International Security* 33, no. 2 (2008): 120–147; Jeffrey Pickering and

Mark Peceny, "Forging Democracy at Gunpoint," *International Studies Quarterly* 50, no. 3 (2006): 556.

69. Matthew Kroenig: "Nuclear Superiority and the Balance of Resolve: Explaining Nuclear Crisis Outcomes," *International Organization* 67, no. 1 (2013): 141–171, and *The Logic of American Nuclear Strategy;* Kyle Beardsley and Victor Asal, "Winning with the Bomb," *Journal of Conflict Resolution* 53, no. 2 (2009): 278–301.

70. Todd S. Sechser and Matthew Fuhrmann, *Nuclear Weapons and Coercive Diplomacy* (New York: Cambridge University Press, 2017), 7–9, 132–231. See also Gary Goertz and Stephan Haggard, "Generalization, Case Studies, and Within-Case Causal Inference: Large-N Qualitative Analysis (LNQA)," University of Notre Dame and University of California, San Diego, unpublished manuscript, 2020.

71. Walt, *The Origins of Alliances,* 19–21.

72. Jerome Slater: "The Domino Theory and International Politics: The Case of Vietnam," *Security Studies* 3, no. 2 (1993): 186–224, and "Dominos in Central America: Will They Fall? Does It Matter?" *International Security* 12, no. 2 (1987): 105–134; Walt, *The Origins of Alliances,* ch. 5.

73. Steven Weinberg, *To Explain the World: The Discovery of Modern Science* (New York: Harper Perennial, 2015), xiii.

74. Carroll E. Izard, "The Many Meanings/Aspects of Emotion: Definitions, Functions, Activation, and Regulation," *Emotion Review* 2, no. 4 (2010): 363–370; Andrea Scarantino and Ronald de Sousa, "Emotion," *The Stanford Encyclopedia of Philosophy* (Winter 2018 edition), ed. Edward N. Zalta; https://plato.stanford.edu/archives/win2018/entries/emotion/.

75. Robin Markwica, *Emotional Choices: How The Logic of Affect Shapes Coercive Diplomacy* (New York: Oxford University Press, 2020): 4–5, 17.

76. Antonio R. Damasio, *Descartes' Error: Emotion, Reason and the Human Brain* (New York: Putnam's, 1994). For a philosophical treatment that makes a similar argument, see Ronald de Sousa, *The Rationality of Emotion* (Cambridge, MA: MIT Press, 1987).

77. Scarantino and de Sousa, "Emotion."

78. Janice Gross Stein, "Threat Perception in International Relations," in *The Oxford Handbook of Political Psychology,* 2nd ed., ed. Leonie Huddy, David O. Sears, and Jack S. Levy, (New York: Oxford University Press, 2013), 388.

79. Dominic D. P. Johnson, *Strategic Instincts: The Adaptive Advantages of Cognitive Biases in International Politics* (Princeton, NJ: Princeton University Press, 2020), 18; emphasis in original.

80. Markwica, *Emotional Choices,* 20–21.

81. Richard Ned Lebow and Janice Gross Stein, "Beyond Deterrence," *Journal of Social Issues* 43, no. 4 (1987): 17–18; quote on p. 17.

82. Philip E. Tetlock, "Social Psychology and World Politics," in *Handbook of Social Psychology*, ed. Daniel T. Gilbert, Susan T. Fiske, and Gardner Lindzey (New York: McGraw-Hill, 1998), 883–884.

83. Rathbun, *Reasoning of State*, 30–32; quote on p. 32.

84. Jonathan Mercer, "Human Nature and the First Image: Emotion in International Politics," *Journal of International Relations and Development* 9, no. 3 (2006): 299.

85. Ripsman, Taliaferro, and Lobell, *Neoclassical Realist Theory of International Politics*, 23. The other oft-cited case concerns German decision-making during the July Crisis. As discussed below, this is not an instance of policymakers being driven by emotions. That said, we identify a clear example of emotion-driven thinking in chapter 7: Neville Chamberlain's policy for dealing with Nazi Germany from May 1937 to October 1938.

86. Marc Trachtenberg, "The Meaning of Mobilization in 1914," *International Security* 15, no. 3 (1990/91): 120–150. See also Sean McMeekin, *July 1914: Countdown to War* (New York: Basic Books, 2013), 300–302.

87. Annika Mombauer, *Helmuth von Moltke and the Origins of the First World War* (New York: Cambridge University Press, 2005), ch. 5.

88. Neta C. Crawford, "The Passion of World Politics: Propositions on Emotion and Emotional Relationships," *International Security* 24, no. 4 (2000): 138; Ian Kershaw, *Fateful Choices: Ten Decisions That Changed the World, 1940–1941* (New York: Penguin, 2007), 288; Oleg V. Khlevniuk, *Stalin: New Biography of a Dictator* (New Haven: Yale University Press, 2015), 198–208.

89. Tom Segev, *1967: Israel, the War, and the Year That Transformed the Middle East* (New York: Metropolitan, 2007), 236–238, 243–245, 255.

90. Bernard Gwertzman, "Pentagon Kept Tight Rein in Last Days of Nixon Rule," *New York Times,* 25 August 1974.

91. Bob Woodward and Robert Costa, *Peril* (New York: Simon & Schuster, 2021), 128–130.

92. For recent claims that rationality can be understood in terms of outcomes, see Gerd Gigerenzer, "Axiomatic Rationality and Ecological Rationality," *Synthese* 198 (2021): 3547–3564; Anastasia Kozyreva and Ralph Hertwig, "The Interpretation of Uncertainty in Ecological Rationality," *Synthese* 198 (2021): 1517–1547; Gerhard Schurz and Ralph Hertwig, "Cognitive Success: A Consequentialist Account of Rationality in Cognition," *Topics in Cognitive Science* 11, no. 1 (2019): 7–36. The equation of nonrationality with failure is implicit in many theories of great power politics. For a summary of these views, see Mearsheimer, *The Tragedy of Great Power Politics*, 209–213.

93. Angell, *The Great Illusion*.

94. Niccolò Machiavelli, *The Prince*, trans. Harvey C. Mansfield, 2nd ed. (Chicago: University of Chicago Press, 1998), 98–101; Thucydides, *The Landmark Thucydides*, 44; Clausewitz, *On War*, 85.

———

CHAPTER 4. CONTENDING DEFINITIONS

1. The political psychology literature is said to be composed of two waves: the "first wave" focused on analogies, images, schemas, and scripts; the "second wave" focuses on heuristics. On the two waves, see Robert Powell, "Research Bets and Behavioral IR," *International Organization* 71, no. S1 (2017): 273–274; Janice Gross Stein, "The Micro-Foundations of International Relations Theory: Psychology and Behavioral Economics," *International Organization* 71, no. S1 (2017): 249–250.

2. To be clear, we are not arguing that rational choice theorists and political psychologists have not developed credible theories of international politics. Rather, the focus here is on evaluating their definitions of rationality and nonrationality.

3. Bruce Bueno de Mesquita, *The War Trap* (New Haven: Yale University Press, 1983), 29, 31.

4. Donald P. Green and Ian Shapiro, *Pathologies of Rational Choice Theory: A Critique of Applications in Political Science* (New Haven: Yale University Press, 1994), 14; emphasis in original.

5. Arthur A. Stein, "The Limits of Strategic Choice: Constrained Rationality and Incomplete Explanation," in *Strategic Choice and International Relations*, ed. David A. Lake and Robert Powell (Princeton, NJ: Princeton University Press, 1999), 211, n. 41.

6. Emilie M. Hafner-Burton, Stephan Haggard, David A. Lake, and David G. Victor, "The Behavioral Revolution and International Relations," *International Organization* 71, no. S1 (2017): 6.

7. John von Neumann and Oskar Morgenstern, *Theory of Games and Economic Behavior* (Princeton, NJ: Princeton University Press, 1944), ch. 1. The fundamentals of expected utility theory were first articulated in a systematic fashion by Daniel Bernoulli in the eighteenth century. See Peter L. Bernstein, *Against the Gods: The Remarkable Story of Risk* (New York: John Wiley & Sons, 1996), 99–115, 187–189; John Kay and Mervyn King, *Radical Uncertainty: Decision-Making beyond the Numbers* (New York: W. W. Norton, 2020), 114–116.

8. Jon Elster, "Introduction," in *Rational Choice*, ed. Jon Elster (New York: New York University Press, 1986), 1.

9. Charles L. Glaser, *Rational Theory of International Politics: The Logic of Competition and Cooperation* (Princeton, NJ: Princeton University Press, 2010), 23, 27, 30.

10. John C. Harsanyi, "Advances in Understanding Rational Behavior," in *Rational Choice*, ed. Jon Elster (New York: New York University Press, 1986), 83; emphasis in original.

11. Arthur Stein, "The Limits of Strategic Choice," 210. For the view that expected utility theory was initially intended to be a descriptive theory but came to be treated as a normative theory after it failed to stand up to empirical testing, see

Magdalena Malecka, "The Normative Decision Theory in Economics: A Philosophy of Science Perspective. The Case of Expected Utility Theory," *Journal of Economic Methodology* 27, no. 1 (2020): 37–38.

12. David A. Lake and Robert Powell, "International Relations: A Strategic-Choice Approach," in *Strategic Choice and International Relations,* ed. David A. Lake and Robert Powell (Princeton, NJ: Princeton University Press, 1999), 6.

13. Green and Shapiro, *Pathologies of Rational Choice Theory,* 15; emphasis in original.

14. Bueno de Mesquita, *The War Trap,* 20, 173.

15. Powell, "Research Bets and Behavioral IR," 269.

16. Von Neumann and Morgenstern, *Theory of Games and Economic Behavior,* 31.

17. James D. Morrow, *Game Theory for Political Scientists* (Princeton, NJ: Princeton University Press, 1994), 22–25; Bruce Bueno de Mesquita, "The Contribution of Expected Utility Theory to the Study of International Conflict," in *The Origin and Prevention of Major Wars,* ed. Robert I. Rotberg and Theodore K. Rabb (New York: Cambridge University Press, 1988), 629–630; Michael Allingham, *Choice Theory: A Very Short Introduction* (New York: Oxford University Press, 2002), 1–49.

18. Hafner-Burton et al., "The Behavioral Revolution and International Relations," 6.

19. This discussion parallels Morrow's illustration of Nixon's decision to bomb North Vietnam in December 1972, in Morrow, *Game Theory for Political Scientists,* 25–28.

20. Bueno de Mesquita, *The War Trap,* 29, 32; emphasis in original. See also Bueno de Mesquita, "The Contribution of Expected Utility Theory to the Study of International Conflict," 55–56.

21. Christopher H. Achen and Duncan Snidal, "Rational Deterrence Theory and Comparative Case Studies," *World Politics* 41, no. 2 (1989): 164; emphasis added.

22. Milton Friedman, "The Methodology of Positive Economics," in Milton Friedman, *Essays in Positive Economics* (Chicago: University of Chicago Press, 1953), 21; emphasis in original.

23. Herbert A. Simon, "Rationality as Process and as Product of Thought," *American Economic Review* 68, no. 2 (1978): 2.

24. Morrow, *Game Theory for Political Scientists,* 20.

25. Achen and Snidal, "Rational Deterrence Theory and Comparative Case Studies," 164.

26. Milton Friedman, "The Methodology of Positive Economics," 22.

27. Brian C. Rathbun, Joshua D. Kertzer, and Mark Paradis, "*Homo Diplomaticus:* Mixed-Method Evidence of Variation in Strategic Rationality," *International Organization* 71, no. S1 (2017): 36.

28. Bueno de Mesquita, *The War Trap,* 31.

29. Bruce Bueno de Mesquita, *Principles of International Politics,* 5th ed. (Thousand Oaks, CA: Sage/Congressional Quarterly Press, 2014), 28.

30. Glaser, *Rational Theory of International Politics,* 30.

31. Jon Elster, *Alchemies of the Mind* (New York: Cambridge University Press, 1999), 285.

32. Brian C. Rathbun, *Reasoning of State: Realists, Romantics and Rationality in International Relations* (New York: Cambridge University Press, 2019), 15.

33. Arthur Stein, "The Limits of Strategic Choice," 207.

34. Elster, "Introduction," 22.

35. Morrow, *Game Theory for Political Scientists,* 28.

36. Frank H. Knight, *Risk, Uncertainty and Profit* (Boston: Houghton Mifflin, 1921), 233, 235.

37. John Maynard Keynes, "The General Theory of Employment," *Quarterly Journal of Economics* 51, no. 2 (1937): 213–214.

38. Jonathan Kirshner, "The Economic Sins of Modern IR Theory and the Classical Realist Alternative," *World Politics* 67, no. 1 (2015): 174–175. See also Jonathan Kirshner, "Rationalist Explanations for War?" *Security Studies* 10, no. 3 (2000): 143–150.

39. See, for example, Robert Jervis, "Was the Cold War a Security Dilemma?" *Journal of Cold War Studies* 3, no. 1 (2001): 36–60.

40. For two examples of the early seminal work on subjective probability, see Frank P. Ramsey, "Truth and Probability," in *Philosophical Papers,* ed. David H. Mellor (New York: Cambridge University Press, 1990), 52–109, and Leonard J. Savage, *The Foundations of Statistics* (New York: Wiley, 1954).

41. Morrow, *Game Theory for Political Scientists,* 28.

42. Jeffrey A. Friedman, *War and Chance: Assessing Uncertainty in International Politics* (New York: Oxford University Press, 2019), 56. Similarly, Morrow writes, "Under uncertainty, actors form subjective probability estimates that reflect their degree of belief about the underlying state of the world." See Morrow, *Game Theory for Political Scientists,* 29.

43. Elster, "Introduction," 6.

44. J. Peter Scoblic and Philip E. Tetlock, "A Better Crystal Ball: The Right Way to Think about the Future," *Foreign Affairs* 99, no. 6 (2020): 15. See also Michael C. Horowitz, "Forecasting Political Events," in *The Oxford Handbook of Behavioral Political Science* (Oxford Academic 2018 online edition), ed. Alex Mintz and Lesley G. Terris; https://doi.org/10.1093/oxfordhb/9780190634131.001.0001.

45. Rathbun, *Reasoning of State,* 22–23. Rathbun is quoting John T. Cacioppo and his colleagues.

46. David M. Edelstein, *Over the Horizon: Time, Uncertainty, and the Rise of Great Powers* (Ithaca, NY: Cornell University Press, 2017), 18, 20.

47. On this point, see Jeffrey Friedman, *War and Chance,* 58–63.

48. Rathbun, *Reasoning of State,* 20. See also Philip E. Tetlock, *Expert Political Judgment: How Good Is It? How Can We Know?* new ed. (Princeton, NJ: Princeton University Press, 2017).

49. Morrow, *Game Theory for Political Scientists,* 29.

50. Bueno de Mesquita, *The War Trap,* 31.

51. Robert Jervis, "Rational Deterrence: Theory and Evidence," *World Politics* 41, no. 2 (1989): 186.

52. Janice Gross Stein, "Threat Perception in International Relations," in *The Oxford Handbook of Political Psychology,* 2nd ed., ed. Leonie Huddy, David O. Sears, and Jack S. Levy (New York: Oxford University Press, 2013), 369, 371.

53. Dominic D. P. Johnson, *Strategic Instincts: The Adaptive Advantages of Cognitive Biases in International Politics* (Princeton, NJ: Princeton University Press, 2020), 13, 18.

54. Rathbun, *Reasoning of State,* 13.

55. Keren Yarhi-Milo, *Knowing the Adversary: Leaders, Intelligence, and Assessment of Intentions in International Relations* (Princeton, NJ: Princeton University Press, 2014), 9.

56. Richard Ned Lebow, "International Relations Theory and the Ukrainian War," *Analyse and Kritik* 44, no. 1 (2022): 132.

57. Richard H. Thaler, *Misbehaving: The Making of Behavioral Economics* (New York: W. W. Norton, 2015), 4, 6.

58. Daniel Kahneman, *Thinking, Fast and Slow* (New York: Farrar, Straus and Giroux, 2011), 8, 10, 411.

59. Gideon Keren and Karl H. Teigen, "Yet Another Look at the Heuristics and Biases Approach," in *Blackwell Handbook of Judgment and Decision Making,* ed. Derek J. Koehler and Nigel Harvey (Malden, MA: Blackwell, 2004), 89–109.

60. Thaler, *Misbehaving,* 22–23.

61. Yuen Foong Khong, *Analogies at War: Korea, Munich, Dien Bien Phu, and the Vietnam Decisions of 1965* (Princeton, NJ: Princeton University Press, 1992), 3, 20.

62. Robert Jervis, *Perception and Misperception in International Politics* (Princeton, NJ: Princeton University Press, 1976), 281. See also Robert Jervis, "Hypotheses on Misperception," *World Politics* 20, no. 3 (1968): 454–479; Richard Ned Lebow, *Between Peace and War: The Nature of International Crisis* (Baltimore: Johns Hopkins University Press, 1981); Janice Gross Stein, "Building Politics into Psychology: The Misperception of Threat," *Political Psychology* 9, no. 2 (1988): 245–271.

63. Deborah Welch Larson, *Origins of Containment: A Psychological Explanation* (Princeton, NJ: Princeton University Press, 1985), 52.

64. Johnson, *Strategic Instincts,* 1–47; Kahneman, *Thinking, Fast and Slow,* 3–13; Janice Stein, "Threat Perception in International Relations," 370–376;

Herbert A. Simon, "Rational Choice and the Structure of the Environment," *Psychological Review* 63, no. 2 (1956): 129–138; Amos Tversky and Daniel Kahneman, "Judgment under Uncertainty: Heuristics and Biases," *Science* 185, no. 4157 (1974): 1124–1131.

65. Kenneth J. Arrow, "Rationality of Self and Others in an Economic System," *Journal of Business* 59, no. 4, pt. 2 (1986): S397.

66. Herbert A. Simon, "Invariants of Human Behavior," *Annual Review of Psychology* 41 (1990): 7.

67. Herbert A. Simon, "A Behavioral Model of Rational Choice," *Quarterly Journal of Economics* 69, no. 1 (1955): 99, 101.

68. Robert O. Keohane, *After Hegemony: Cooperation and Discord in the World Political Economy* (Princeton, NJ: Princeton University Press, 1984), 111.

69. Janice Stein, "Threat Perception in International Relations," 371.

70. Johnson, *Strategic Instincts*, 3, 15.

71. Rathbun, *Reasoning of State*, 4.

72. Jervis, *Perception and Misperception in International Politics*, 228–229; emphasis in original.

73. Tversky and Kahneman, "Judgment under Uncertainty," 1130–1131.

74. Janice Stein, "Threat Perception in International Relations," 371.

75. Philip E. Tetlock, "Social Psychology and World Politics," in *Handbook of Social Psychology,* ed. Daniel T. Gilbert, Susan T. Fiske, and Gardner Lindzey (New York: McGraw-Hill, 1998), 877.

76. Robert Jervis, *How Statesmen Think: The Psychology of International Politics* (Princeton, NJ: Princeton University Press, 2017), 6.

77. Johnson, *Strategic Instincts*, 3–4.

78. Jonathan Mercer, "Rationality and Psychology in International Politics," *International Organization* 59, no. 1 (2005): 77, 78.

79. There has been a similar trend in the economics literature. See Kahneman, *Thinking, Fast and Slow*, 4–13. For the explicit claim that heuristics lead to success, see Gerd Gigerenzer, "The Bias Bias in Behavioral Economics," *Review of Behavioral Economics* 5, nos. 3–4 (2018): 303–336. Indeed, Gigerenzer maintains that employing heuristics is rational. Political psychologists do not go this far.

80. Johnson, *Strategic Instincts*, 4, 6.

81. Rathbun, *Reasoning of State*, 3.

82. Aristotle, *The Nicomachean Ethics,* trans. David Ross (New York: Oxford University Press, 2009), 11.

83. Janice Stein, "The Micro-Foundations of International Relations Theory," 255.

84. Elizabeth N. Saunders, "No Substitute for Experience: Presidents, Advisers, and Information in Group Decision Making," *International Organization* 71, no. S1 (2017): 219–220.

85. Powell, "Research Bets and Behavioral IR," 274.

86. For a similar argument, see Daryl G. Press, "The Credibility of Power: Assessing Threats during the 'Appeasement' Crises of the 1930s," *International Security* 29, no. 3 (2004/05): 138–139.

87. Mercer, "Rationality and Psychology in International Politics," 88.

88. Kenneth Schultz, Review of Keren Yarhi-Milo, *Who Fights for Reputation: The Psychology of Leaders in International Conflict,* H-Diplo ISSF Roundtable 11, no. 10 (2019): 13.

89. Janice Stein, "The Micro-Foundations of International Relations Theory," 257–258.

90. Jervis, *How Statesmen Think,* 6.

91. Khong, *Analogies at War;* Larson, *Origins of Containment;* Rose McDermott, *Risk-Taking in International Politics: Prospect Theory in American Foreign Policy* (Ann Arbor: University of Michigan Press, 1998), ch. 6. There is also a substantial body of case study, survey, and experiment-based literature where scholars pay careful attention to how statesmen think, including how they form their beliefs and how those beliefs affect their behavior. But those works do not focus on the rational actor assumption.

CHAPTER 5. RATIONALITY AND GRAND STRATEGY

1. On the use of "least likely" cases to test theories, see Harry Eckstein, "Case Study and Theory in Political Science," in *Handbook of Political Science,* vol. 7: *Strategies of Inquiry,* ed. Fred I. Greenstein and Nelson W. Polsby (Reading, MA: Addison-Wesley, 1975), 113–120; Alexander L. George and Andrew Bennett, *Case Studies and Theory Development in the Social Sciences* (Cambridge, MA: MIT Press, 2005), 120–123; John Gerring, *Case Study Research: Principles and Practices* (New York: Cambridge University Press, 2007), 115–121; Aaron Rapport, "Hard Thinking about Hard and Easy Cases in Security Studies," *Security Studies* 24, no. 3 (2015): 433–457.

2. Jack Snyder, *Myths of Empire: Domestic Politics and International Ambition* (Ithaca, NY: Cornell University Press, 1993), 66, 74, 75.

3. Michelle English, "Stephen Van Evera Revisits World War I, One Century after Its Bitter End," MIT Center for International Studies, 1 November 2018; https://cis.mit.edu/publications/analysis-opinion/2018/stephen-van-evera-revisits-world-war-i-one-century-after-its; Stephen Van Evera, "Why States Believe Foolish Ideas: Non-Self-Evaluation by States and Societies," Massachusetts Institute of Technology, unpublished ms., January 2002, 23–24.

4. Ludwig Dehio, *Germany and World Politics in the Twentieth Century,* trans. Dieter Pevsner (New York: W. W. Norton, 1967), 13.

5. This case is based on Volker R. Berghahn, *Germany and the Approach of War in 1914*, 2nd ed. (New York: St. Martin's, 1993); Christopher Clark, *The Sleepwalkers: How Europe Went to War in 1914* (New York: Penguin, 2013), chs. 4–6; Dale C. Copeland, *The Origins of Major War* (Ithaca, NY: Cornell University Press, 2000), ch. 3; Gordon A. Craig, *Germany, 1866–1945* (New York: Oxford University Press, 1978), chs. 8–9; Jack R. Dukes, "Militarism and Arms Policy Revisited: The Origins of the German Army Law of 1913," in *Another Germany: A Reconsideration of the Imperial Era*, ed. Jack R. Dukes and Joachim Remak (Boulder, CO: Westview, 1988), 19–39; Klaus Epstein, "German War Aims in the First World War," *World Politics* 15, no. 1 (1962): 163–185; Fritz Fischer, *War of Illusions: German Policies from 1911 to 1914*, trans. Marian Jackson (New York: W. W. Norton, 1975); David G. Herrmann, *The Arming of Europe and the Making of the First World War* (Princeton, NJ: Princeton University Press, 1996), chs. 4–7; James Joll, *The Origins of the First World War* (New York: Longman, 1992); David E. Kaiser, "Germany and the Origins of the First World War," *Journal of Modern History* 55, no. 3 (1983): 442–474; Jack S. Levy and William Mulligan, "Why 1914 but Not Before? A Comparative Study of the July Crisis and Its Precursors," *Security Studies* 30, no. 2 (2021): 213–244; David Stevenson: "Militarization and Diplomacy in Europe before 1914," *International Security* 22, no. 1 (1997): 125–161, and *Armaments and the Coming of War: Europe, 1904–1914* (Oxford: Clarendon, 1996), chs. 3–6.

6. Quoted in Herrmann, *The Arming of Europe and the Making of the First World War*, 168.

7. Quoted in Stevenson, *Armaments and the Coming of War*, 210.

8. Quoted in Stevenson, *Armaments and the Coming of War*, 203.

9. Quoted in Herrmann, *The Arming of Europe and the Making of the First World War*, 166, 169–170.

10. Herrmann, *The Arming of Europe and the Making of the First World War*, 162–170; Stevenson, *Armaments and the Coming of War*, 163, 201–204.

11. Quoted in Herrmann, *The Arming of Europe and the Making of the First World War*, 181.

12. Quoted in Stevenson, *Armaments and the Coming of War*, 286.

13. Quoted in Herrmann, *The Arming of Europe and the Making of the First World War*, 182, 183, 191–192; Copeland, *The Origins of Major War*, 68.

14. Quoted in Stevenson, *Armaments and the Coming of War*, 296.

15. Quoted in Herrmann, *The Arming of Europe and the Making of the First World War*, 179–180.

16. Quoted in Clark, *The Sleepwalkers*, 332, 333.

17. Copeland, *The Origins of Major War*, 67–69; Herrmann, *The Arming of Europe and the Making of the First World War*, 179–182; Stevenson, *Armaments and the Coming of War*, 285–293.

18. Snyder, *Myths of Empire*, 113, 114, 120.

19. Charles A. Kupchan, *The Vulnerability of Empire* (Ithaca, NY: Cornell University Press, 1994), 325, 357.

20. Robert J. C. Butow, *Tojo and the Coming of War* (Princeton, NJ: Princeton University Press, 1961), 315.

21. Saburō Ienaga, *The Pacific War, 1931-1945: A Critical Perspective on Japan's Role in World War II* (New York: Pantheon, 1978), 33.

22. Van Evera, "Why States Believe Foolish Ideas," 32, 34.

23. This case is based on Sadao Asada, *From Mahan to Pearl Harbor: The Imperial Japanese Navy and the United States* (Annapolis, MD: Naval Institute, 2006), chs. 5-10; Michael A. Barnhart, *Japan Prepares for Total War: The Search for Economic Security, 1919-1941* (Ithaca, NY: Cornell University Press, 1987); Butow, *Tojo and the Coming of War,* chs. 1-8; Dale C. Copeland, *Economic Interdependence and War* (Princeton, NJ: Princeton University Press, 2015), chs. 4-5; James B. Crowley, *Japan's Quest for Autonomy: National Security and Foreign Policy, 1930-1938* (Princeton, NJ: Princeton University Press, 1966); Ienaga, *The Pacific War, 1931-1945,* chs. 1-8; Akira Iriye, *The Origins of the Second World War in Asia and the Pacific,* 4th ed. (London: Longman, 1989); Kupchan, *The Vulnerability of Empire,* ch. 5; Rana Mitter, *Forgotten Ally: China's World War II, 1937-1945* (Boston: Mariner, 2013); James W. Morley, ed., *The China Quagmire: Japan's Expansion on the Asian Continent, 1933-1941* (New York: Columbia University Press, 1983); Ian Nish, *Japanese Foreign Policy in the Interwar Period* (Westport, CT: Praeger, 2002), chs. 2-8; Sadako N. Ogata, *Defiance in Manchuria: The Making of Japanese Policy, 1931-1932* (Berkeley: University of California Press, 1964); Mark A. Peattie, *Ishiwara Kanji and Japan's Confrontation with the West* (Princeton, NJ: Princeton University Press, 1975), chs. 3-4; Jeffrey W. Taliaferro, *Balancing Risks: Great Power Intervention in the Periphery* (Ithaca, NY: Cornell University Press, 2004), ch. 4; Louise Young, *Japan's Total Empire: Manchuria and the Culture of Wartime Imperialism* (Berkeley: University of California Press, 1998), chs. 1-2.

24. Quoted in Herbert P. Bix, *Hirohito and the Making of Modern Japan* (New York: HarperCollins, 2000), 227.

25. Quoted in W. G. Beasley, *Japanese Imperialism, 1894-1905* (Oxford: Clarendon, 1987), 189.

26. Quoted in Yamamuro Shin'ichi, *Manchuria under Japanese Domination,* trans. Joshua A. Fogel (Philadelphia: University of Pennsylvania Press, 2006), 17, 20.

27. Kikijuro Ishii, "The Permanent Bases of Japanese Foreign Policy," *Foreign Affairs* 11, no. 2 (1933): 228-229.

28. Rustin Gates, "Solving the 'Manchurian Problem': Uchida Yasuya and Japanese Foreign Affairs before the Second World War," *Diplomacy & Statecraft* 23, no. 1 (2012): 25-26.

---

29. Joyce C. Lebra, ed., *Japan's Greater East Asia Co-Prosperity Sphere in World War II: Selected Readings and Documents* (New York: Oxford University Press, 1975), 58–64.

30. Butow, *Tojo and the Coming of War,* 80–86; Crowley, *Japan's Quest for Autonomy,* 279–300; Copeland, *Economic Interdependence and War,* 164–167.

31. Snyder, *Myths of Empire,* 116.

32. Quoted in Nish, *Japanese Foreign Policy in the Interwar Period,* 126.

33. Copeland notes that not only were the Japanese restrained, but they were also deliberative: "Through a series of meetings and conferences that began in 1937, and that dominated the decision-making process after June 1940, Japanese officials of all stripes actively discussed the pros and cons of various options, including peaceful diplomatic solutions. The shift toward harder-line policies was done gradually and by consensus, and in full awareness of great risks to the Japanese state." Copeland, *Economic Interdependence and War,* 146.

34. Robert J. Young, *In Command of France: French Foreign Policy and Military Planning, 1933–1940* (Cambridge, MA: Harvard University Press, 1978), 3, 6.

35. Randall L. Schweller, *Unanswered Threats: Political Constraints on the Balance of Power* (Princeton, NJ: Princeton University Press, 2006), 1, 77–78.

36. Ernest R. May, *Strange Victory: Hitler's Conquest of France* (New York: Hill and Wang, 2000), 454, 458–459, 464.

37. This case is based on Anthony Adamthwaite: *France and the Coming of the Second World War, 1936–1939* (London: Frank Cass, 1977), and "Bonnet, Daladier and French Appeasement, April–September 1938," *International Relations* 3, no. 3 (1968): 226–241; Martin S. Alexander, *The Republic in Danger: General Maurice Gamelin and the Politics of French Defence, 1933–1940* (New York: Cambridge University Press, 1992), chs. 9–10; Patrice Buffotot, "The French High Command and the Franco-Soviet Alliance, 1933–1939," trans. John Gooch, *Journal of Strategic Studies* 5, no. 4 (1982): 546–559; Susan B. Butterworth, "Daladier and the Munich Crisis: A Reappraisal," *Journal of Contemporary History* 9, no. 3 (1974): 191–216; Michael Jabara Carley: *1939: The Alliance That Never Was and the Coming of World War II* (Chicago: Ivan R. Dee, 1999), and "Prelude to Defeat: Franco-Soviet Relations, 1919–1939," *Historical Reflections* 22, no. 1 (1996): 159–188; Mark L. Haas: *The Ideological Origins of Great Power Politics, 1789–1989* (Ithaca, NY: Cornell University Press, 2005), ch. 4, and *Frenemies: When Ideological Enemies Ally* (Ithaca, NY: Cornell University Press, 2022), ch. 2; Peter Jackson, *France and the Nazi Menace: Intelligence and Policy Making, 1933–1939* (New York: Oxford University Press, 2000), chs. 7–10; Elizabeth Kier, *French and British Military Doctrine between the Wars* (Princeton, NJ: Princeton University Press, 1997), chs. 3–4; Norrin M. Ripsman and Jack S. Levy, "The Preventive War That Never Happened: Britain, France, and the Rise of Germany in the 1930s," *Security Studies* 16, no. 1 (2007): 32–67; Arnold Wolfers, *Britain and France between Two Wars:*

Conflicting Strategies of Peace since Versailles (New York: Harcourt, Brace, 1940), chs. 1–10; Robert Young: *In Command of France*, chs. 8–9; *France and the Origins of the Second World War* (New York: St. Martin's, 1996), ch. 1–3; and "A. J. P. Taylor and the Problem with France," in *The Origins of the Second World War Reconsidered: The A. J. P. Taylor Debate after Twenty-Five Years,* ed. Gordon Martel (Boston: Allen & Unwin, 1986), 97–118.

38. Quoted in Jackson, *France and the Nazi Menace,* 249, 317, 322.

39. Quoted in Adamthwaite, *France and the Coming of the Second World War,* 294.

40. Quoted in Carley, *1939,* 94.

41. Quoted in Jackson, *France and the Nazi Menace,* 316.

42. Quoted in Butterworth, "Daladier and the Munich Crisis," 199.

43. Quoted in Jackson, *France and the Nazi Menace,* 328.

44. Quoted in Carley, *1939,* 85.

45. Quoted in Adamthwaite, *France and the Coming of the Second World War,* 273.

46. Quoted in Robert Young, *In Command of France,* 228.

47. Quoted in Haas, *The Ideological Origins of Great Power Politics,* 124.

48. Quoted in Adamthwaite, *France and the Coming of the Second World War,* 109.

49. Robert Young, *In Command of France,* 2.

50. Quoted in Adamthwaite, *France and the Coming of the Second World War,* 301.

51. Quoted in Carley, *1939,* 122. For the argument that ideological theories influenced French policy but were ultimately subordinated to realist reasoning, see Haas, *The Ideological Origins of Great Power Politics,* 120–135.

52. Quoted in Michael MccGwire, "NATO Expansion: 'A Policy Error of Historic Importance,'" *Review of International Studies* 24, no. 1 (1998): 23. Similarly, George Kennan, a key architect of containment, said, "Expanding NATO would be the most fateful error of American policy in the entire post-cold-war era." See George F. Kennan, "A Fateful Error," *New York Times,* 5 February 1997.

53. Michael Mandelbaum, "The New NATO: Bigger Isn't Better," *Wall Street Journal,* 9 July 1997.

54. MccGwire, "NATO Expansion," 25, 26, 40.

55. Kenneth N. Waltz, "NATO Expansion: A Realist's View," *Contemporary Security Policy* 21, no. 2 (2000): 31.

56. Quoted in Joshua R. Iskowitz Shifrinson, "Deal or No Deal? The End of the Cold War and the U.S. Offer to Limit NATO Expansion," *International Security* 40, no. 4 (2016): 36.

57. Timothy A. Sayle, *Enduring Alliance: A History of NATO and the Postwar Global Order* (Ithaca, NY: Cornell University Press, 2019), ch. 10; Joshua R.

Iskowitz Shifrinson, "Eastbound and Down: The United States, NATO Enlarge-ment, and Suppressing the Soviet and Western European Alternatives, 1990–1992," *Journal of Strategic Studies* 43, nos. 6–7 (2020): 816–846.

58. This case is based on Ronald D. Asmus, *Opening NATO's Door: How the Alliance Remade Itself for a New Era* (New York: Columbia University Press, 2002); James M. Goldgeier, *Not Whether but When: The U.S. Decision to Enlarge NATO* (Washington, DC: Brookings Institution, 1999). On the Russian dimension of the issue as seen from Washington, see James M. Goldgeier and Michael McFaul, *Power and Purpose: U.S. Policy toward Russia after the Cold War* (Washington, DC: Brookings Institution, 2003).

59. Quoted in Asmus, *Opening NATO's Door,* 34. Asmus notes that the National Security Council harbored similar fears at the time.

60. Quoted in Asmus, *Opening NATO's Door,* 62; Goldgeier, *Not Whether but When,* 50.

61. Quoted in Asmus, *Opening NATO's Door,* 45, 89, 97.

62. North Atlantic Treaty Organization, "The Partnership for Peace Pro-gramme"; available at https://www.sto.nato.int/Pages/partnership-for-peace.aspx.

63. Quoted in Walter B. Slocombe, "A Crisis of Opportunity: The Clinton Ad-ministration and Russia," in *In Uncertain Times: American Foreign Policy after the Berlin Wall and 9/11,* ed. Melvyn P. Leffler and Jeffrey W. Legro (Ithaca, NY: Cor-nell University Press, 2011), 87.

64. Asmus, *Opening NATO's Door,* 48–52; quote on p. 51. For details of the meeting, see also Goldgeier, *Not Whether but When,* 38–42; Mary E. Sarotte, "How to Enlarge NATO: The Debate Inside the Clinton Administration, 1993–95," *In-ternational Security* 44, no. 1 (2019): 18–21.

65. Goldgeier, *Not Whether but When,* 54–58; Clinton quotes on pp. 55, 57. See also Asmus, *Opening NATO's Door,* 64–68; Sarotte, "How to Enlarge NATO," 22–24.

66. Asmus, *Opening NATO's Door,* 72–79; Goldgeier, *Not Whether but When,* 62–71.

67. Goldgeier, *Not Whether but When,* 71–72.

68. Asmus, *Opening NATO's Door,* 77–78.

69. Quoted in Douglas Jehl, "Clinton Offers Poland Hope, but Little Aid," *New York Times,* 8 July 1994.

70. Goldgeier, *Not Whether but When,* 74–75; Holbrooke quote on p. 74; As-mus, *Opening NATO's Door,* 88, 97; Sarotte, "How to Enlarge NATO," 29–31, 35–36.

71. "Transcript: Donald Trump's Foreign Policy Speech," *New York Times,* 27 April 2016.

72. Stephen M. Walt, *The Hell of Good Intentions: America's Foreign Policy Elite and the Decline of U.S. Primacy* (New York: Farrar, Straus and Giroux, 2018), 13.

73. Andrew J. Bacevich, *The Age of Illusions: How America Squandered Its Cold War Victory* (New York: Picador, 2020), 5.

74. David C. Hendrickson, *Republic in Peril: American Empire and the Liberal Tradition* (New York: Oxford University Press, 2018), 4.

75. Patrick Porter, "A Dangerous Myth," Lowy Institute; available at https://interactives.lowyinstitute.org.

76. To be clear, although we believe that liberal theories of international politics are credible—that is, they are logically coherent explanations derived from reasonable assumptions and supported by significant empirical evidence—we also think they are flawed. See John J. Mearsheimer, *The Great Delusion: Liberal Dreams and International Realities* (New Haven: Yale University Press, 2018), ch. 7; Sebastian Rosato, "The Flawed Logic of Democratic Peace Theory," *American Political Science Review* 97, no. 4 (2003): 585–602.

77. Mary E. Sarotte, *1989: The Struggle to Create Post-War Europe* (Princeton, NJ: Princeton University Press, 2009).

78. Quoted in Hal Brands, *Making the Unipolar Moment: U.S. Foreign Policy and the Rise of the Post-Cold War Order* (Ithaca, NY: Cornell University Press, 2016), 327, 329.

79. Eric S. Edelman, "The Strange Career of the 1992 Defense Planning Guidance," in *In Uncertain Times: American Foreign Policy after the Berlin Wall and 9/11*, ed. Melvyn P. Leffler and Jeffrey W. Legro (Ithaca, NY: Cornell University Press, 2011), 63–77; quote on p. 66. See also Brands, *Making the Unipolar Moment*, 323–329.

80. Quoted in Derek Chollet and James Goldgeier, *America between the Wars, from 11/9 to 9/11: The Misunderstood Years between the Fall of the Berlin Wall and the Start of the War on Terror* (New York: PublicAffairs, 2008), 48–49. See also Robert B. Zoellick, "An Architecture of U.S. Strategy after the Cold War," in *In Uncertain Times: American Foreign Policy after the Berlin Wall and 9/11*, ed. Melvyn P. Leffler and Jeffrey W. Legro (Ithaca, NY: Cornell University Press, 2011), 26–29.

81. On these strategic options, see Nuno P. Monteiro, "Unrest Assured: Why Unipolarity Is Not Peaceful," *International Security* 36, no. 3 (2011/12): 9–40.

82. James D. Boys, *Clinton's Grand Strategy* (London: Bloomsbury, 2015), 85–96; Chollet and Goldgeier, *America between the Wars*, 68–70.

83. Remarks of Anthony Lake, "From Containment to Enlargement," Johns Hopkins University School of Advanced International Studies, Washington, DC, 21 September 1993.

84. Address by President Bill Clinton to the U.N. General Assembly, New York, 27 September 1993.

85. Madeleine Albright, "Use of Force in a Post-Cold War World," *U.S. Department of State Dispatch* 4, no. 39, 27 September 1993.

86. Chollet and Goldgeier, *America between the Wars*, ch. 6.

---

87. To illustrate the breadth and depth of this consensus, consider the case of Peter Tarnoff, the under secretary of state for political affairs. In a meeting with reporters in May 1993, several months before the Clinton administration rolled out its grand strategy, Tarnoff cast doubt on the notion that the United States had the wherewithal to implement liberal hegemony. The response from his colleagues in the administration was immediate and fierce, causing him to back off and fall into line. See Owen Harries and Tom Switzer, "Leading from Behind: Third Time a Charm?" *The American Interest,* 12 April 2013.

88. Chollet and Goldgeier, *America between the Wars,* 79, 99–102.

CHAPTER 6. RATIONALITY AND CRISIS MANAGEMENT

1. Richard Ned Lebow, *Between Peace and War: The Nature of International Crisis* (Baltimore: Johns Hopkins University Press, 1981), 119–124; quote on p. 119.

2. Richard Ned Lebow and Janice Gross Stein, "Beyond Deterrence," *Journal of Social Issues* 43, no. 4 (1987): 17–18.

3. Jack Snyder, "Civil-Military Relations and the Cult of the Offensive, 1914 and 1984," *International Security* 9, no. 1 (1984): 110; Stephen Van Evera: "Why Cooperation Failed in 1914," *World Politics* 38, no. 1 (1985): 116, and *Causes of War: Power and the Roots of Conflict* (Ithaca, NY: Cornell University Press, 1999), 194. Regarding the origins of the plan, Snyder writes that "Schlieffen's bias against the defensive is the main indication that his war planning for the western front was dominated by nonrational processes." See Jack Snyder, *Ideology of the Offensive: Military Decisionmaking and the Disasters of 1914* (Ithaca, NY: Cornell University Press, 1984), 145.

4. Van Evera, "Why Cooperation Failed in 1914," 81, 117.

5. Jack Snyder, "Better Now Than Later: The Paradox of 1914 as Everyone's Favored Year for War," *International Security* 39, no. 1 (2014): 88.

6. Richard Ned Lebow, *Nuclear Crisis Management: A Dangerous Illusion* (Ithaca, NY: Cornell University Press, 1987), 34.

7. John C. G. Röhl, "The Curious Case of the Kaiser's Disappearing War Guilt: Wilhelm II in July 1914," in *An Improbable War? The Outbreak of World War I and European Political Culture before 1914,* ed. Holger Afflerbach and David Stevenson (New York: Berghahn, 2007), 77.

8. This case relies on Christopher Clark, *The Sleepwalkers: How Europe Went to War in 1914* (New York: Penguin, 2013), chs. 7–12; Dale C. Copeland, *The Origins of Major War* (Ithaca, NY: Cornell University Press, 2000), chs. 3–4; Jack S. Levy and William Mulligan, "Why 1914 but Not Before? A Comparative Study of the July Crisis and Its Precursors," *Security Studies* 30, no. 2 (2021): 213–244; Sean McMeekin, *July 1914: Countdown to War* (New York: Basic Books, 2013);

Annika Mombauer, *Helmuth von Moltke and the Origins of the First World War* (Cambridge: Cambridge University Press, 2001), chs. 3-4; T. G. Otte, *July Crisis: The World's Descent into War, Summer 1914* (New York: Cambridge University Press, 2014); John C. G. Röhl, *Wilhelm II: Into the Abyss of War and Exile, 1900-1941* (New York: Cambridge University Press, 2014), chs. 36-41; Marc Trachtenberg: "The Meaning of Mobilization in 1914," *International Security* 15, no. 3 (1990/91): 120-150, and "The Coming of the First World War: A Reassessment," in *History and Strategy* (Princeton, NJ: Princeton University Press, 1991), 47-99, and "A New Light on 1914?" H-Diplo|ISSF Forum, no. 16 (2017); Alexander Watson, *Ring of Steel: Germany and Austria-Hungary in World War I* (New York: Basic, 2014), ch. 1.

9. Röhl, "The Curious Case of the Kaiser's Disappearing War Guilt," 78.

10. Quoted in Röhl, "The Curious Case of the Kaiser's Disappearing War Guilt," 79.

11. Bethmann is quoted in Watson, *Ring of Steel*, 36, and Konrad H. Jarausch, "The Illusion of Limited War: Chancellor Bethmann Hollweg's Calculated Risk, July 1914 [1969]," *Historical Social Research/Historische Sozialforschung* 24 (2012): 54.

12. Quoted in Stephen Van Evera, "The Cult of the Offensive and the Origins of the First World War," *International Security* 9, no. 1 (1984): 80.

13. Quoted in Copeland, *The Origins of Major War*, 71.

14. Quoted in Snyder, "Better Now Than Later," 76.

15. Scott D. Sagan, "1914 Revisited: Allies, Offense, and Instability," *International Security* 11, no. 2 (1986): 151-175.

16. On the Schlieffen Plan, see Hans Ehlert, Michael Epkenhans, and Gerhard P. Gross, eds., *The Schlieffen Plan: International Perspectives on the German Strategy for World War I* (Lexington: University of Kentucky Press, 2014); Gerhard Ritter, *The Schlieffen Plan: Critique of a Myth* (New York: Praeger, 1958).

17. Quoted in Van Evera, *Causes of War*, 204.

18. Michael Howard, "Men against Fire: Expectations of War in 1914," *International Security* 9, no. 1 (1984): 43. See also Holger H. Herwig, "Germany and the 'Short-War' Illusion: Toward a New Interpretation?" *Journal of Military History* 66, no. 3 (2002): 681-693; Keir A. Lieber, "The New History of World War I and What It Means for International Relations Theory," *International Security* 32, no. 2 (2007): 177-183.

19. Clark, *The Sleepwalkers*, 332.

20. Röhl, "The Curious Case of the Kaiser's Disappearing War Guilt," 78.

21. Mombauer, *Helmuth von Moltke and the Origins of the First World War*, 285-286.

22. Trachtenberg, "The Coming of the First World War," 96. For a similar assessment, see Stephen A. Schuker, "Dust in the Eyes of Historians: A Comment on Marc Trachtenberg's 'New Light,'" H-Diplo|ISSF Forum, no. 16 (2017): 70-99.

23. Lebow and Stein, "Beyond Deterrence," 13, 15.

24. Jack Snyder, *Myths of Empire: Domestic Politics and International Ambition* (Ithaca, NY: Cornell University Press, 1991), 148.

25. Charles A. Kupchan, *The Vulnerability of Empire* (Ithaca, NY: Cornell University Press, 1994), 345–346.

26. Jeffrey Record, *A War It Was Always Going to Lose: Why Japan Attacked America in 1941* (Washington, DC: Potomac, 2011), 6.

27. Dale C. Copeland, *Economic Interdependence and War* (Princeton, NJ: Princeton University Press, 2015), 144.

28. Robert Jervis, "Deterrence and Perception," *International Security* 7, no. 3 (1982): 30.

29. Snyder, *Myths of Empire*, 148.

30. Stephen Van Evera, "Why States Believe Foolish Ideas: Non-Self-Evaluation by States and Societies," unpublished ms., Massachusetts Institute of Technology, January 2002, 33.

31. This case is based on Sadao Asada, *From Mahan to Pearl Harbor: The Imperial Japanese Navy and the United States* (Annapolis, MD: Naval Institute, 2006), chs. 10–11; Michael A. Barnhart, *Japan Prepares for Total War: The Search for Economic Security, 1919–1941* (Ithaca, NY: Cornell University Press, 1987), chs. 12–13; Herbert P. Bix, *Hirohito and the Making of Modern Japan* (New York: HarperCollins, 2000), ch. 11; Robert J. C. Butow, *Tojo and the Coming of War* (Princeton, NJ: Princeton University Press, 1961), chs. 9–12; Copeland, *Economic Interdependence and War*, chs. 4–5; Nobutaka Ike, *Japan's Decision for War: Records of the 1941 Policy Conferences* (Stanford, CA: Stanford University Press, 1967); Akira Iriye, *The Origins of the Second World War in Asia and the Pacific*, 4th ed. (London: Longman, 1989), chs. 5–6; Kupchan, *The Vulnerability of Empire*, ch. 5; Bruce M. Russett, *No Clear and Present Danger: A Skeptical View of the United States Entry into World War II* (Boulder, CO: Westview, 1997), ch. 3; Scott D. Sagan, "The Origins of the Pacific War," in *The Origin and Prevention of Major Wars*, ed. Robert I. Rotberg and Theodore K. Rabb (New York: Cambridge University Press, 1989), 323–352; Jeffrey W. Taliaferro, *Balancing Risks: Great Power Intervention in the Periphery* (Ithaca, NY: Cornell University Press, 2004), ch. 4.

32. Quoted in Ike, *Japan's Decision for War*, 130–131, 138.

33. Quoted in Ike, *Japan's Decision for War*, 236, 238. See Butow, *Tojo and the Coming of War*, 280, for Tojo's making a similar argument.

34. Quoted in Ike, *Japan's Decision for War*, 131, 139, 207.

35. Quoted in Ike, *Japan's Decision for War*, 139–140.

36. Ike, *Japan's Decision for War*, xxiii–xxiv.

37. Copeland, *Economic Interdependence and War*, 228.

38. Sagan, "The Origins of the Pacific War," 324.

39. Russett, *No Clear and Present Danger*, 56.

40. Rolf-Dieter Müller, *Enemy in the East: Hitler's Secret Plans to Invade the Soviet Union* (London: I. B. Tauris, 2014), x.

41. Volker Ullrich, *Hitler: Downfall, 1939–1945,* trans. Jefferson Chase (New York: Alfred A. Knopf, 2020), 2.

42. Norrin M. Ripsman, Jeffrey W. Taliaferro, and Steven E. Lobell, *Neoclassical Realist Theory of International Politics* (New York: Oxford University Press, 2016), 23.

43. Alex Schulman, "Testing Ideology against Neorealism in Hitler's Drive to the East," *Comparative Strategy* 25, no. 1 (2006): 34.

44. Daniel L. Byman and Kenneth M. Pollack, "Let Us Now Praise Great Men: Bringing the Statesman Back In," *International Security* 25, no. 4 (2001): 115.

45. Klaus Hildebrand, *The Foreign Policy of the Third Reich,* trans. Anthony Fothergill (Berkeley: University of California Press, 1973), 111.

46. Michael Geyer, "German Strategy in the Age of Machine Warfare, 1914–1945," in *Makers of Modern Strategy from Machiavelli to the Nuclear Age,* ed. Peter Paret (Princeton, NJ: Princeton University Press, 1986), 575, 584.

47. Alan Bullock, *Hitler: A Study in Tyranny,* rev. ed. (New York: Harper Torch, 1964), 806.

48. This case is based on Matthew Cooper, *The German Army, 1933–1945: Its Political and Military Failure* (New York: Stein and Day, 1978), chs. 1–18; Copeland, *The Origins of Major War,* ch. 5; James Ellman, *Hitler's Great Gamble: A New Look at German Strategy, Operation Barbarossa, and the Axis Defeat in World War II* (Guilford, CT: Stackpole, 2019), chs. 1–7; David C. Gompert, Hans Binnendijk, and Bonny Lin, *Blinders, Blunders, and War: What America and China Can Learn* (Santa Monica, CA: RAND Corporation, 2014), ch. 7; Ian Kershaw, *Fateful Choices: Ten Decisions That Changed the World, 1940–1941* (New York: Penguin, 2007), ch. 2; Barry A. Leach, *German Strategy against Russia, 1939–1941* (Oxford: Oxford University Press, 1973); Williamson Murray and Allan R. Millett, *A War to Be Won: Fighting the Second World War* (Cambridge, MA: Belknap, 2000), ch. 6; David Stahel, *Operation Barbarossa and Germany's Defeat in the East* (New York: Cambridge University Press, 2009), part I; Adam Tooze, *The Wages of Destruction: The Making and Breaking of the Nazi Economy* (New York: Penguin, 2008), part II; Barton Whaley, *Codeword BARBAROSSA* (Cambridge, MA: MIT Press, 1973).

49. Franz Halder, *Kriegstagebuch,* vol. 2: *Von der geplanten Landung in England bis zum Beginn des Ostfeldzuges* (Stuttgart: W. Kohlhammer, 1963), 212.

50. Quoted in Copeland, *The Origins of Major War,* 141.

51. Quoted in Whaley, *Codeword BARBAROSSA,* 14.

52. Quoted in Stahel, *Operation Barbarossa and Germany's Defeat in the East,* 65.

53. Quoted in Copeland, *The Origins of Major War,* 128–129.

54. Quoted in Anthony Read and David Fisher, *The Deadly Embrace: Hitler, Stalin and the Nazi-Soviet Pact, 1939–1941* (New York: W. W. Norton, 1988), 498–499.

55. Cooper, *The German Army, 1933–1945,* 252.

56. Quoted in Copeland, *The Origins of Major War,* 140.

57. Quoted in Leach, *German Strategy against Russia, 1939–1941,* 132.

58. For a comprehensive account of those meetings, see Stahel, *Operation Barbarossa and Germany's Defeat in the East,* 33–104.

59. Leach, *German Strategy against Russia, 1939–1941,* appendix IV.

60. Stahel, *Operation Barbarossa and Germany's Defeat in the East,* 38–39, 72, 79–81; quotes on pp. 72, 80.

61. Stahel, *Operation Barbarossa and Germany's Defeat in the East,* 33–95.

62. Stahel, *Operation Barbarossa and Germany's Defeat in the East,* 39, 73. See also Copeland, *The Origins of Major War,* 142.

63. Robert Cecil, *Hitler's Decision to Invade Russia, 1941* (New York: David McKay, 1975), 121; Copeland, *The Origins of Major War,* 142; Ellman, *Hitler's Great Gamble,* 90–91.

64. This was not the first time Hitler and his generals disagreed about strategic plans. In fact, they clashed in the planning process for the invasion of France in May 1940. See Ernest R. May, *Strange Victory: Hitler's Conquest of France* (New York: Hill and Wang, 2000).

65. Copeland, *The Origins of Major War,* 119–123. We distinguish between ideological and racial theories. In the case of Nazi Germany, they coexisted. But this need not be true. For example, the Cold War was in part an ideological struggle between liberalism and communism, and it had no racial dimension.

66. Brendan Simms and Charlie Laderman, *Hitler's American Gamble: Pearl Harbor and Germany's March to Global War* (New York: Basic Books, 2021), x; Ripsman, Taliaferro, and Lobell, *Neoclassical Realist Theory of International Politics,* 23.

67. Ian O. Johnson, "Review of Brendan Simms and Charlie Laderman, *Hitler's American Gamble: Pearl Harbor and Germany's March to Global War,*" H-Diplo Review Essay, no. 409, 17 February 2022; Ian Kershaw: *Hitler, 1936–45: Nemesis* (New York: W. W. Norton, 2000), 442–446, and *Fateful Choices,* ch. 9; Randall L. Schweller, *Deadly Imbalances: Tripolarity and Hitler's Strategy of World Conquest* (New York: Columbia University Press, 1998), chs. 4–6; Simms and Laderman, *Hitler's American Gamble;* Tooze, *The Wages of Destruction,* 501–506; Marc Trachtenberg, *The Craft of International History: A Guide to Method* (Princeton, NJ: Princeton University Press, 2006), 80–88; Gerhard L. Weinberg, "Why Hitler Declared War on the United States," *Historynet,* Spring 1992, historynet.com.

68. Janice Gross Stein, "Threat Perception in International Relations," in *The Oxford Handbook of Political Psychology,* 2nd ed., ed. Leonie Huddy, David O. Sears, and Jack S. Levy (New York: Oxford University Press, 2013), 375.

69. Ripsman, Taliaferro, and Lobell, *Neoclassical Realist Theory of International Politics,* 23.

70. Kershaw, *Fateful Choices,* ch. 6; Stephen Kotkin, *Stalin: Waiting for Hitler, 1929–1941* (New York: Penguin, 2018), ch. 14 and coda; Stephen Kotkin, "When Stalin Faced Hitler: Who Fooled Whom?" *Foreign Affairs* 96, no. 6 (2017): 55–64; Roger Moorhouse, *The Devil's Alliance: Hitler's Pact with Stalin, 1939–1941* (London: Bodley Head, 2014), ch. 8; David E. Murphy, *What Stalin Knew: The Enigma of Barbarossa* (New Haven: Yale University Press, 2008).

71. For studies that treat the Kennedy administration's decision-making as rational, see Irving L. Janis, *Groupthink: Psychological Studies of Policy Decisions and Fiascoes,* 2nd rev. ed. (Boston: Houghton Mifflin, 1983), ch. 6; John Kay and Mervyn King, *Radical Uncertainty: Decision-Making beyond the Numbers* (New York: W. W. Norton, 2020), 278–282.

72. Mark L. Haas, "Prospect Theory and the Cuban Missile Crisis," *International Studies Quarterly* 45, no. 2 (2001): 260, 267.

73. James A. Nathan, "The Missile Crisis: His Finest Hour Now," *World Politics* 27, no. 2 (1975): 260.

74. Noam Chomsky, "Cuban Missile Crisis: How the US Played Russian Roulette with Nuclear War," *Guardian,* 15 October 2012.

75. Richard Ned Lebow, "The Cuban Missile Crisis: Reading the Lessons Correctly," *Political Science Quarterly* 98, no. 3 (1983): 458. See also Lebow, *Between Peace and War,* 302–303.

76. David A. Welch, "Crisis Decision Making Reconsidered," *Journal of Conflict Resolution* 33, no. 3 (1989): 443.

77. Graham T. Allison, *Essence of Decision: Explaining the Cuban Missile Crisis* (New York: HarperCollins, 1971); Graham T. Allison and Philip Zelikow, *Essence of Decision: Explaining the Cuban Missile Crisis,* 2nd ed. (New York: Longman, 1999). See also Barton J. Bernstein, "Understanding Decisionmaking, U.S. Foreign Policy, and the Cuban Missile Crisis: A Review Essay," *International Security* 25, no. 1 (2000): 134–164.

78. Ronald Steel, "Endgame," *New York Review of Books,* 13 March 1969.

79. This case relies on Allison and Zelikow, *Essence of Decision;* Michael Dobbs, *One Minute to Midnight: Kennedy, Khrushchev, and Castro on the Brink of Nuclear War* (New York: Alfred A. Knopf, 2008); Aleksandr Fursenko and Timothy Naftali, *One Hell of a Gamble: Khrushchev, Castro, and Kennedy, 1958–1964* (New York: W. W. Norton, 1997); Max Frankel, *High Noon in the Cold War: Kennedy, Khrushchev, and the Cuban Missile Crisis* (New York: Presidio, 2005); Alice L. George, *The Cuban Missile Crisis: The Threshold of Nuclear War* (New York: Routledge, 2013); Janis, *Groupthink,* ch. 6.

80. For a discussion of American strategic thinking during the crisis, see Marc Trachtenberg, "The Influence of Nuclear Weapons in the Cuban Missile Crisis," *International Security* 10, no. 1 (1985): 137–163.

---

81. Quoted in Raymond L. Garthoff, *A Journey through the Cold War: A Memoir of Containment and Coexistence* (Washington, DC: Brookings Institution, 2001), 236.

82. Vernon V. Aspaturian, "Soviet Foreign Policy at the Crossroads: Conflict and/or Collaboration?" *International Organization* 23, no. 3 (1969): 589–592.

83. Fred H. Eidlin, *The Logic of "Normalization": The Soviet Intervention in Czechoslovakia of 21 August 1968 and the Czechoslovak Response* (New York: Columbia University Press, 1980), 23, 26.

84. Jiri Valenta, *Soviet Intervention in Czechoslovakia, 1968: Anatomy of a Decision*, rev. ed. (Baltimore: John Hopkins University Press, 1991), 4.

85. David W. Paul, "Soviet Foreign Policy and the Invasion of Czechoslovakia: A Theory and a Case Study," *International Studies Quarterly* 15, no. 2 (1971): 159.

86. This case relies on Laurien Crump, *The Warsaw Pact Reconsidered: International Relations in Eastern Europe, 1955–69* (New York: Routledge, 2015), ch. 6; Karen Dawisha, *The Kremlin and the Prague Spring* (Berkeley: University of California Press, 1984); Eidlin, *The Logic of "Normalization"*; Mark Kramer, "The Kremlin, the Prague Spring, and the Brezhnev Doctrine," in *Promises of 1968: Crisis, Illusion, and Utopia*, ed. Vladimir Tismăneanu (New York: Central European University Press, 2011), 285–370; Matthew J. Ouimet, *The Rise and Fall of the Brezhnev Doctrine in Soviet Foreign Policy* (Chapel Hill: University of North Carolina Press, 2003), ch. 1; Mikhail Prozumenshchikov, "Politburo Decision-Making on the Czechoslovak Crisis in 1968," in *The Prague Spring and the Warsaw Pact Invasion of Czechoslovakia in 1968*, ed. Günter Bischof, Stefan Karner, and Peter Ruggenthaler (Lanham, MD; Lexington, 2010); Valenta, *Soviet Intervention in Czechoslovakia, 1968*.

87. Janis, *Groupthink*, 9, 11. See also Mark Schafer and Scott Crichlow, *Groupthink Versus High-Quality Decision Making in International Relations* (New York: Columbia University Press, 2010).

88. Janis, *Groupthink*, 48–49.

89. David Halberstam, *The Coldest Winter: America and the Korean War* (New York: Hyperion, 2007), part 7; Max Hastings, *The Korean War* (New York: Simon & Schuster, 1987), ch. 6; Janis, *Groupthink*, ch. 3; Allen S. Whiting, *China Crosses the Yalu: The Decision to Enter the Korean War* (New York: Macmillan, 1960), ch. 6.

90. Janis, *Groupthink*, 107, 115.

91. Janis, *Groupthink*, 97, 129–130; quotes on p. 97.

92. Janis, *Groupthink*, 97.

93. Leslie H. Gelb and Richard K. Betts, *The Irony of Vietnam: The System Worked* (Washington, DC: Brookings Institution, 2016), 2–3; emphasis in original. See also Daniel Ellsberg, "The Quagmire Myth and the Stalemate Machine," *Public Policy* 19, no. 2 (1971): 217–274; Fredrik Logevall, *Choosing War: The Lost*

Chance for Peace and the Escalation of War in Vietnam (Berkeley: University of California Press, 1999).

CHAPTER 7. NONRATIONAL STATE BEHAVIOR

1. This case relies on Michael Epkenhans, *Tirpitz: Architect of the High Seas Fleet* (Washington, DC: Potomac, 2008), chs. 3–4; Carl-Axel Gemzell, *Organization, Conflict, and Innovation: A Study of German Naval Strategic Planning, 1888–1940* (Lund: Berlingska Boktryckeriet, 1973), ch. 2; Holger H. Herwig, *Luxury Fleet: The Imperial German Navy, 1888–1918* (London: Allen & Unwin, 1980), ch. 3; Rolf Hobson, *Imperialism at Sea: Naval Strategic Thought, the Ideology of Sea Power and the Tirpitz Plan, 1875–1914* (Boston: Brill, 2002), chs. 6–7; Patrick J. Kelly, *Tirpitz and the Imperial German Navy* (Bloomington: Indiana University Press, 2011), chs. 7–11; Paul Kennedy: *Strategy and Diplomacy, 1870–1945* (London: George Allen & Unwin, 1983), chs. 4–5, and "Tirpitz, England and the Second Navy Law of 1900: A Strategical Critique," *Militaergeschichtliche Zeitschrift* 8, no. 2 (1970): 33–57; Michelle Murray, "Identity, Insecurity, and Great Power Politics: The Tragedy of German Naval Ambition before the First World War," *Security Studies* 19, no. 4 (2010): 656–688; Peter Padfield, *The Great Naval Race: The Anglo-German Naval Rivalry, 1900–1914* (New York: David McKay, 1974), chs. 1–5; Stephen R. Rock, "Risk Theory Reconsidered: American Success and German Failure in the Coercion of Britain, 1890–1914," *Journal of Strategic Studies* 11, no. 3 (1988): 342–364; Jonathan Steinberg, *Yesterday's Deterrent: Tirpitz and the Birth of the German Battle Fleet* (London: Macdonald, 1965), chs. 2–5.

2. Quoted in Kennedy, *Strategy and Diplomacy, 1870–1945*, 139.

3. Quoted in Robert Jervis, *Perception and Misperception in International Politics* (Princeton, NJ: Princeton University Press, 1976), 85.

4. Kennedy, *Strategy and Diplomacy, 1870–1945*, 151.

5. Quoted in Kennedy, *Strategy and Diplomacy*, 142.

6. Hobson, *Imperialism at Sea*, 222–225, 242–244; Kelly, *Tirpitz and the Imperial German Navy*, 112, 115, 185–186, 195.

7. Hobson, *Imperialism at Sea*, 236. See also Kelly, *Tirpitz and the Imperial German Navy*, 112.

8. Kelly, *Tirpitz and the Imperial German Navy*, 164.

9. This case relies on Brian Bond, *British Military Policy between the Two World Wars* (Oxford: Clarendon, 1980), chs. 6–11; Peter Dennis, *Decision by Default: Peacetime Conscription and British Defence, 1919–39* (Durham, NC: Duke University Press, 1972), chs. 3–11; Norman H. Gibbs, *Grand Strategy*, vol. 1: *Rearmament Policy* (London: Her Majesty's Stationary Office, 1976); Michael Howard, *The Continental Commitment: The Dilemma of British Defence Policy in the Era of the*

Two World Wars (London: Temple Smith, 1972), ch. 5; Gaines Post, Jr., *Dilemmas of Appeasement: British Deterrence and Defense, 1934–1937* (Ithaca, NY: Cornell University Press, 1993); Robert Paul Shay, Jr., *British Rearmament in the Thirties: Politics and Profits* (Princeton, NJ: Princeton University Press, 1977).

10. Howard, *The Continental Commitment*, 117.

11. Gibbs, *Grand Strategy*, 515.

12. Nicholas Milton, *Neville Chamberlain's Legacy: Hitler, Munich and the Path to War* (Barnsley: Pen & Sword, 2019), 37.

13. Bond, *British Military Policy between the Two World Wars*, 255.

14. Shay, *British Rearmament in the Thirties*, 182.

15. Quoted in Gibbs, *Grand Strategy*, 469.

16. Shay, *British Rearmament in the Thirties*, 196.

17. Shay, *British Rearmament in the Thirties*, 200.

18. Brian Bond, ed., *Chief of Staff: The Diaries of Lieutenant-General Sir Henry Pownall*, vol. 1: *1933–1940* (Hamden, CT: Archon, 1973), 197.

19. Keren Yarhi-Milo, *Knowing the Adversary: Leaders, Intelligence, and Assessment of Intentions in International Relations* (Princeton, NJ: Princeton University Press, 2014), 91–92.

20. Quoted in Jervis, *Perception and Misperception in International Politics*, 78. For a summary of the common claim that Britain "was highly instrumentally rational" not only at Munich, but also throughout the late 1930s, see Brian Rathbun, *Reasoning of State: Realists, Romantics and Rationality in International Relations* (New York: Cambridge University Press, 2019), 176. As should be apparent, we agree with Rathbun about Munich but not about the British decision to pursue "no liability."

21. This case relies on Phil Carradice, *Bay of Pigs: CIA's Cuban Disaster, April 1961* (Barnsley: Pen & Sword Military, 2018), chs. 1–6; Rebecca R. Friedman, "Crisis Management at the Dead Center: The 1960–1961 Presidential Transition and the Bay of Pigs Fiasco," *Presidential Studies Quarterly* 41, no. 2 (2011): 307–333; Irving L. Janis, *Groupthink: Psychological Studies of Policy Decisions and Fiascoes*, 2nd rev. ed. (Boston: Houghton Mifflin, 1983); Howard Jones, *The Bay of Pigs* (New York: Oxford University Press, 2008), chs. 1–4; Peter Kornbluh, ed., *Bay of Pigs Declassified: The Secret CIA Report on the Invasion of Cuba* (New York: New Press, 1998); Jim Rasenberger, *The Brilliant Disaster: JFK, Castro, and America's Doomed Invasion of Cuba's Bay of Pigs* (New York: Scribner, 2012); Joshua H. Sandman, "Analyzing Foreign Policy Crisis Situations: The Bay of Pigs," *Presidential Studies Quarterly* 16, no. 2 (1986): 310–316; Peter Wyden, *The Bay of Pigs: The Untold Story* (New York: Simon & Schuster, 1980).

22. Friedman, "Crisis Management at the Dead Center," 313–315; quotes on pp. 314, 315.

23. Quoted in Friedman, "Crisis Management at the Dead Center," 321.

24. Jones, *The Bay of Pigs,* 37, 55; quote on p. 55.

25. Quoted in Friedman, "Crisis Management at the Dead Center," 326.

26. Jones, *The Bay of Pigs,* 59.

27. Friedman, "Crisis Management at the Dead Center," 318.

28. Janis, *Groupthink,* 22.

29. Memorandum Prepared in the Central Intelligence Agency to General Maxwell D. Taylor, 26 April 1961, in *Foreign Relations of the United States, 1961–1963,* vol. X: *Cuba, January 1961–September 1962* (Washington, DC: U.S. Government Printing Office, 1997), document 98.

30. Quoted in Jones, *The Bay of Pigs,* 70.

31. Janis, *Groupthink,* 23.

32. Jones, *The Bay of Pigs,* 58–59.

33. Memorandum Prepared in the Central Intelligence Agency to General Maxwell D. Taylor.

34. Quoted in Jones, *The Bay of Pigs,* 49. See also ibid., 62.

35. Jones, *The Bay of Pigs,* 50, 54–55.

36. Jones, *The Bay of Pigs,* 56–57, 60–61; Friedman, "Crisis Management at the Dead Center," 325–326.

37. Friedman, "Crisis Management at the Dead Center," 319–320.

38. Quoted in Jones, *The Bay of Pigs,* 65.

39. Jones, *The Bay of Pigs,* 65.

40. Janis, *Groupthink,* 41–42.

41. Friedman, "Crisis Management at the Dead Center," 321.

42. Jones, *The Bay of Pigs,* 57.

43. This case relies on Robert Draper, *To Start a War: How the Bush Administration Took America into Iraq* (New York: Penguin, 2020); James Fallows, "Blind into Baghdad," *Atlantic Monthly,* 15 February 2004; Michael R. Gordon and Bernard E. Trainor, *Cobra II: The Inside Story of the Invasion and Occupation of Iraq* (New York: Pantheon, 2006), chs. 1–8; James Mann, *Rise of the Vulcans: The History of Bush's War Cabinet* (New York: Penguin, 2004); George Packer, *The Assassins' Gate: America in Iraq* (New York: Farrar, Straus and Giroux, 2005), chs. 1–3; Thomas E. Ricks, *Fiasco: The American Military Adventure in Iraq* (New York: Penguin, 2006), chs. 1–6; Bob Woodward, *Plan of Attack: The Definitive Account of the Decision to Invade Iraq* (New York: Simon & Schuster, 2004).

44. Quoted in Packer, *The Assassins' Gate,* 61.

45. Quoted in John T. Correll, "What Happened to Shock and Awe?" *Air Force Magazine,* 1 November 2003.

46. Quoted in Draper, *To Start a War,* 191.

47. Quoted in Ricks, *Fiasco,* 96.

48. Quoted in Draper, *To Start a War,* 166, 318.

49. Quoted in Draper, *To Start a War*, 162–163.

50. Packer, *The Assassins' Gate*, 58.

51. Jeffrey Pickering and Mark Peceny, "Forging Democracy at Gunpoint," *International Studies Quarterly* 50, no. 3 (2006): 539–559. See also William Easterly, Shanker Satyanath, and Daniel Berger, "Superpower Interventions and Their Consequences for Democracy: An Empirical Inquiry," (Cambridge, MA: National Bureau of Economic Research, Working Paper no. 13992, May 2008), 1.

52. Jerome Slater, "Dominos in Central America": Will They Fall? Does It Matter?" *International Security* 12, no. 2 (1987): 112. For a relevant analysis that looks at the Middle East, see Stephen M. Walt, *The Origins of Alliances* (Ithaca, NY: Cornell University Press, 1987), ch. 5.

53. On this point, see also Mark Schafer and Scott Crichlow, *Groupthink Versus High-Quality Decision Making in International Relations* (New York: Columbia University Press, 2010), ch. 8.

54. Quoted in Packer, *The Assassins' Gate*, 45.

55. Draper, *To Start a War*, 238–240.

56. Quoted in Draper, *To Start a War,* 316.

57. Quoted in Draper, *To Start a War,* 313.

58. Quoted in Ricks, *Fiasco,* 106.

59. Quoted in Ricks, *Fiasco,* 109–110.

60. Quoted in Ricks, *Fiasco,* 99; emphasis in original.

61. Quoted in Draper, *To Start a War,* 320.

62. The quotes in this paragraph are all in Ricks, *Fiasco,* 71–73. For a description of a prewar State Department report that threw cold water on the notion that removing Saddam would lead to democracy throughout the Middle East, see Oliver Burkeman, "Secret Report Throws Doubt on Democracy Hopes," *Guardian,* 14 March 2003.

63. Quoted in Ricks, *Fiasco,* 97, 104.

64. Quoted in Draper, *To Start a War,* 84.

65. Quoted in Draper, *To Start a War,* 155–156.

CHAPTER 8. GOAL RATIONALITY

1. Quoted in Karin Edvardsson and Sven Ove Hansson, "When Is a Goal Rational?" *Social Choice and Welfare* 24, no. 2 (2005): 344.

2. For a related discussion, see John J. Mearsheimer, *The Great Delusion: Liberal Dreams and International Realities* (New Haven: Yale University Press, 2018), 28–33.

3. Quoted in Stephen Kalberg, "Max Weber's Types of Rationality: Cornerstones for the Analysis of Rationalization Processes in History," *American Journal of Sociology* 85, no. 5 (1980): 1156; emphasis in original.

4. Thomas Hobbes, *Leviathan,* ed. David Johnston (New York: W. W. Norton, 2021), 104.

5. John J. Mearsheimer, *The Tragedy of Great Power Politics,* updated ed. (New York: W. W. Norton, 2014), 31; Sebastian Rosato, *Intentions in Great Power Politics: Uncertainty and the Roots of Conflict* (New Haven: Yale University Press, 2021), 25.

6. On the components of a state's base and institutions, see Barry Buzan, *People, States, and Fear: The National Security Problem in International Relations* (Chapel Hill: University of North Carolina Press, 1983), 53-65.

7. Kenneth N. Waltz, *Theory of International Politics* (New York: McGraw-Hill, 1979), 126. See also Robert Gilpin, "The Richness of the Tradition of Political Realism," *International Organization* 38, no. 2 (1984): 290-291.

8. As should be apparent, our definition of goal rationality differs from that employed by rational choice theorists. For them, states are rational as long as they can identify and rank order their various goals. See Andrew H. Kydd, *International Relations Theory: The Game Theoretic Approach* (New York: Cambridge University Press, 2015), 12-14; David A. Lake and Robert Powell, "International Relations: A Strategic-Choice Approach," in *Strategic Choice and International Relations,* ed. David A. Lake and Robert Powell (Princeton, NJ: Princeton University Press, 1999), 6-7; James Morrow, *Game Theory for Political Scientists* (Princeton, NJ: Princeton University Press, 1994), 18-19. We impose the additional requirement that rationality involves ranking survival as the number one goal.

9. James D. Fearon, "Domestic Politics, Foreign Policy, and Theories of International Relations," *Annual Review of Political Science* 1 (1998): 294.

10. Fearon's discussion of survival directly engages with Kenneth Waltz's work, which is widely recognized as stressing the primacy of survival as a state goal. It is worth noting, however, that Waltz is inconsistent on the matter. On the one hand, he argues that "survival is a prerequisite to achieving any goals that states may have," and on the other hand, he argues that "some states may persistently seek goals that they value more highly than survival." See Waltz, *Theory of International Politics,* 91-92.

11. Fearon, "Domestic Politics, Foreign Policy, and Theories of International Relations," 294.

12. Charles Tilly, *Coercion, Capital, and European States, AD 990-1992,* revised ed. (Malden, MA: Blackwell, 1992), 1-2.

13. See Peter H. Wilson, "Dynasty, Constitution, and Confession: The Role of Religion in the Thirty Years War," *International History Review* 30, no. 3 (2008): 494-502, 512-514. For a more detailed treatment, see Peter H. Wilson, *The Thirty Years War: Europe's Tragedy* (Cambridge, MA: Belknap, 2009).

14. Dale C. Copeland, *The Origins of Major War* (Ithaca, NY: Cornell University Press, 2000), chs. 3-4.

15. Thomas Friedman, *The Lexus and the Olive Tree: Understanding Globalization* (New York: Farrar, Straus and Giroux, 1999), 202.

16. Quoted in Stephen M. Walt, *The Origins of Alliances* (Ithaca, NY: Cornell University Press, 1987), 38.

17. Zeev Maoz and Bruce Russett, "Normative and Structural Causes of Democratic Peace, 1946–1986," *American Political Science Review* 87, no. 3 (1993): 625. See also Michael W. Doyle, "Kant, Liberal Legacies, and Foreign Affairs, Part 2," *Philosophy and Public Affairs* 12, no. 4 (1983): 324.

18. Nobuyasu Abe, "The NPT at Fifty: Successes and Failures," *Journal for Peace and Nuclear Disarmament* 3, no. 2 (2020): 224–233.

19. Alexander B. Downes, *Targeting Civilians in War* (Ithaca, NY: Cornell University Press, 2012).

20. Jack Snyder, *Myths of Empire: Domestic Politics and International Ambition* (Ithaca, NY: Cornell University Press, 1991), 1. See also Randall L. Schweller, "Neorealism's Status Quo Bias: What Security Dilemma?" *Security Studies* 5, no. 3 (1996): 107, 113.

21. Randall L. Schweller, *Unanswered Threats: Political Constraints on the Balance of Power* (Princeton, NJ: Princeton University Press, 2006), 1–2, 69–79.

22. Quoted in Copeland, *The Origins of Major War,* 83, 141, 230–231.

23. Quoted in Scott D. Sagan, "The Origins of the Pacific War," in *The Origin and Prevention of Major Wars,* ed. Robert I. Rotberg and Theodore K. Rabb (New York: Cambridge University Press, 1989), 325.

24. On French and British policies in the late 1930s, see chapters 5 and 7 respectively.

25. Quoted in Zachary Keck, "China's Mao Zedong 'Seemed to Welcome a Nuclear Holocaust,'" *The National Interest,* 14 December 2017.

26. Kenneth N. Waltz, "Why Iran Should Get the Bomb: Nuclear Balancing Would Mean Stability," *Foreign Affairs* 91, no. 4 (2012): 4.

27. Dustin Ells Howes, "When States Choose to Die: Reassessing Assumptions about What States Want," *International Studies Quarterly* 47, no. 4 (2003): 669, 671–672.

28. Mariya Grinberg, "Unconstrained Sovereignty: Delegation of Authority and Reversibility"; available at https://ssrn.com/abstract=3725113, 4 November 2020.

29. Joseph M. Parent, *Uniting States: Voluntary Union in World Politics* (New York: Oxford University Press, 2011); Sebastian Rosato, *Europe United: Balance of Power Politics and the Making of the European Community* (Ithaca, NY: Cornell University Press, 2011).

30. Michael Geyer, "Endkampf 1918 and 1945: German Nationalism, Annihilation, and Self-Destruction," in *No Man's Land of Violence: Extreme Wars in the*

20th Century, ed. Richard Bessel, Alf Lüdtke, and Bernd Weisbrod (Munich: Max-Planck-Institut für Geschichte/Wallstein Verlag, 2006), 39.

CHAPTER 9. RATIONALITY IN INTERNATIONAL POLITICS

1. See, for example, Robert Jervis, *Perception and Misperception in International Politics* (Princeton: Princeton University Press, 1976); Richard Ned Lebow, *Between Peace and War: The Nature of International Crisis* (Baltimore: Johns Hopkins University Press, 1981); Janice Gross Stein, "Building Politics into Psychology: The Misperception of Threat," *Political Psychology* 9, no. 2 (1988): 245–271; Philip E. Tetlock and Charles McGuire, Jr., "Cognitive Perspectives on Foreign Policy," in *Political Behavior Annual,* vol. 1, ed. Samuel Long (Boulder, CO: Westview, 1986), 147–179.

2. See, for example, Christopher H. Achen and Duncan Snidal, "Rational Deterrence Theory and Comparative Case Studies," *World Politics* 41, no. 2 (1989): 143–169; Bruce Bueno de Mesquita, *The War Trap* (New Haven: Yale University Press, 1983); James D. Morrow, *Game Theory for Political Scientists* (Princeton, NJ: Princeton University Press, 1994).

3. For a summary, see Emilie Hafner-Burton, Stephan Haggard, David A. Lake, and David G. Victor, "The Behavioral Revolution and International Relations," *International Organization* 71, no. S1 (2017): 1–31.

4. See, for example, James D. Fearon, "Rationalist Explanations for War," *International Organization* 49, no. 3 (1995): 379–414; Charles L. Glaser, *Rational Theory of International Politics: The Logic of Competition and Cooperation* (Princeton, NJ: Princeton University Press, 2010).

5. On this point, see Kenneth N. Waltz, *Man and the State of War: A Theoretical Analysis* (New York: Columbia University Press, 1959), 169.

6. For the contrary view that liberalism and realism are poor guides to understanding international politics, see David A. Lake, "Why 'isms' Are Evil: Theory, Epistemology, and Academic Sects as Impediments to Understanding and Progress," *International Studies Quarterly* 55, no. 2 (2011): 465–480; Rudra Sil and Peter J. Katzenstein, "Analytic Eclecticism in the Study of World Politics: Reconfiguring Problems and Mechanisms across Research Traditions," *Perspectives on Politics* 8, no. 2 (2010): 411–431.

7. Steven Pinker, *The Better Angels of Our Nature: Why Violence Has Declined* (New York: Viking, 2011), 292. See also Steven Pinker, *Rationality: What It Is, Why It Seems Scarce, Why It Matters* (New York: Viking, 2021). For an early description of this optimistic perspective, see E. H. Carr, *The Twenty Years' Crisis, 1919–1939: An Introduction to the Study of International Relations,* 2nd ed. (London: Macmillan, 1962), ch. 4.

INDEX

Notes and tables are indicated by n and t following the page number.

INDEX

Christopher, Warren, 131
Churchill, Winston, 216
CIA (Central Intelligence Agency): U.S. invasion of Cuba (1961) and, 196, 197–200; U.S. invasion of Iraq (2003) and, 208–9
Clark, Wesley, 132, 133
clash of civilizations theory, 55
Clausewitz, Carl von, 25, 41, 68
Clinton, Bill: NATO expansion and, 127–33, 139; post–Cold War liberal hegemony strategy and, 135–38
Coase, Ronald, 45
coercion: Cuban Missile Crisis and, 34, 164–67; nuclear weapons and, 51, 58; realist approach and, 51–52; Soviet Union's invasion of Czechoslovakia and, 170–74; theories of, 51
Cold War: containment strategy and, 30–31; expected utility maximization and, 75–76, 83, 87–88; U.S. policy decisions during, 75–76, 83, 87–88. *See also* Soviet Union
collective rationality, 6, 19, 22–23
Colombia, 58
containment: NATO expansion and, 251n52; U.S. liberal hegemony strategy after Cold War and, 135, 137–38; U.S. policy toward East Asia after Cold War and, 30–31; U.S. policy toward Europe after World War II and, 28
Cooper, Duff, 190, 191
Copeland, Dale, 147–48, 153, 250n33
Co-Prosperity Sphere, 147
Coulondre, Robert, 121, 124, 125
Crane, Conrad, 207
credible theories: defined, 44–48; inventory of, 48–54; as probabilistic, 48, 86; strategic rationality and, 7–9, 37–38, 63–66, 68–69

crisis management, 140–79; defined, 25–26
Cross, Tim, 207
Cuba: Cuban Missile Crisis (1962), 33–35, 58, 61, 103t, 162–67, 178; U.S. invasion of (Bay of Pigs, 1961), 181t, 195–200
Czechoslovakia and Czech Republic: Germany's invasion of, 120, 124–126, 187, 194; NATO expansion and, 128; Soviet invasion of, 103t, 168–75; state death and, 222

Dahl, Robert, 43–44
Daladier, Édouard, 120–26
Damasio, Antonio, 60, 61
Dearlove, Richard, 201
decision maker rationality, 2, 4, 7–8, 19, 37, 63–64, 67
deductive reasoning, 40
Defense Planning Guidance (U.S. 1992), 135–36
Dehio, Ludwig, 104
deliberation: defined, 8–9, 65–66; state nonrationality and, 2, 9, 13, 37, 65, 69; state rationality and, 2, 7, 8, 12, 37, 65, 68–69, 224
democratic peace theory, 38–39, 43, 47, 52–53
democratization and war theory, 56–57
Desch, Michael, 41
deterrence: Britain's no-liability strategy before World War II and, 188, 189, 220; conventional, 51; France's grand strategy before World War II and, 126; Germany's grand strategy before World War I and, 106–109; goal rationality and, 221; nuclear, 29, 48, 51; Soviet crisis management in World War II and, 161–62; theories, 51; U.S. provision of, 29

strategy before World War I, 181*t*,
181–87; U.S. policy toward Europe
after World War II and, 26–29

Geyer, Michael, 155, 222

Gigerenzer, Gerd, 246n79

Glaser, Charles, 72, 80, 235n38

goal rationality, 4, 16, 211–22; defining,
211–15, 265n8; ignoring survival,
220–21; in practice, 215–21;
privileging survival, 215–18; risking
survival, 218–20; survival imperative
of, 213–15; 221–22; ubiquity of,
212, 221–22

Goldstein, Judith, 231n1

Gomulka, Wladyslaw, 171

Gore, Al, 130, 132

Graham, Bob, 209

grand strategy formulation, 101–39;
defined, 26

Gray, David, 199

Great Depression, 113

Grechko, Andrey, 170, 173

Greece, France's grand strategy before
World War II and, 126

Green, Donald, 72, 73

Gromyko, Andrey, 170

groupthink, 97, 98, 175–77

Gulf War (1990–91), 61

Haas, Mark, 162

Haass, Richard, 205

Hadley, Stephen, 205, 206

Hafner-Burton, Emilie, 72

Halder, Franz, 156, 158

Halifax, Viscount, 192, 193

Hara Yoshimichi, 150

Harsanyi, John, 73

Hawkins, Jack, 198

Heeringen, August von, 186

Heeringen, Josias von, 107–8, 109, 110

Hendrickson, David, 134

Herriot, Édouard, 124

heuristics: bias and, 14–15, 71, 91, 94;
cognitive limits and, 14, 91, 92–93;
data-driven thinking and, 59–60;
defined, 60, 62; in international
relations, 97–100; nonrationality and,
14–15, 71, 91, 94; nontheoretical
thinking and, 54; outcomes and,
94–95; theories versus, 14, 93–94.
See also analogies

Hildebrand, Klaus, 154

Hilsman, Roger, 41–42, 200

Hiranuma Kiichirō, 114

Hirohito (emperor), 114, 150

Hirota Kōki, 117

Hitler, Adolf: Britain's no-liability strategy
before World War II and, 187–88,
193; deliberation and, 258n64;
expected utility maximization and, 74;
France's grand strategy before World
War II and, 121–22, 124, 127;
Germany's decision to invade Soviet
Union and, 153–62; goal rationality,
219; Munich analogy and, 91; as
poster child of nonrationality, 1

Hobbes, Thomas, 213

Holbrooke, Richard, 132, 133

Holeman, Frank, 167

homo theoreticus, 7, 15, 63, 179

Hore-Belisha, Leslie, 191, 192, 193

Howard, Michael, 145, 188

Howes, Dustin, 221

Hughes, Paul, 207

Hungary, NATO expansion and, 128

Hussein, Saddam, 1, 61, 200–202, 209,
264n62

Ienaga Saburō, 112

Ike Nobutaka, 152–53

individual rationality, 5, 19, 20–21

inductive reasoning, 40

INDEX

INDEX